THE METHOD AND MESSAGE
OF JESUS' TEACHINGS

THE METHOD
AND MESSAGE
OF JESUS' TEACHINGS

By

ROBERT H. STEIN

THE WESTMINSTER PRESS
Philadelphia

Scripture quotations from the Revised Standard Version of the Bible are copyrighted 1946, 1952, © 1971, 1973 by the Division of Christian Education of the National Council of the Churches of Christ in the U.S.A., and are used by permission.

Book Design by Dorothy Alden Smith

First edition

Published by The Westminster Press®
Philadelphia, Pennsylvania

PRINTED IN THE UNITED STATES OF AMERICA

9 8 7 6 5 4 3 2 1

Library of Congress Cataloging in Publication Data

Stein, Robert H., 1935–
The method and message of Jesus' teachings.

Includes bibliographical references and indexes.
1. Jesus Christ—Teaching methods. 2. Jesus Christ—Teachings. I. Title.
BT590.T5S73   232.9′54   78–16427
ISBN 0–664–24216–2

To my wife
JOAN

A good wife who can find?
    She is far more precious than jewels.
The heart of her husband trusts in her,
    and he will have no lack of gain.
She does him good, and not harm,
    all the days of her life.
                            PROVERBS 31:10–12

Contents

Abbreviations

b. Sanhedrin	The tractate "Sanhedrin" in the Babylonian Talmud
CBQ	*The Catholic Biblical Quarterly*
ExpT	*The Expository Times*
JBL	*Journal of Biblical Literature*
JTS	*Journal of Theological Studies*
KJV	The King James Version of the Bible
L	Material unique to the Gospel of Luke
LUKE	Material in the Gospel of Luke that is also found in the Gospel of Matthew, i.e., the Q material in Luke
Luke	Material that is found only in the Gospel of Luke, i.e., the L material
Loeb	The Loeb Classical Library
LXX	The Greek translation of the Old Testament, called the Septuagint
M	Material unique to the Gospel of Matthew
MATT	Material in the Gospel of Matthew that is also found in the Gospel of Luke, i.e., the Q material in Matthew
Matt	Material that is found only in the Gospel of Matthew, i.e., the M material
MARK	Material in the Gospel of Mark that is also found in either the Gospel of Matthew, the Gospel of Luke, or both
Mark	Material unique to the Gospel of Mark
NTS	*New Testament Studies*
Q	A hypothetical source used by Matthew and Luke in writing their Gospels, i.e., the material common to Matthew and Luke but not found in Mark

1QH	The Thanksgiving Hymns of the Dead Sea Scrolls
1QS	The Manual of Discipline of the Dead Sea Scrolls
RQ	*Revue de Qumran*
RSV	The Revised Standard Version of the Bible
TDNT	*Theological Dictionary of the New Testament*
ZNW	*Zeitschrift für die Neutestamentliche Wissenschaft*

Preface

IT IS THE COMMON EXPERIENCE of many teachers that they never find exactly the right text to use for their classes. This was my experience also in teaching classes in "The Life and Teachings of Jesus." The present volume makes no pretense of being breathtakingly original. Rather, it is an attempt to place into the hands of students certain material that I believe important for dealing with the teachings of Jesus. Their affirmation of the helpfulness of this work has encouraged me to believe that it may fill a similar need of other teachers as well. It is even my hope that it will help any interested student or general reader to understand better the form and content of Jesus' teaching.

Some readers may object that in Chapter 2 especially no attempt has been made to establish which of the examples listed should be attributed to Jesus and which to the Evangelist or to the church. This omission was intentional. I thought it would be more valuable to place before the reader as large a representative sample as possible from the various Gospel strata. In so doing, I have presented the place in the Gospels where these various forms are found, and the reader must judge in regard to the issue of their *Sitz im Leben*.

In the present work I have used an unusual method to refer to the materials found in the Synoptic Gospels. Through the use of the forms MARK, Mark, MATT, Matt, LUKE, and Luke the reader can see at a glance whether the material referred to is unique to that Gospel or whether it is found in another Synoptic Gospel as well. The reader should review the list of Abbreviations in order to understand the system used in this work. I fully realize that this system may be somewhat confusing at first, but I believe that in a short time the reader will find this system of reference helpful. There are some instances, of course, when it is uncertain whether a passage in Matthew should be attributed to MARK, Q, or M. As a result, it may appear at times that a particular designation is somewhat arbitrary, but in the vast majority of instances such a designation will tell the reader at a glance whether the material in Matthew (or Mark and Luke) has a parallel in another Synoptic Gospel. This system is valid regardless of what solution the reader holds with regard to the Synoptic Problem.

I would like to thank some of the persons who helped to prepare the manuscript for publication. To the faculty secretary, Jean Lindblom, I am especially indebted for the loving care she exercised in the preparation of the original manuscript. I would also like to thank my various teaching assistants for their aid in retyping the manuscript in its final form and for their care in reading the final draft. Lastly, I want to thank my wife, Joan, for her typing and reading of the final manuscript. Above all, however, I want to thank her for her encouragement and help throughout the preparation of the manuscript, for without her assistance the manuscript would never have been written.

All Biblical quotations in this work come from the Revised Standard Version of the Bible unless otherwise specified.

R.H.S.

Chapter 1

JESUS THE TEACHER

IN THE NEW TESTAMENT we find numerous titles used to describe the person and work of Jesus. The total number of titles used is well over forty.[1] Within certain circles some titles tend to be more emphasized than others, and frequently the choice of titles given to Jesus reveals a great deal about the views of that particular circle. One group may emphasize that Jesus was/is the "Prophet"; another the "Savior"; another "Lord"; another the "Messiah"; etc. In some circles, however, the role of Jesus as a teacher has been minimized, partly perhaps because of a reaction to the portrait of Jesus as a teacher which characterized nineteenth-century liberalism. Nevertheless, within the four Gospels one of the titles most frequently used to describe Jesus is "Teacher." This title is used of Jesus forty-five times.[2] Although it is usually used as a title of address, at times it is found on the lips of Jesus as a self-designation:

> But you are not to be called rabbi, for you have one teacher, and you are all brethren. (Matt 23:8; cf. also MATT 10:24–25; John 13:13–14)

The more original Aramaic title of "Rabbi" is used of Jesus some fourteen times.[3] It is the unanimous witness of the Gospel tradition and redaction that one of the prominent functions of Jesus during his public ministry was teaching (Matt 4:23—the Markan parallel in 1:39 uses the word "preaching") and that despite his lack of formal training (MARK 6:2–3; cf. John 7:15) he was correctly recognized as a "Rabbi" (MARK 12:14; cf. John 3:2). Although Jesus had not gone through the normal prescribed course of instruction,[4] his wisdom and manner of teaching resembled that of the other rabbis, so that it was not unnatural to ascribe this title to him.[5] Like other rabbis, Jesus proclaimed the divine law (MARK 12:28–34), taught in the synagogues (MARK 1:21–28, 39; 3:1–6; 6:1–6), gathered disciples (MARK 1:16–20; 3:13–19; cf. John 1:35–51; I Cor 15:5), debated with the scribes (MARK 7:5f.; 11:27–33; 12:13–17,

1

18–27), was asked to settle legal disputes (MARK 12:13–17; Luke 12: 13–15; cf. the postcanonical tradition found in John 7:53 to 8:11), sat as he taught (MARK 4:1; Mark 9:35; Luke 4:20; Matt 5:1; cf. also Luke 2:46), supported his teaching with Scripture (MARK 2:25–26; 4:12; 10:6–8, 19; 12:26, 29–31, 36; Matt 12:40; 18:16), used poetic-didactic techniques to help his disciples memorize,[6] etc.

There were also differences between Jesus and the rabbis in the way he taught, for Jesus often taught in the open fields and countryside as well as in the synagogues (MARK 4:1; 6:32–44; 8:1–9; Mark 2:13; Matt 5:1), and his association with women, tax collectors, sinners, and children (MARK 2:14–17; 10:13–16; MATT 11:16–19; Luke 7:39; 15:1–2) was quite "unrabbinic." The relationship between Jesus and his disciples also differed from that between the rabbis and their disciples. Normally a pupil *(talmid)* was a disciple of the tradition of his teacher, but the disciples of Jesus were exactly that—disciples *of Jesus*. Their message was not just the words of Jesus, although they did "receive" and thus now "delivered" his words; but their message consisted of the person of their teacher as well.

JESUS THE SAGE

The teachings of Jesus possess qualities in common with the teachings of both the wise men and the prophets of the Old Testament, but whereas the prophetic aspect of the teachings of Jesus usually receives its due recognition, there is a tendency to overlook and underestimate the role of Jesus as a sage. The evidence in the Gospels that Jesus taught as a wise man, however, is impressive. His abundant use of proverbs, parables, paradox, metaphor, etc.,[7] witnesses to a similarity between the form of his teachings and that of the wise men. One need only compare the following passages to see that often there is a similarity in content as well:

MATT 5:42

Give to him who begs from you, and do not refuse him who would borrow from you.

Sirach 4:4–6

Do not reject an afflicted suppliant, nor turn your face away from the poor. Do not avert your eye from the needy. (Cf. also 29:1f.; Prov 28:27; Tobit 4:7.)

MATT 24:28

Wherever the body is, there the eagles will be gathered together.

Job 39:30

His [the eagle's] young ones suck up blood; and where the slain are, there is he.

MARK 4:25   IV Ezra 7:25 (II Esdras)

For to him who has will more be   Therefore, Ezra, empty things are for
given; and from him who has not,   the empty, and full things are for the
even what he has will be taken away.   full.

Other examples are: Matt 6:34 with b. Sanhedrin 100b.; MATT 7:1f. with
Pirke Aboth 1:6; 2:4; Luke 14:7–11 with Prov 25:6–7; Matt 11:28–30 with
Sirach 51:23f.; 24:19f.; Prov 1:20f.; 8:1f.[8] Jesus also filled the role of a
wise man, for like the wise men of old he answered questions (cf. I Kings
4:34; 10:1–5; Dan 1:19–21; 2:17–49 with Luke 2:46–47; MARK 10:2;
12:13–34, especially v. 28) and challenged his audience to be wise
(MATT 7:24–27).[9]

Finally, we should note that Jesus spoke of himself as a wise man. In
MATT 12:38–42 we read:

Then some of the scribes and Pharisees said to him, "Teacher, we
wish to see a sign from you." But he answered them, "An evil and
adulterous generation seeks for a sign; but no sign shall be given to
it except the sign of the prophet Jonah. For as Jonah was three days
and three nights in the belly of the whale, so will the Son of man be
three days and three nights in the heart of the earth. The men of
Nineveh will arise at the judgment with this generation and condemn
it; for they repented at the preaching of Jonah, and behold, something greater than Jonah is here. The queen of the South will arise
at the judgment with this generation and condemn it; for she came
from the ends of the earth to hear the wisdom of Solomon, and
behold, something greater than Solomon is here."

In this passage Jesus is portrayed as one greater than both the prophet
Jonah and the wise man Solomon.[10] He is greater than Jonah because
even as Jonah was three days and three nights in a whale and lived, so
Jesus will be three days and three nights in the heart of the earth, i.e., shall
experience death and the grave, and live. In a similar way the parallel
between Jesus and Solomon is best understood as follows: Jesus is greater
than Solomon because even as the wisdom of Solomon was renowned
throughout the world, so the wisdom of Jesus is greater still. Something
greater than Solomon is present because the kingdom of God has come
and its bearer possesses greater wisdom than Solomon.[11]

JESUS THE PROPHET

During his ministry Jesus was also considered by many to be a
prophet[12] (MARK 6:15; 8:28; 14:65; Luke 7:16; Matt 21:11, 46), and Jesus
referred to himself as a prophet when he said:

A prophet is not without honor, except in his own country, and among his own kin, and in his own house. (MARK 6:4)

The people attributed the role of prophet to Jesus for several reasons. One reason is that he worked miracles and signs (Luke 7:16; cf. John 3:2). He also claimed the possession of the Spirit (Matt 12:18; MARK 3:28–30; Luke 4:16–30; cf. John 14:17) by which he was aware that he possessed a divine calling and anointing (Luke 4:18f.; 10:21). Because of this anointing, his message, unlike that of the scribes, was not derived but was immediate. In Jesus once again the people heard the authority of a "Thus says the Lord," for in Jesus one encountered God's new word for that day, "You have heard that it was said. . . . But I say . . ." (Matt 5:21–22, 27–28, 31–32, 33–34, 38–39, 43–44). The message of Jesus was likewise prophetic in the sense that it was concerned with the relationship of God to the course of history both now (MARK 1:15; MATT 16:1–3) and in the future (MARK 13:1f.). Like Jeremiah he could warn of the destruction of Jerusalem (Jer 13; 19; MARK 13:1f.); like Micah he could castigate those who concentrated upon the externals of religion and lost sight of love and justice toward both God and man (Micah 6:6–8; MATT 23:23–28); and like Amos he could become angry at the hypocrisy of the leaders of the nation (Amos 4:1–2; MARK 7:1f.; Mark 3:5, cf. also Isa 29:13). Like the prophets Jesus could foresee that his message would not be greeted any more favorably than theirs, and he likened his future prospects to the fate of the prophets before him:

"Nevertheless I must go on my way today and tomorrow and the day following; for it cannot be that a prophet should perish away from Jerusalem." O Jerusalem, Jerusalem, killing the prophets and stoning those who are sent to you! How often would I have gathered your children together as a hen gathers her brood under her wings, and you would not! (LUKE 13:33–34)

THE LANGUAGE OF JESUS

Although the sayings of Jesus recorded in the New Testament appear in the Greek language, it is apparent from the Gospels that Greek was not his mother tongue. Gustaf Dalman at the turn of the century clearly demonstrated that the native tongue of Jesus was Aramaic. To be more exact, we can say that he spoke *"a Galilean version of western Aramaic"*[13] which differed somewhat from the Aramaic of Judea (MATT 26:73; cf. Acts 2:7). That Jesus spoke Aramaic is evident for several reasons. One reason is that we still possess even in the Greek New Testament a number of Aramaic terms and phrases that come from the lips of Jesus:

Talitha cumi—"Little girl, I say to you, arise" (Mark 5:41)
Eloi, Eloi, lama sabachthani—"My God, my God, why hast thou forsaken me?" (MARK 15:34)
Abba—"Father" (Mark 14:36; cf. Gal 4:6 and Rom 8:15)
Bar—"Son [of Jonah]" (Matt 16:17)
Beel—"Beel [zebul]" (Matt 10:25; MATT 12:27)
Gehenna—"Hell" (MARK 9:47; Mark 9:43, 45; MATT 10:28; Matt 5:22, 29; 23:15, 33)
Cephas—"Peter" (John 1:42)
Mammon—"Money/Property" (MATT 6:24; Luke 16:9, 11)
Pascha—"Passover" (MARK 14:14; Matt 26:2; Luke 22:8, 15)[14]
Rabbi—"Rabbi/Teacher" (Matt 23:7, 8)
Boanerges—"Boanerges/Sons of Thunder" (Mark 3:17)
Raca—"You fool!" (Matt 5:22)
Sabbata—"Sabbath" (MARK 3:4; Matt 12:5, 11)[15]
Sata—"Measures" (MATT 13:33)
Satan—"Satan" (MARK 3:26; 8:33; Mark 3:23; Luke 10:18; 13:16; 22:31)

Along with these Aramaic terms which are still preserved in the Greek New Testament[16] it is also evident to the Aramaic scholar that certain expressions in the Gospels are "Aramaisms" or Greek translations of sayings that were originally Aramaic.[17] A final argument from silence can also be put forward. It is generally accepted that Aramaic was the native tongue of Palestine in the first century. If this is true, then the burden of proof is clearly upon anyone who would seek to deny that the mother tongue of Jesus was Aramaic.

Along with Aramaic, Jesus could also speak and read Hebrew. At one time it was thought that Hebrew was for the most part a dead language in the first century and limited to rabbinic circles, but the discovery of the Dead Sea Scrolls, which are primarily in Hebrew, and of the Bar Cochba correspondence,[18] which is also in Hebrew, has demonstrated that Hebrew was still used extensively at least in certain circles.[19] That Jesus could read Hebrew is evident from Luke 4:16–20, where Jesus read the Hebrew Scriptures in the synagogue at Nazareth. His familiarity with the Hebrew Old Testament[20] also indicates that he must have been able at least to read Hebrew. Furthermore, it is doubtful that Jesus would have been addressed as "Rabbi"[21] unless he were capable of discussing the Hebrew texts.

There have been several attempts to discover certain Hebrew terms on the lips of Jesus which are still preserved in the Greek New Testament. Success has been far more limited here than in the case of Aramaic terms. Some have argued that *amen* (MARK 14:30; Matt 5:26), *Eli* (Matt 27:46 —the Markan parallel in 15:34 has the Aramaic *Eloi*), and *ephphatha* ("Be opened," Mark 7:34) are Hebrew terms, but Joachim Jeremias has pointed out that the former two terms had been absorbed into Aramaic,[22] and thus they have no more significance for understanding the native tongue of the speaker than the use of "eucharist" or "kosher" in America. *Ephphatha* could be a Hebrew term, but this is still not certain. The most certain Hebrew terms in the Gospels are *corban* ("Given to God" [Mark 7:11]) and *-zebul* ("house" [MATT 12:27; Matt 10:25]), but even here it should be noted that the latter term is joined to *Beel*, which is clearly Aramaic, and that *corban* occurs some eighty times in the Old Testament and was a technical term that non-Hebrew-speaking Jews could very well have used.

The third major language spoken in Palestine was Greek. Since the time of Alexander the Great, Hellenistic influence was present in Palestine, and by the first century B.C. the Mediterranean was a "Greek sea." In Egypt already in the second century B.C. the Jewish community there could no longer read the Hebrew Old Testament and thus it was translated into Greek. This famous translation, the Septuagint, or LXX, became the Bible of the Diaspora and the early church. When Paul wrote to the churches in Rome and Galatia he wrote in Greek. In Rome itself, the church fathers wrote in Greek until the time of Tertullian (ca. 150–ca. 220). It is not surprising therefore to discover that Jesus, raised in Galilee of the Gentiles and living only three or four miles from the Greek city of Sepphoris, could probably speak some Greek. There are several incidents during his ministry where his listeners would not have been able to understand either Aramaic or Hebrew, so that he would have had to converse with them in Greek or through an interpreter. Yet we never read in the Gospels of any interpreter being involved. Some occasions when Jesus probably could not have spoken Aramaic or Hebrew are: his visit to Tyre, Sidon, and the Decapolis (Mark 7:31f.); his discussion with the centurion concerning his sick servant (MATT 8:5–13); his conversation with the Syrophoenician woman (MARK 7:24–30), who is described as a Canaanite (Matt 15:22) and a Greek (Mark 7:26), which almost certainly could not have taken place in Aramaic or Hebrew; and his conversation with Pontius Pilate (MARK 15:2f.), which according to the text was carried on without an interpreter and thus must have occurred in Greek.[23]

In summary, it appears certain that the native tongue of Jesus was Aramaic and that this Aramaic differed somewhat from the Aramaic spoken in Judea. It seems also probable that Jesus could read and speak Hebrew and at least speak Greek. It is most doubtful that he would have known Latin, although he might have known certain Latin terms associated with the army and the administration of Rome.[24]

Chapter 2

THE FORM OF JESUS' TEACHING

IT IS EVIDENT from what we have said in the preceding chapter that Jesus was, among other things, an outstanding teacher. Without the use of modern-day audiovisual materials and props he captured the attention of his audience. This ability of Jesus at times even created problems for him. According to MARK 4:1,[1] on one occasion Jesus attracted such a large crowd by his teaching that he had to enter a boat on the Sea of Galilee and teach from it. The miracle of the feeding of the five thousand recorded in MARK 6:30f. was due in part to the fact that the crowd simply forgot about their need for food because of their fascination and interest in the teaching of Jesus (cf. vs. 35–36). The same appears to be true with regard to the feeding of the four thousand (cf. MARK 8:2–3). In the above examples we should note that the crowds are portrayed as gathering not because of any miracles Jesus was performing, for none are mentioned, but because of their interest in the teaching of Jesus.

Why was Jesus such a fascinating teacher? What caused these large crowds to follow him? In reply one might say that it was *what* Jesus said that drew the crowds. With Jesus the voice of prophecy had once again returned to Israel after four hundred years.[2] In the ministry of Jesus the Spirit of God was once again active in Israel (cf. MATT 12:28; Luke 4:16–21). God was once again visiting his people and proclaiming his will. One reason people came to hear Jesus was that many were convinced that God was speaking through Jesus of Nazareth and that what he was saying was indeed the Word of God (cf. Luke 5:1; 11:28; MARK 4:14–20). Yet every Christian teacher and preacher must confess that at times he has proclaimed the same *what*, the same Word of God, that Jesus taught and has been less than exciting. There must therefore be other factors which together with the *what* made Jesus the exciting teacher that he was.

No doubt an additional factor that enters the picture involves the personality of Jesus, for the personality of Jesus gave life and vitality to

7

his message. It was the Word made flesh (John 1:14) which was the medium through which and by which the Word of God came. People loved to listen to Jesus because of the kind of person he was. Publicans, sinners, children, the crowds—all found in Jesus one whom they enjoyed being near. It was therefore not only *what* he taught but also *who* he was that attracted people to hear him. Closely related to this was the authority with which Jesus taught (cf. MARK 1:21–28). Jesus' message, unlike that of the scribes and the rabbis, did not possess a derivative authority from the rabbis of the past but possessed an immediate authority (cf. Matt 5:21–22, 27–28, 31–32, 33–35, 38–39, 43–45), and we should note that the message of Jesus was frequently accompanied by signs and wonders (MARK 1:22, 27, 39; 3:10–11; cf. John 3:2). All of this is of course true. The *what* of his message and the *who*, i.e., the "personality" and "authority," of the messenger all played a part in making Jesus an exciting teacher.

There is still another factor that made Jesus a great teacher, however, which is frequently overlooked. This is the *how*, or the exciting manner in which Jesus taught. The purpose of this chapter is to investigate some of the forms and techniques that Jesus used as the medium for his message.

OVERSTATEMENT

One means by which Jesus sought to capture the attention of his listeners was by overstating a truth in such a way that the resulting exaggeration forcefully brought home the point he was attempting to make. Such overstatement is a characteristic of Semitic speech, and we possess numerous examples of this in the Gospels. In LUKE 14:26, Jesus says:

> If any one comes to me and does not hate his own father and mother and wife and children and brothers and sisters, yes, and even his own life, he cannot be my disciple.

It should be clear to us today, just as it was to Jesus' listeners in the first century, that Jesus was not teaching here that his followers should hate their parents, wives, husbands, children, brothers, sisters, etc. It would be foolish for someone to tell his parents after reading this verse that because of his commitment to Jesus Christ he will seek henceforth to hate them. One need only read Jesus' scathing denunciation of the Pharisees in MARK 7:9f. for dishonoring their parents to see how foolish this would be. Furthermore, the command to love one's enemies (LUKE 6:27) must also include one's parents and friends! The meaning of these words must lie elsewhere. Jesus is using overstatement to make his point. The point he is making is that even natural affection for our loved ones dare not interfere or take precedence over loyalty to him. Most times love and loyalty for Jesus and love and loyalty for parents go hand in hand, but when a choice must be made, natural affections must be set aside out of love for Jesus.[3] Love for Jesus must be so great that any human love, even the most intimate human love, will so pale in comparison that it will appear as "hate." As an off-white paint looks white when compared to a dark color but when compared to a very bright white gives the impression of being "grayish," so too the love of a child for his parents when compared to the love one must have for Jesus becomes "grayish" or "hatish."

Another example of the use of overstatement by Jesus is found in Matt 5:29–30 (cf. also the parallel passage in MARK 9:43–47), where we read:

If your right eye causes you to sin, pluck it out and throw it away; it is better that you lose one of your members than that your whole body be thrown into hell. And if your right hand causes you to sin, cut it off and throw it away; it is better that you lose one of your members than that your whole body go into hell.

Tragically there have been instances in the history of the church in which Christians have interpreted these words literally and mutilated themselves. Yet self-mutilation clearly does not solve the problem, for if one removes his right eye, he is still able to lust.[4] Even the removal of the left eye will not solve the problem, for blind people can still remember and lust, for it is not the eyes that cause us to lust but the "heart."[5] What Jesus was seeking to convey to his listeners by this use of overstatement was the need to remove from their lives anything that might cause them to sin. There is no sin in life worth perishing over. Better to repent of that sin, even if it is as painful as tearing out an eye or tearing off a hand, and enter as a result into the kingdom of God than to cherish that sin and be thrown into hell. Jesus is saying in effect, "Tear out anything in your life that is causing you to sin and keeping you from God."

At this point it may be profitable to consider the question of whether one should interpret the Bible "literally." On occasion we may hear someone claim that the Bible must always be interpreted literally. Yet this itself is an overstatement, for the absence of eye patches on the men in our churches indicates either that they do not interpret Matt 5:29–30 literally or, and this seems less likely, that they have never lusted. What we must be careful to do at times is to distinguish between the "words" of Jesus and the "meaning" Jesus intended to convey by those words. The words Jesus spoke were not intended to be an end in themselves but rather were intended to serve as a vehicle to convey his message. In the majority of instances the words and the meaning are the same, so that a literal fulfillment is meant. In the two examples given above, however, the "words" and the "meaning" are not synonymous, for to take the words literally would be to lose sight of the meaning that Jesus intended those words to convey. To understand the meaning of Jesus' words in certain instances therefore requires that we not take the words literally. Should one interpret the Bible literally? The answer to this question is that we are to take the meaning of the Bible literally. Our conscience is to be bound by the Word of God! Yet the language Jesus used in this teaching was not an end in itself. It was an instrument by which he sought to convey what he meant. It is the meaning of these words, therefore, which we are to seek and which we are to apply to our lives. In this regard it may be appropriate to warn against discovering overstatement on the part of Jesus whenever his statements become unpalatable to us. One can only make effective use of overstatement as a communicative tool when in the great majority of instances there is a close correspondence between word and meaning.[6] Furthermore, we must be careful not to read into the teaching of Jesus our own desires and wishes. We shall only deceive ourselves if we seek to remove the cross of discipleship which Jesus so clearly taught by claiming that Jesus is "overstating" in these instances.[7]

In MATT 5:38–42 we have several examples of overstatement placed side by side:

> You have heard that it was said, "An eye for an eye and a tooth for a tooth." But I say to you, Do not resist one who is evil. But if any one strikes you on the right cheek, turn to him the other also; and if any one would sue you and take your coat, let him have your cloak as well; and if any one forces you to go one mile, go with him two miles. Give to him who begs from you, and do not refuse him who would borrow from you.

With regard to the reference about the coat and cloak it should be noted that in the time of Jesus the normal dress consisted of a tunic, or *chiton*, which in the text above is called a coat but which was worn next to the skin, and an outer garment, or *himation*, which is called a cloak.[8] The literal interpretation of this commandment would result in nudity. Yet Jesus is not primarily concerned here with advocating a style of dress or undress, but by use of overstatement he gives an example of what he means by saying, "Do not resist one who is evil." The disciples of Jesus cannot apply the *ius talionis* but must be willing to endure insult and contempt for their Lord.

Another example of the use of overstatement by Jesus is:

> Judge not, that you be not judged. (MATT 7:1)

Compare, however, Matt 7:6, which says, "Do not give dogs what is holy; and do not throw your pearls before swine, lest they trample them under foot and turn to attack you." How can one be careful not to cast pearls before swine or not to give dogs what is holy unless in some way one judges who the "swine" and the "dogs" are? In another place Jesus says:

Do not think that I have come to bring peace on earth; I have not come to bring peace, but a sword. (MATT 10:34)

Contrast, however, MARK 5:34; Matt 5:9; MATT 10:12–13; Luke 19:42. To these examples can be added:
MARK 10:11 (Certainly the "exception clause" in Matt 5:32 and 19:9 reveals that MARK 10:11 is an overstatement in the eyes of Matthew); 11:24; 13:2
MATT 5:18, 48(?); 6:24; 7:7–8; 10:30(?)
Matt 5:23–24 (Not every Jew lived close enough to Jerusalem to do this), 34a(?); 6:6, 17; 17:20; 18:19; 23:3; 26:52
Luke 10:19

HYPERBOLE

Closely related to Jesus' use of overstatement is his use of hyperbole, for both have in common the use of exaggeration. We shall distinguish the two, however, by the degree of exaggeration involved and define as overstatement a saying that could be understood, although of course incorrectly, as literal in its application or portrayal. In hyperbole the gross exaggeration makes such a literal fulfillment or portrayal impossible. Thus Matt 5:29–30 and MATT 5:38–42 are examples of overstatement, for one could follow literally the advice to cut off his right hand and to give up his coat as well as his cloak. Matt 23:23–24 on the other hand is an example of hyperbole:

Woe to you, scribes and Pharisees, hypocrites! for you tithe mint and dill and cummin, and have neglected the weightier matters of the law, justice and mercy and faith; these you ought to have done, without neglecting the others. You blind guides, straining out a gnat and swallowing a camel!

It is clear that in this statement of Jesus we find once again exaggeration, but here the degree of exaggeration is so great that we have passed beyond overstatement, for one cannot in any way "swallow a camel." Another example of hyperbole is Matt 7:3–5:

Why do you see the speck that is in your brother's eye, but do not notice the log that is in your own eye? Or how can you say to your brother, "Let me take the speck out of your eye," when there is a log in your own eye? You hypocrite, first take the log out of your own eye, and then you will see clearly to take the speck out of your brother's eye.

Although the meaning of Jesus' words is clear and the impression most forceful, it is evident that the example is impossible even to imagine, for who possesses an eye large enough to contain a "log"?

A third example is found in Matt 6:2–4:

Thus, when you give alms, sound no trumpet before you, as the hypocrites do in the synagogues and in the streets, that they may be praised by men. Truly, I say to you, they have their reward. But when you give alms, do not let your left hand know what your right hand is doing, so that your alms may be in secret; and your Father who sees in secret will reward you.

Again it is evident that we are dealing here with an example of hyperbole, for how can the left hand be ignorant of what the right hand is doing? Ultimately, of course, we must acknowledge that the "right hand" and the "left hand" do not refer to parts of man's anatomy but to man as a totality considered from the particular aspect of his giving alms, for "hands" cannot know anything. It is man as a thinking and reasoning unity who knows. Understood in this way, the hyperbole becomes almost a paradox, for the believer acting consciously in the giving of alms should not know consciously what he is doing!

A final example that can be mentioned is MARK 10:24b–25:

Children, how hard it is to enter the kingdom of God! It is easier for a camel to go through the eye of a needle than for a rich man to enter the kingdom of God.

The hyperbolic element in this passage involves the comparison between a rich man entering the kingdom of God and a camel going through the eye of a needle. The numerous attempts that have been made to soften the force of this saying by arguing that the eye of the needle was the name of a small gate in the walls of Jerusalem through which a camel could only pass with great difficulty or that the term "camel" (kamelos) is a mistranslation of the Aramaic word Jesus used and should really be "cable" (kamilos) are quite unnecessary and beside the point. Jesus is clearly using hyperbolic language,[9] for while it is simply impossible for a large animal to go through the eye of a needle, it is not altogether impossible for a rich man to be saved.[10]

PUN

Another form Jesus used in his teaching was the pun. A pun is a play on words in which either homonyms (like-sounding words) suggest two or more different meanings or the same word may have two different meanings. The term "paronomasia" is sometimes used to describe the former aspect of a pun. The use of puns by Jesus is frequently not evident in an English, or for that matter any other, translation of the Bible. In fact, such puns are not usually evident in the Greek New Testament in the case of homonyms, since the pun was originally uttered by Jesus in Aramaic and the corresponding homonyms in Aramaic rarely remain homonyms in translation. In order to discover such puns, the scholar must translate the sayings in our Gospels back into the Aramaic which Jesus spoke. When this is done we discover several possible examples of puns in the Gospels. One such example is Matt 23:23–24:

> Woe to you, scribes and Pharisees, hypocrites! for you tithe mint and dill and cummin, and have neglected the weightier matters of the law, justice and mercy and faith; these you ought to have done, without neglecting the others. You blind guides, straining out a gnat and swallowing a camel!

In this saying, which we also discussed as an example of hyperbole, Jesus contrasts the meticulous concern of the Pharisees in straining their beverages lest they swallow a gnat and become ceremonially unclean, for the gnat was unclean according to the law of Moses (cf. Lev 11:41f.), with their rejection of mercy, justice, and love in their dealings with their fellowman. The pun in this saying is not at all evident in an English translation, but in the corresponding Aramaic there is a clear play on words. Jesus in his example is not merely contrasting the size of a camel with the size of a gnat, for why not contrast a gnat with a tree or with an elephant? Jesus' use of the term "camel" is due to the fact that in Aramaic "camel" and "gnat" both look alike and sound alike. In Aramaic the word for gnat is *galma* and the word for camel is *gamla*. Jesus in his example made a pun. What he said was, "You blind guides, you strain out a *galma* but turn around and swallow a *gamla!*"

A second example of the use of puns by Jesus is found in Matt 16:18:

> And I tell you, you are Peter, and on this rock I will build my church, and the powers of death shall not prevail against it.

The play on words in this saying is evident also in Greek, where the terms *petros* and *petra* are used respectively for "Peter" and "rock." In Aramaic, however, the play on words is even more pronounced, since the same term *kepha* served as both the proper name and the word for rock. A third example is found in John 3:8:

The wind blows where it wills, and you hear the sound of it, but you do not know whence it comes or whither it goes; so it is with every one who is born of the Spirit.

In Aramaic the word for "wind" and the word for "spirit" are the same —*ruha*.[11] Jesus therefore is saying, "The *ruha* blows where it wills, and you hear the sound of it . . . ; so it is with every one who is born of the *ruha.*" Another example is found in LUKE 9:59–60:

To another he said, "Follow me." But he said, "Lord, let me first go and bury my father." But he said to him, "Leave the dead to bury their own dead."

In this difficult saying the same word "dead" is used with a double meaning and means: "Let the spiritually dead bury their own physically dead." A similar kind of pun is found in MARK 1:17, where a play is made on the idea of "fishers [of fish]" and "fishers [of men]" and MARK 8:35, where "save" and "lose" have a physical meaning and a spiritual meaning. Other possible examples of puns are: MARK 4:9 (The term "hear" is used in the double sense of "hearing" and "heeding"); MARK 9:35b–37 (It has been suggested that since the Aramaic word *talya* can mean both "child" and "servant" this figurative action of Jesus may contain a pun);[12] MARK 10:31 (The terms "first" and "last" possess a double meaning); and MARK 13:28 (Since the Aramaic term *qayta*, which is translated "summer," can also mean "summer harvest," some scholars believe that the term may indicate both a time of year and a time of judgment along the lines of Amos 8:1–2).[13]

SIMILE

A simile is an explicit comparison between two things that are essentially unlike each other and that are introduced by a connective such as "like," "as," or "than" or by a verb such as "seems." In our discussion of parables[14] it will become evident that some similes in the Gospels are parables, for a parable in essence is a simile. When a simile is expanded into a picture, the result is a similitude. When it is expanded into a story, the result is a story-parable.[15] It is obvious, therefore, that our division between a simile and a parable will be somewhat arbitrary. What we have included here as examples of simile are those similes not usually listed as parables.[16] Some examples of simile are:

Behold, I send you out as sheep in the midst of wolves; so be wise as serpents and innocent as doves. (MATT 10:16)

For as Jonah was three days and three nights in the belly of the whale, so will the Son of man be three days and three nights in the heart of the earth. (MATT 12:40)

If you had faith as a grain of mustard seed, you could say to this sycamine tree, "Be rooted up, and be planted in the sea," and it would obey you. (LUKE 17:6)

O Jerusalem, Jerusalem, killing the prophets and stoning those who are sent to you! How often would I have gathered your children together as a hen gathers her brood under her wings, and you would not! (LUKE 13:34)

Woe to you, scribes and Pharisees, hypocrites! for you are like white-washed tombs, which outwardly appear beautiful, but within they are full of dead men's bones and all uncleanness. (MATT 23:27)

In the above examples the elements of comparison and dissimilarity are quite clear. The believer is likened to sheep and told to be like serpents in wisdom and doves in their blamelessness, whereas the unbelievers are likened to wolves; Jesus' resurrection is likened to Jonah's stay in the belly of a fish; the believer's faith is likened to a seed; Jesus' desire to gather the people of Jerusalem to himself is likened to a mother hen gathering her chicks to herself; and the stately appearance of the Pharisees with their inner spiritual corruption is likened to tombs that outwardly are impressive but inwardly contain corruption! Other examples of the use of simile by Jesus can be found in:
MARK 10:15 (?); 14:48
MATT 6:29; 24:27
Matt 13:40, 43; 25:32–33
Luke 10:18; 11:36; 21:34–35; 22:31
Cf. John 15:6
MATT 24:37; Matt 18:17; Luke 17:28–30 might also be listed here, but there is a question as to whether the "unlikeness" or dissimilarity in the comparison is great enough to warrant their being described as similes.

METAPHOR

A metaphor, like a simile, is a comparison between two essentially unlike things. In contrast to a simile, however, where an explicit comparison is made ("The eye is like a lamp for the body"), the metaphor makes an implicit comparison ("The eye is the lamp of the body").[17] The Gospels contain numerous examples of such figures of speech, for Jesus was fond of using analogies. As in the case of the simile, so here also it is evident that some metaphors can also be defined as parables, so that any absolute distinction between the two is impossible.[18] The following are some examples of metaphors in the Gospels:

Take heed, beware of the leaven of the Pharisees and the leaven of Herod. (MARK 8:15)

You are the salt of the earth; but if salt has lost its taste, how shall its saltness be restored? (Matt 5:13; cf. MARK 9:49–50)

You are the light of the world. A city set on a hill cannot be hid. Nor do men light a lamp and put it under a bushel, but on a stand, and it gives light to all in the house. Let your light so shine before men, that they may see your good works and give glory to your Father who is in heaven. (Matt 5:14–16)

The harvest is plentiful, but the laborers are few; pray therefore the Lord of the harvest to send out laborers into his harvest. (MATT 9:37–38)

You serpents, you brood of vipers, how are you to escape being sentenced to hell? (Matt 23:33; cf. also Matt 12:34)

At that very hour some Pharisees came, and said to him, "Get away from here, for Herod wants to kill you." And he said to them, "Go and tell that fox, 'Behold, I cast out demons and perform cures today and tomorrow, and the third day I finish my course.'" (Luke 13: 31–32)

In the above examples the point of comparison is evident. Although they are things essentially unlike, Jesus compares the teaching (Matt 16:12) and the hypocrisy (Luke 12:1) of the Pharisees to leaven or sour dough. In the other examples, Jesus likens: his followers to salt and the light of the world; the masses who follow him to a harvest; the scribes and Pharisees to serpents and vipers; and Herod to a fox. As in a simile, there is here a comparison of unlike things, but the omission of the connectives "as," "like," "than," etc., makes the comparison even more forceful. Other examples of metaphors can be found in:

MARK 1:17; 2:17, 19–20; 3:34–35; 7:26–27; 8:34; 10:38–39; 14:22, 24, 36

MATT 6:22; 7:13–14, 16–20; 10:16, 34; 11:7

Matt 7:6, 15; 10:6; 11:29–30; 15:13; 16:18; 19:12

Luke 9:62; 12:35, 49; 15:32; 23:31.[19]

It should be pointed out that in some of the examples listed above, there may be a question as to whether a specific comparison contains sufficiently unlike figures to be properly considered a metaphor. In such cases the decision is of course somewhat arbitrary.

Another type of metaphor found in the Gospels that should be mentioned at this point is the familiar "I am" sayings found in the Gospel of John.[20] Some of these are:

I am the bread of life; he who comes to me shall not hunger, and he who believes in me shall never thirst. (John 6:35)

I am the light of the world; he who follows me will not walk in darkness, but will have the light of life. (John 8:12)

I am the vine, you are the branches. He who abides in me, and I in him, he it is that bears much fruit, for apart from me you can do nothing. (John 15:5)

Other examples are found in John 6:41, 48, 51; 9:5; 10:7, 9, 11, 14; 14:6; 15:1.

PROVERB

As has been mentioned above,[21] the teaching of Jesus stands at times in continuity with the wisdom tradition of the Middle East. Nowhere is this more evident than in his use of proverbs. For our purpose we shall speak of "proverbs" in a broad sense and include proverbs, maxims, and aphorisms. We shall therefore define a proverb as a terse pithy saying that contains in a striking manner a memorable statement. At times such a statement gives advice on moral behavior and becomes an ethical maxim (cf. MATT 6:22, 24; 7:12; Luke 16:10). At times such a statement is an ingeniously worded paradox (cf. MARK 4:25; 10:43; Luke 14:11). Generally a proverb is characterized by succinctness and consists of one sentence.

Judging what sayings of Jesus are proverbs again involves an element of arbitrariness, but it would appear that the following could be considered proverbs:

For where your treasure is, there will your heart be also. (MATT 6:21)

Therefore do not be anxious about tomorrow, for tomorrow will be anxious for itself. Let the day's own trouble be sufficient for the day. (Matt 6:34)

. . . all who take the sword will perish by the sword. (Matt 26:52)

If a kingdom is divided against itself, that kingdom cannot stand. (MARK 3:24)

A prophet is not without honor, except in his own country, and among his own kin, and in his own house. (MARK 6:4)

No one who puts his hand to the plow and looks back is fit for the kingdom of God. (Luke 9:62)

In addition to these can be listed:

MARK 2:17, 21, 22; 3:27; 4:21, 22, 25; 7:15; 8:35, 36, 37; 9:40, 50; 10:25, 27, 31, 43–44

Mark 2:27

MATT 6:22–23a, 23b, 24, 27; 7:12, 17–18; 8:22; 10:24, 26, 27; 11:19c; 12:30, 34b, 35; 15:14; 24:28; 25:29

Matt 5:14; 10:16b

Luke 4:23 (The term "proverb" translates the Greek word *parabole* here); 5:39; 9:62; 11:47; 12:15, 48b; 14:11; 16:10; 20:18; the Agrapha in Acts 20:35

Cf. John 3:3, 12, 20; 4:23; 12:25, 36; 15:14

RIDDLE

The use of riddles by Jesus has numerous parallels in the Old Testament. The most famous example of a riddle in the Bible is probably Samson's riddle in Judg. 14:14:

Out of the eater came something to eat.
Out of the strong came something sweet.

It is evident from Prov 1:5–6 that the riddle, which involves a match of wits in which the individual is challenged to discover the concealed meaning of the saying, is a typical form of wisdom saying. It is also clear that riddles can have certain similarities with proverbs, metaphors, similes, and parables.[22] Yet since the term *parabole* is never used with regard to the riddles listed below, we shall list them as a separate category.

From the days of John the Baptist until now the kingdom of heaven has suffered violence, and men of violence take it by force. (MATT 11:12)

I will destroy this temple that is made with hands, and in three days I will build another, not made with hands. (MARK 14:58)

Go and tell that fox, "Behold, I cast out demons and perform cures today and tomorrow, and the third day I finish my course. Nevertheless I must go on my way today and tomorrow and the day following; for it cannot be that a prophet should perish away from Jerusalem." (Luke 13:32b–33)

Other riddles can be found in:

MARK 2:19; 9:12–13
MATT 10:34; 11:11 (This is also a paradox.)
MATT 13:52; 19:12
LUKE 22:36[23]

PARADOX

In the sayings of Jesus we possess several statements that are paradoxical in nature. By this we mean that the statements appear contradictory. This apparent contradiction must be understood in the light of the beliefs and values present in Jesus' day among his contemporaries, for in another context with different values and beliefs his statements might not appear contradictory. The words of Jesus in MARK 10:43–44 concerning the "greatest" being a servant and the "first" being slave of all are not necessarily paradoxical in certain Christian circles where the values and example of Jesus have been accepted and promoted, but in a context of "might makes right" they certainly are. In Nazi Germany with its superman concept it is therefore a paradox; in a deaconess order that is dedicated to service for mankind it would not necessarily appear so. For some Christians, therefore, several sayings of Jesus may not appear as paradoxical as they must have appeared in their original situation in the life of Jesus. That is, to the degree that our values and beliefs correspond to Christian teaching some of these statements may not appear paradoxical, but spoken in a context that is not shaped by Christian values they are. We therefore shall define a paradox as a statement that may appear to be self-contradictory, absurd, or at variance with common sense but that, upon investigation or when explained, may prove to be logical.

We have already seen in our discussion of the proverbial sayings of Jesus that some of them are paradoxical in nature.[24] To these can also be added:

MARK 4:22, 25; 6:4; 8:35; 10:43–44
MATT 25:29
Luke 4:23; 14:11

Some other examples of Jesus' use of paradox are:

And he sat down opposite the treasury, and watched the multitude putting money into the treasury. Many rich people put in large sums. And a poor widow came, and put in two copper coins, which make a penny. And he called his disciples to him, and said to them, "Truly,

I say to you, this poor widow has put in more than all those who are contributing to the treasury. For they all contributed out of their abundance; but she out of her poverty has put in everything she had, her whole living." (MARK 12:41-44)

Woe to you, scribes and Pharisees, hypocrites! for you are like white-washed tombs, which outwardly appear beautiful, but within they are full of dead men's bones and all uncleanness. So you also outwardly appear righteous to men, but within you are full of hypocrisy and iniquity. (Matt 23:27-28)

In the two examples given, the paradox is apparent. Despite the apparent contradiction, the gift of a penny was greater in God's sight than the much larger sums contributed by the rich, and the beautiful veneer of dress and outward piety of the Pharisees and scribes, who were the religious leaders of Israel, was at variance with their inner corruption and spiritual poverty. Other examples of paradox can be found in:

MARK 10:14, 31, 45 (We must be careful not to let our Christian environment and background dull the paradox of the Son of man–Messiah being a servant.)

Mark 9:35

MATT 10:34-36 (In the context of such teaching as the beatitudes this does appear to be contradictory); 10:39; 11:11, 22-24; 23:25

Matt 5:5, 6:17; 7:15; 18:3-4 (One must keep in mind that children were not thought of in Judaism as innocent unspoiled children of God. On the contrary, they were thought of as under the fall of Adam, possessing an evil inclination [yetzer] and without help until they became a bar mitzvah at the age of thirteen and received the help of the law[25]); 21:31; 23:11, 24 ("blind guides")

Luke 12:3 (cf. Matt 10:27), 32 (?); 14:11, 24; 18:14

Cf. John 12:25

A FORTIORI

An a fortiori statement is not so much a figure of speech as a type of argument in which the conclusion follows with even greater logical necessity than the already accepted fact or conclusion previously given. In other words, granted the first fact or conclusion, the subsequent conclusion is more certain and inescapable still. An example of this is found in MATT 7:9-11:

Or what man of you, if his son asks him for bread, will give him a stone? Or if he asks for a fish, will give him a serpent? If you then, who are evil, know how to give good gifts to your children, how much

more will your Father who is in heaven give good things to those who
ask him!

In this example Jesus moves from the accepted fact that those present
who are evil (due to Adam's fall, in contrast to God's holiness, as the Day
of Atonement reveals, etc.) still manage to do good for their children to
the more certain conclusion that God, who is wholly good and is in fact
their heavenly Father, will even more certainly do what is good for his
children. In Matt 10:25 (cf. John 15:20) Jesus states:

It is enough for the disciple to be like his teacher, and the servant
like his master. If they have called the master of the house Beelzebul,
how much more will they malign those of his household.

Here the argument is also clear. If the Jewish leadership (cf. v. 17) and
the political authorities (cf. v. 18) have persecuted the master of the
house, how much more free will they feel to persecute the less powerful
members of his household. In other words, if Jesus' authority and influence were not enough to protect him from persecution, how much more
will his followers who have less authority and influence be persecuted.
A third, even more familiar example is found in MATT 6:28–30:

Consider the lilies of the field, how they grow; they neither toil nor
spin; yet I tell you, even Solomon in all his glory was not arrayed like
one of these. But if God so clothes the grass of the field, which today
is alive and tomorrow is thrown into the oven, will he not much more
clothe you, O men of little faith?

Here we once again find the "If . . ., how much more . . ." which so
frequently characterizes the *a fortiori* argument. The contrast between the
lowly flower and the pinnacle of God's creation clearly indicates that the
God who so carefully adorns and cares for these lowly flowers will of
course adorn and care for his children! Other examples of this type of
argument can be found in:
MARK 2:23–28 (If David did something even more forbidden than
plucking grain on the Sabbath and was not rebuked, how much more
can the Son of man, who is greater than David and Lord of the Sabbath,
allow his disciples to pluck grain.)
MATT 6:23 (?), 26; 10:28, 29–31; 12:11–12
Luke 13:15–16; 14:1–6 (Here the final conclusion is not stated but
implied); 18:1–8
Cf. John 13:14

IRONY

Defined narrowly, irony is the subtle use of contrast between what is actually stated and what is more or less wryly suggested. Frequently there is present a feigned sense of ignorance. When such a contrast becomes crude or heavy-handed and as a result loses much of its cleverness it becomes sarcasm. In this narrow sense a statement or expression is ironic when its intended meaning is the opposite of the literal meaning of the statement. A possible example of irony in this narrow sense may be LUKE 7:35 (cf. also John 10:32). In a broader sense, however, irony can refer to an event or result that is opposite to what one would normally expect. In this last respect irony resembles and may make use of paradox. We shall somewhat arbitrarily distinguish between irony and paradox by including in the former a comic element, even if that element is sometimes tragic. It is primarily in this second broader sense that we can speak of Jesus' use of irony. Some possible examples of irony in the Gospels are:

> When it is evening, you say, "It will be fair weather; for the sky is red." And in the morning, "It will be stormy today, for the sky is red and threatening." You know how to interpret the appearance of the sky, but you cannot interpret the signs of the times. (MATT 16:2–3)

> And he told them a parable, saying, "The land of a rich man brought forth plentifully; and he thought to himself, 'What shall I do, for I have nowhere to store my crops?' And he said, 'I will do this: I will pull down my barns, and build larger ones; and there I will store all my grain and my goods. And I will say to my soul, Soul, you have ample goods laid up for many years; take your ease, eat, drink, be merry.' But God said to him, 'Fool! This night your soul is required of you; and the things you have prepared, whose will they be?' " (Luke 12:16–20)

In the former passage we have an example of irony and not just paradox, because an amusing, if nevertheless tragic, element is present in that the Pharisees and the Sadducees, though religious, are able to interpret the physical signs and predict their implications but are unable to see God's signs in the ministry of Jesus and interpret their significance. In the latter passage there is an unexpected and surprising conclusion to the elaborately made plans of the rich man. He never reckoned that he might not live as long as his plans demanded! Other possible examples of irony are:

MARK 2:17c (Some scholars see this as ironic in the light of Jesus' call of all men to repentance. Cf. also Luke 15:7.)

Mark 7:9
MATT 11:16–19; 22:1–10; 23:29–35
Luke 10:29–37 (The irony here is the reversal of roles—the devout of Israel [the Levite and the priest] are the villains and the despicable half-breed and rebel [the Samaritan] is the hero); 13:33; 15:7; 16:1–9, 19–31 (The irony of this parable may be lost on us if we forget that in Israel wealth was often thought of as a sign of divine blessing and poverty a sign of the absence of such blessing); 18:9–14
Cf. John 3:10; 5:43[26]

THE USE OF QUESTIONS

Several centuries before the time of Jesus, Socrates made famous the use of questions as a method of instruction. Socrates was well aware that by his use of questions he forced his audience to become involved in the learning process. Jesus also knew the merits of this "Socratic" method and frequently used questions in his teaching. He used questions in a variety of ways and in a variety of situations. One way in which Jesus used questions was by drawing from his audience the correct answer he sought. By being drawn out from the listeners rather than by simply being declared by Jesus, the correct answer was more convincingly and permanently impressed upon their minds. The turning point of his entire ministry centered around an incident in Caesarea Philippi, where Jesus asked his disciples:

"Who do men say that I am?" And they told him, "John the Baptist; and others say, Elijah; and others one of the prophets." And he asked them, "But who do you say that I am?" Peter answered him, "You are the Christ." And he charged them to tell no one about him.
And he began to teach them that the Son of man must suffer many things, and be rejected by the elders and the chief priests and the scribes, and be killed, and after three days rise again. And he said this plainly. (MARK 8:27–32)

Other examples of this use of the question by Jesus are:
MARK 8:19–20; 10:38
Matt 17:25; 21:31
Luke 10:36; 22:35
A more polemical use of this method of teaching was Jesus' use of the counterquestion. Like a fortiori, the counterquestion is a method of argumentation. The counterquestion shall be defined here as a question raised by Jesus in response to (a) a question which is either stated or implied, or (b) a situation to which he is expected or feels constrained to

reply. In contrast, however, to his use of rhetorical questions, Jesus always expected from his audience a verbal or at least a mental response to his counterquestion. Generally Jesus made use of the counterquestion as a response to a hostile attitude or question from his audience. Some examples of this are:

> Again he entered the synagogue, and a man was there who had a withered hand. And they watched him, to see whether he would heal him on the sabbath, so that they might accuse him. And he said to the man who had the withered hand, "Come here." And he said to them, "Is it lawful on the sabbath to do good or to do harm, to save life or to kill?" (MARK 3:1–4)[27]

> And they came again to Jerusalem. And as he was walking in the temple, the chief priests and the scribes and the elders came to him, and they said to him, "By what authority are you doing these things, or who gave you this authority to do them?" Jesus said to them, "I will ask you a question; answer me, and I will tell you by what authority I do these things. Was the baptism of John from heaven or from men? Answer me." And they argued with one another, "If we say, 'From heaven,' he will say, 'Why then did you not believe him?' But shall we say 'From men'?"—they were afraid of the people, for all held that John was a real prophet. So they answered Jesus, "We do not know." And Jesus said to them, "Neither will I tell you by what authority I do these things." (MARK 11:27–33)

Other examples of Jesus' use of the counterquestion are:
MARK 2:6–9, 19, 25–26; 3:23–24; 10:3, 37–39 (In this instance no hostility is present in the question that Jesus is asked); 12:14–16
MATT 12:27–29
Matt 12:11–12
Luke 7:39–42; 10:26 (?); 13:15–16; 14:1–5

The most frequent use Jesus made of the question was as a rhetorical device. By using a rhetorical question Jesus sought not so much to draw a verbal response from his audience as to produce an effect. At times the effect sought was the assent of his listeners to what he was saying, for Jesus assumed that only one answer was possible (cf. MARK 3:23; MATT 7:16; Luke 15:8). At times the rhetorical question sought to add solemnity and weight to a statement (cf. MARK 8:36–37; MATT 5:13). On occasion Jesus used this device to force his listeners to think about what he or they were saying (cf. MARK 3:33; 10:18; 12:35–37), and on occasion Jesus even used it as a method of revealing his exasperation and frustration (cf. MARK 9:19; Luke 12:14). Some examples of Jesus' use of the rhetorical question are:

And he said, "With what can we compare the kingdom of God, or what parable shall we use for it?" (MARK 4:30)

Salt is good; but if the salt has lost its saltness, how will you season it? (MARK 9:50)

Or what man of you, if his son asks him for bread, will give him a stone? Or if he asks for a fish, will give him a serpent? (MATT 7:9-10)

Additional examples can be found in:
MARK 4:13, 21, 40; 7:18-19; 8:12, 17-18, 21; 11:17; 12:9, 24-26; 13:2; 14:6, 37, 41, 48
MATT 5:46-47; 6:25-30; 7:3-4; 10:29; 11:7-9, 23; 18:12; 24:45
Matt 12:34; 14:31; 23:17-19, 33; 26:53-54
LUKE 6:39; 11:40; 12:51, 56; 13:20
Luke 2:49; 6:34, 46; 11:5-7; 13:2-4; 14:28, 31; 16:11-12; 17:7-9, 17-18; 18:7-8; 22:27

PARABOLIC OR FIGURATIVE ACTIONS

There are a number of occasions in the Gospels where the teaching of Jesus was mediated through a particular action. On these occasions the action of Jesus was not simply an illustration to support a verbal utterance, but the teaching was nonverbal and contained in the action itself. The action of Jesus in these instances was often carefully planned and thought out in order to serve as an instructive tool for his disciples and his audience. A verbal commentary or explanation might follow, but the action itself was parabolic and was meant to teach. An example of such an action is found in Luke 19:1-6:

He entered Jericho and was passing through. And there was a man named Zacchaeus; he was a chief tax collector, and rich. And he sought to see who Jesus was, but could not, on account of the crowd, because he was small of stature. So he ran on ahead and climbed up into a sycamore tree to see him, for he was to pass that way. And when Jesus came to the place, he looked up and said to him, "Zacchaeus, make haste and come down; for I must stay at your house today." So he made haste and came down, and received him joyfully.

Jesus' action in eating at the home of Zacchaeus, a tax collector, is not to be thought of as simply an act of friendship. Verse 5 implies that Jesus knew who Zacchaeus was and in the light of MATT 11:5 Jesus' behavior must be understood as a prophetic action and sign of the coming of the kingdom of God. According to MATT 11:4-5, all the examples of Jesus' healing and of his preaching to the rejected of Israel are symbolic actions claiming both the presence of the kingdom of God and the messianic character of Jesus. The kingdom of God has come in the ministry of Jesus, for the forgiveness of God is now offered even to tax collectors! The protest of the crowd in Luke 19:7 indicates that they saw in Jesus' action symbolic significance:

> And when they saw it they all murmured, "He has gone in to be the guest of a man who is a sinner."

In a parallel incident recorded in MARK 2:15–16 this is brought out even more clearly by the question "Why does he eat with tax collectors and sinners?" Although the scribes and the Pharisees (MARK 2:16) did not understand the significance of Jesus' action, they did know that the action was significant!

Another example of such a parabolic action on the part of Jesus is found in MARK 3:14–19:

> And he appointed twelve, to be with him, and to be sent out to preach and have authority to cast out demons: Simon whom he surnamed Peter; James the son of Zebedee and John the brother of James, whom he surnamed Boanerges, that is, sons of thunder; Andrew, and Philip, and Bartholomew, and Matthew, and Thomas, and James the son of Alphaeus, and Thaddaeus, and Simon the Cananaean, and Judas Iscariot, who betrayed him.

The selection of the twelve disciples is, of course, symbolic and has as its background the twelve sons of Jacob from whom the twelve tribes of Israel stem. By his action Jesus indicated that he was now establishing a "new Israel" which was both a continuation of the old and yet the beginning of a new people of God. It was important that there be twelve disciples and not seven or ten, and it is therefore not surprising that the first action of the early church was to choose a replacement for Judas (Acts 1:15–26), for the symbolic significance of the number must be retained.

Other examples of such parabolic actions are found in:
MARK 1:9 (Whatever the difficulties that the question "Why did Jesus experience John's baptism of repentance?" may raise, the symbolic significance of the action is evident); 2:18; 4:10–12; 6:32–44 and 8:1–10; 10:33–34 (This must be viewed in the light of Luke 13:33); 11:1–10; 11:12–14;[28] 11:15–17; 14:61a and 15:5; cf. also MARK 6:11 (Here Jesus tells his disciples to perform the symbolic act of shaking the dust off their feet if a village refuses to hear their message) and 9:36–37 (Here the action may be more illustrative in nature)

Cf. also John 2:1–11; 4:4–42 (Note v. 27); 11:38–44 (Note vs. 25–27); 13:1–11 (Note vs. 12–17)[29]

POETRY

In the Gospels there are numerous examples of poetry in the sayings of Jesus. This poetry is frequently unrecognized because these sayings lack rhyme, but what is basic to poetry is not so much rhyme but rhythm. The poetry of Jesus is to be found not in its rhyme but in its rhythmic balance. The expression frequently used to describe this kind of poetry is *parallelismus membrorum,* or parallelism in the members. Generally four kinds of parallelism are listed. These are: synonymous, antithetical, synthetic, and step or climactic parallelism.[30] To these shall be added one additional classification—chiasmic parallelism.

SYNONYMOUS PARALLELISM

In this form of parallelism there is a correspondence between the various lines or strophes, and the following lines are essentially synonymous repetitions of the first. Some examples of this are:

If a kingdom is divided against itself, that kingdom cannot stand. And if a house is divided against itself, that house will not be able to stand. (MARK 3:24–25)

Ask, and it will be given you;
seek, and you will find;
knock, and it will be opened to you.
For every one who asks receives,
and he who seeks finds,
and to him who knocks it will be opened. (MATT 7:7–8)

But I say to you that hear,
Love your enemies,
do good to those who hate you,
bless those who curse you,
pray for those who abuse you. (LUKE 6:27–28)

In each of these examples it is evident that the following line (or lines) essentially repeats the meaning of the first line. In the first example we have a twofold parallelism, whereas in the second example we have a threefold parallelism that is repeated twice, and in the third example we have a fourfold parallelism. In most instances, however, the parallelism is twofold. Other examples of this kind of parallelism are found in:
MARK 2:21–22; 3:4, 28; 4:22, 30; 8:17, 18; 9:43–47; 10:38, 43–44;

13:24–25
MATT 5:39–40, 46–47; 6:25; 12:30, 41–42; 13:16
Matt 7:6; 10:24–25, 41; 23:29
LUKE 17:26–29
Luke 6:37, 38; 12:48b; 13:2–5; 15:32; 19:43–44; 23:29
Cf. also John 3:11; 6:35, 55; 12:31; 13:16

ANTITHETICAL PARALLELISM

In antithetical parallelism the second line contrasts with the first and instead of providing a synonymous parallel provides an antithetical one. Examples of this type of rhythmic parallelism are more numerous than that of all the others combined.[31] Some examples of this type of poetry are:

For whoever would save his life will lose it;
and whoever loses his life for my sake and the gospel's will save it.
(MARK 8:35)

He who is faithful in a very little is faithful also in much;
and he who is dishonest in a very little is dishonest also in much.
(Luke 16:10)

So, every sound tree bears good fruit,
but the bad tree bears evil fruit. (Matt 7:17)
A sound tree cannot bear evil fruit,
nor can a bad tree bear good fruit. (MATT 7:18)

In the latter example it should be noted that each verse is an example of antithetical parallelism and that together both verses are also an example of such parallelism. From the examples given above and those listed below it is clear that whereas in synonymous parallelism we may have two, three, or even four parallel strophes, in antithetical parallelism we usually have just two. Some additional examples of this kind of parallelism can be found in:

MARK 2:19–20; 3:28–29 (Whereas each individual verse is an example of synonymous parallelism, together they provide an example of antithetical parallelism); 4:25; 7:8, 15
MATT 6:22–23, 24; 10:32–33; 13:16–17
Matt 5:19; 6:2–3, 5–6; 22:14
Luke 6:21a and 25a; 21b and 25b; 7:44, 45, 46, 47
Cf. also John 3:6, 12, 17, 20–21[32]

SYNTHETIC PARALLELISM

In this form of parallelism, which is sometimes called formal or constructive parallelism, the thought of the second line neither repeats nor contrasts the thought of the first line but rather supplements and brings it to completion. As a result, in this form of parallelism the second line causes the thought of the first line to continue and flow on further. C. F. Burney[33] gives as examples of this kind of parallelism:

They do all their deeds to be seen by men;
for they make their phylacteries broad and their fringes long,
and they love the place of honor at feasts and the best seats in the
   synagogues,
and salutations in the market places,
and being called rabbi by men.
But you are not to be called rabbi, for you have one teacher, and you
   are all brethren.
And call no man your father on earth, for you have one Father, who
   is in heaven.
Neither be called masters, for you have one master, the Christ. (Matt
   23:5–10—The Matthean account is dependent here on both
   MARK 12:38b–39 and Matthew's special source M.)

I came to cast fire upon the earth; and would that it were already
   kindled!
I have a baptism to be baptized with; and how I am constrained until
   it is accomplished!
Do you think that I have come to give peace on earth? No, I tell you,
   but rather division. (Luke 12:49–51)[34]

STEP OR CLIMACTIC PARALLELISM

In step parallelism the second strophe takes up the thought of the first strophe and advances the thought one additional step. As a result, the second line is not simply a synonymous repetition of the first but is an additional, although related, statement that brings the entire saying to its climax and completion. Step parallelism is therefore similar to synthetic parallelism in that the second strophe advances the thought of the first, but in step parallelism the thought is brought to a climax. Some examples of step parallelism are:

Whoever receives one such child in my name receives me;

and whoever receives me, receives not me but him who sent me. (MARK 9:37)

Think not that I have come to abolish the law and the prophets;

I have come not to abolish them but to fulfill them. (Matt 5:17)

He who receives you receives me,

and he who receives me receives him who sent me. (MATT 10:40)

Other examples can be found in:
Mark 2:27–28
MATT 6:22, 23 (Together MATT 6:22–23 are an example of antithetical parallelism); 10:34; 12:28 (?), 29 (?)
Matt 6:6, 34
LUKE 10:16 (The LUKAN parallel to MATT 10:40 is listed because it is somewhat different from MATT 10:40.)
Cf. John 6:37; 8:32; 10:11; 11:25; 13:20; 14:2–3, 21; 16:7, 22

CHIASMIC PARALLELISM

The fifth and final form of *parallelismus membrorum* that should be mentioned is chiasmic parallelism. A chiasmus is an inversion of parallel statements that results in a pattern a b // B A. Such patterns are frequently found in the letters of Paul,[35] but the appearance of such chiasmic parallelism in the Gospels frequently goes unnoticed. Often such parallelism is also antithetical in nature and is listed therefore as an example of antithetical parallelism. Examples of chiasmic parallelism are shown on the opposite page.

In the first two examples below it is clear that we have examples of chiasmic parallelism as well as antithetical parallelism, for in MATT 23:12 the (a) = "exalts," (b) = "humbled," (B) = "humbles," and (A) = "exalted," and in MARK 8:35 (a) = "save his life," (b) = "lose it," (B) = "loses his life," and (A) = "save it." The third example is also chiasmic parallelism, for the "dogs" of (a) corresponds with "turn to attack you" of (A) whereas the "swine" of (b) corresponds to "trample them under foot" of (B).

whoever exalts himself (a)

will be humbled, (b)

and whoever humbles himself (B)

will be exalted. (A) (MATT 23:12)

For whoever would save his life (a)

will lose it; (b)

and whoever loses his life for my

sake and the gospel's (B)

will save it. (A) (MARK 8:35)

Do not give dogs what is holy; (a)

and do not throw your pearls before

swine, (b)

lest they trample them under foot (B)

and turn to attack you. (A)

(Matt 7:6)

Other examples of such parallelism can be found in:
MARK 2:22 (wine—old wineskins // the skins burst—wine lost); 9:43 (hand—cut it off // maimed—two hands), 47; 10:31 (first—last // last —first)
Mark 2:27 (sabbath—man // man—sabbath); 9:45
MATT 6:24 (hate—love // devoted—despise)
One cannot help being impressed with the numerous examples of parallelism found in the Gospels. That at times an Evangelist or the church modified the sayings of Jesus in both form and content is of course true, but certainly Burney and Jeremias are correct in emphasizing that such parallelism, especially antithetical parallelism, is characteristic of the teaching of Jesus. One can also conclude that Jesus must have spent time in organizing his teaching and preparing its form, for unless we conclude

that this poetic parallelism simply popped into his mind on the spur of the moment, we must conclude that Jesus carefully prepared "for his classes."[36] Perhaps some of the time that he sought to be alone was not only for the purpose of prayer (cf. MARK 1:35; 6:46; Luke 5:16; 6:12; 9:28) but also to prepare *what* and *how* he would teach.

Another conclusion that can be drawn from Jesus' use of parallelism is that he no doubt used such forms in order to help his listeners remember more easily what he taught. The extent to which Jesus taught as a rabbi is much debated,[37] but it is clear from his use of various kinds of parallelism that he did place his teaching in a form that would be easy to memorize. It is evident that in so doing Jesus intended that his listeners would not only be challenged to decision by his words but also retain them in their memory. For the disciples as well as the multitudes, this was important in that both before his resurrection[38] and after it the disciples would proclaim the Gospel "of" (both in the sense of "from" as well as "about") Jesus. By placing his message in such poetic form Jesus demonstrated that his listeners were to preserve and retain his teachings in their minds as well as in their hearts.

CONCLUSION

The purpose of this chapter was to describe some of the forms Jesus used to present his message.[39] In seeking to understand his message, we must keep in mind that Jesus was born, raised, and lived in a culture quite different from the scientific culture of our day. In an age that is concerned with computer accuracy we must be careful not to demand the same kind of interest and concern on the part of Jesus. Jesus' words were not meant to be photographic portraits or laboratory descriptions for a scientific culture but rather impressionistic stories and sayings that sought in a storytelling culture to describe the arrival of the kingdom of God.[40] Scientific description is merely one method of describing reality. At times and in certain contexts it is no doubt the best method, but in other contexts it is inappropriate, or, at least, less suitable than others. A scientist does not use scientific terminology to describe his love to his beloved even if she, too, is a scientist! His language is far more impressionistic and must be understood as impressionistic language.

The form or vehicle that Jesus used to convey his message is clearly not the language of twentieth-century science but rather the metaphorical, exaggerating, impressionistic language of a culture that loved to tell stories. The vehicle that Jesus used to convey his message is, however, not an end in itself. It is the message far more than the medium that is paramount, for that message was and is the Word of God. To understand that Word correctly, however, requires us to understand the vehicle that Jesus used. This does not mean, as some maintain, that we are to distinguish between the message of Jesus and the divine message contained in Jesus' message.[41] We are not dealing here with different levels of revelation in Jesus' message but rather with the need to distinguish the form of that message and its content. This distinction is most evident in Jesus' use of overstatement and hyperbole, but to varying degrees it is also applicable in his use of other forms as well. It is evident that Jesus thought that his hearers were capable of making this distinction and expected them to do so, and it is likewise evident that the Gospel writers thought the same and expected the same from their readers.

Chapter 3

THE PARABLES OF JESUS

THE MOST FAMOUS FORM used by Jesus in his teaching is the parable. It has frequently been pointed out that this is the most characteristic element of his teaching, for not less than thirty-five percent of his teaching in the Synoptic Gospels is found in parabolic form.[1] The fame and popularity of the parables of Jesus is such that we possess in the English language many expressions whose origins are clearly derived from the parables. We speak of "being a good Samaritan" (Luke 10:29–37), "wheat and tares" (Matt 13:24–30), "counting the cost" (Luke 14:28), wasting one's livelihood in "riotous living" (Luke 15:13), leaving things until the "eleventh hour" (Matt 20:6), hiding one's light "under a bushel" (MARK 4:21), "burying one's talent" (MATT 25:25), "passing by on the other side" (Luke 10:31–32), etc., frequently without realizing that in so doing we are actually quoting from the parables of Jesus.[2]

THE DEFINITION OF A PARABLE

The importance of the parables and the amount of parabolic teaching we possess in the Gospels is generally recognized. To most people, however, it is far from clear what a parable is! In church school we frequently teach that a parable is "an earthly story with a heavenly meaning." Sometimes a parable is defined as a "short fictitious story that teaches a moral or religious principle." The Greek word *parabole* means essentially "a comparison." The two most basic forms of comparison are the simile and the metaphor. The difference between the two lies in the fact that whereas a metaphor contains an implied comparison or likeness (The fox knew just what to do), the simile contains a stated likeness (The thief like a fox knew just what to do).[3] Another way of stating this is that a metaphor suggests a comparison, whereas a simile explicitly states such a comparison. If one expands a simile, the result is a similitude. If one

34

strings together a series of metaphors, the result is an allegory. Basic to the classical Greek understanding of a parable is this idea of analogy. A parable, by this way of thinking, is an analogy. It may be brief or extended but it is generally an analogy used in an illustrative way.

In seeking to understand the way in which Jesus defined or understood a parable, however, we find it more profitable to understand the Old Testament and rabbinic idea of what a parable is than that of the classical Greek writers, for Jesus was far more influenced by the former than by the latter. In the Septuagint the term *parabole* translated the Hebrew word *mashal* in all but two instances (Eccl 1:17; Sirach 47:11). Since the term that Jesus used for parable was *mashal*, not *parabole*, it is therefore from the Hebrew conception of what a *mashal* is that we should seek to understand how Jesus would have understood a parable. In the Old Testament the term *mashal* had a wide range of meanings and could refer to any of the following:

Proverb. In I Sam 24:13 we read:

As the proverb [*mashal*] of the ancients says, "Out of the wicked comes forth wickedness. . . ."

Compare also I Sam 10:12; Ezek 12:22–23; 16:44; 18:2–3.

Satire, Taunt, or *Word of Derision.* When the Lord appeared to Solomon in I Kings 9, he warned Solomon that if the people of Israel turned aside from following him, they would

. . . become a proverb [*mashal*] and a byword among all peoples. (I Kings 9:7)

Compare also Deut 28:37; Num 21:27–30; II Chron 7:20; Ps 69:11; Isa 14:4; Hab 2:6.

Riddle. In Ezek 17:2 the Lord speaks to the writer and says:

Son of man, propound a riddle, and speak an allegory [*mashal*] to the house of Israel.

Compare also Ps 49:4; 78:2; Prov 1:6; and especially Hab 2:6, where *mashal*, or "taunt," is almost a synonym for the Hebrew *hidah*, or "riddle."

Story Parable or *Allegory.* In Ezek 24:2–5 we read:

Son of man, write down the name of this day, this very day. The king of Babylon has laid siege to Jerusalem this very day. And utter an allegory [*mashal*] to the rebellious house and say to them, Thus says the Lord GOD:

Set on the pot, set it on,
   pour in water also;
put in it the pieces of flesh,
   all the good pieces, the thigh and the shoulder;
   fill it with choice bones.
Take the choicest one of the flock,
   pile the logs under it;
boil its pieces,
   seethe also its bones in it.

Compare also Ezek 20:49 to 21:5; 17:2–10; and II Sam 12:1–4; 14:1–11; Isa 5:1–7. In the latter three examples the term *mashal* does not appear. Nevertheless, it is evident that they are all examples of story parables or allegory, and if defined would have been called *mashal*. The presence of allegory in the Old Testament *mashal* should be especially noted since the question of whether any of the parables of Jesus are allegories or contain allegorical details is much debated.[4]

In the light of the broad usage of the term *mashal* in the Old Testament as well as in the rabbinic writings it is not surprising to find that the term *parabole* in the Gospels also refers to a great variety of different figures of speech. It can refer to:

Metaphor or *Figurative Saying*. In his debate with the Pharisees over the issue of ritual cleanness Jesus states:

Hear me, all of you, and understand: there is nothing outside a man which by going into him can defile him; but the things which come out of a man are what defile him. (MARK 7:14–16)

In the next verse we read:

And when he had entered the house, and left the people, his disciples asked him about the *parable*. (MARK 7:17, italics added)

Compare also Luke 5:36–39, where the term *parabole* is used even though it does not appear in the Markan or Matthean parallel.

Proverb. In Luke 4:23 we find a proverb that is specifically referred to as a parable:

And he said to them, "Doubtless you will quote to me this *proverb* [*parabole*], 'Physician, heal yourself. . . .' " (Italics added)

Compare also MARK 3:23–24 and Luke 6:39.

Similitude. The similitude is in essence an expanded simile. Whereas in a simile Jesus compares an object (faith) to a grain of mustard seed (MATT 17:20), in a similitude Jesus compares an object (the kingdom of God) to a grain of mustard seed which . . . (MARK 4:30–32). Here rather than a simple simile we have a simile that is now expanded into a picture. We shall follow Eta Linnemann's description of a similitude as a comparison involving typical regular events, i.e., a likening of something (like the kingdom of God) to daily occurrences.[5] The manner in which many of these similitudes begin should be noted in this regard: "What man of you" (LUKE 15:4), "Which of you" (Luke 11:5), "What father among you" (LUKE 11:11), etc. This clearly reveals their general nature. An example of a similitude is found in Mark 4:26–29:

> The kingdom of God is as if a man should scatter seed upon the ground, and should sleep and rise night and day, and the seed should sprout and grow, he knows not how. The earth produces of itself, first the blade, then the ear, then the full grain in the ear. But when the grain is ripe, at once he puts in the sickle, because the harvest has come.

Compare also MARK 4:30–32; MATT 13:33; 18:12–14; LUKE 11:11–13; Luke 15:8–10; 17:7–10.

Story Parable. In contrast to the similitude the story parable refers to an interesting singular incident that occurred one time.[6] The manner in which many of these stories begin should also be noted: "There was a rich man" (Luke 16:1), "A man had two sons" (Matt 21:28), "A man once gave a great banquet" (LUKE 14:16), "In a certain city there was a judge" (Luke 18:2), etc. Here it is evident that in contrast to the similitude we are dealing with a specific rather than a general occurrence. An example of a story parable is found in Matt 21:28–31:

> What do you think? A man had two sons; and he went to the first and said, "Son, go and work in the vineyard today." And he answered, "I will not"; but afterward he repented and went. And he went to the second and said the same; and he answered, "I go, sir," but did not go. Which of the two did the will of his father?

Compare also MATT 25:14–30; Matt 25:1–13; LUKE 14:16–24; Luke 15:11–32; 16:1–9; 18:2–8.

Example Parable. There is a great deal of similarity between the story parable and the example parable, so that they could be combined together under the former designation, but we shall again follow Linnemann's description and distinguish between a parable that is used as an analogy (a story parable) and one that is used as an example.[7] An example of this type of parable is found in Luke 12:16–21:

> The land of a rich man brought forth plentifully; and he thought to himself, "What shall I do, for I have nowhere to store my crops?" And he said, "I will do this: I will pull down my barns, and build

larger ones; and there I will store all my grain and my goods. And I will say to my soul, Soul, you have ample goods laid up for many years; take your ease, eat, drink, be merry." But God said to him, "Fool! This night your soul is required of you; and the things you have prepared, whose will they be?" So is he who lays up treasure for himself, and is not rich toward God.

Compare also Matt 18:23–35; Luke 10:29–37; 14:7–14; 16:19–31; 18: 9–14.

Allegory. In an allegory the subject is described by circumstances and details that indicate that the subject as well as the circumstances and details refer to something else. An allegory is therefore a guise under which the intention of the story is different from what it first appears. In an allegory the details of the story are not simply local coloring to fill out the story, as in the story and example parables, but are of great importance and must be "interpreted." There has been a great deal of resistance since the work of Adolf Jülicher[8] to seeing any allegorical elements in the parables of Jesus. This was a natural overreaction to the allegorical method of interpretation of the early church.[9] It is now generally recognized that the *a priori* exclusion of allegory from Jesus' teaching is illegitimate. Whether or not Jesus used allegory cannot be determined on *a priori* grounds but can be determined only by observing the text. It would appear that some parables possess undeniable allegorical elements. Linnemann lists MATT 22:2–14 as the only sure example of allegory in the Gospels:[10]

> The kingdom of heaven may be compared to a king who gave a marriage feast for his son, and sent his servants to call those who were invited to the marriage feast; but they would not come. Again he sent other servants, saying, "Tell those who are invited, Behold, I have made ready my dinner, my oxen and my fat calves are killed, and everything is ready; come to the marriage feast." But they made light of it and went off, one to his farm, another to his business, while the rest seized his servants, treated them shamefully, and killed them. The king was angry, and he sent his troops and destroyed those murderers and burned their city. Then he said to his servants, "The wedding is ready, but those invited were not worthy. Go therefore to the thoroughfares, and invite to the marriage feast as many as you find." And those servants went out into the streets and gathered all whom they found, both bad and good; so the wedding hall was filled with guests.
>
> But when the king came in to look at the guests, he saw there a man who had no wedding garment; and he said to him, "Friend, how did you get in here without a wedding garment?" And he was speechless. Then the king said to the attendants, "Bind him hand and foot, and

cast him into the outer darkness; there men will weep and gnash their teeth." For many are called but few are chosen.

Compare also MARK 4:3–9 and 13–20; 12:1–12; Matt 13:24–30 and 36–43. In contrast to the Old Testament (Judg 9:8f.; II Kings 14:9), the parables of Jesus include no fables.

It is evident from the above that while the most famous parables of Jesus are either story or example parables, not all parables are "earthly stories with heavenly meanings." On the contrary, a parable may be a simile, a metaphor, or a proverb in brief or expanded form. This makes defining what is and what is not a parable difficult if not impossible. It might be convenient to limit the term *parabole* to story and example parables, but the New Testament does not do so. It might be more reasonable, on the other hand, to list all similes and metaphors as parables, since every metaphor presupposes a simile, a similitude and a story parable result from the expansion of a simile, and an allegory results from running together several metaphors. But then what about proverbs? Are all proverbs to be considered parables as well? It would seem best therefore to define a parable somewhat loosely to include proverbs, similes, metaphors, and similitudes, as well as story and example parables and allegories, thus allowing an overlapping of the various forms.[11] An estimate of the number of parables in the Synoptic Gospels will of course vary according to the estimate of how many similes, metaphors, and proverbs are legitimate parables. In general the estimates range somewhere between fifty-five and sixty-five.[12]

JESUS' USE OF PARABLES

A critical question that must be raised at this point, because the Gospels themselves raise it, is why Jesus taught in parables. According to the popular definition of a parable as an illustratory story, one would have to answer this question by saying that Jesus used parables primarily to illustrate his message. That some parables are illustratory is of course self-evident. We have even defined one group of parables as "example parables." There is an extremely important passage in Mark, however, that seems to contradict this explanation. This *crux interpretum*, found in MARK 4:10–12, reads as follows:

And when he was alone, those who were about him with the twelve asked him concerning the parables. And he said to them, "To you has been given the secret of the kingdom of God, but for those outside everything is in parables; so that [*hina*] they may indeed see but not perceive, and may indeed hear but not understand; lest [*mepote*] they should turn again, and be forgiven."

It is evident why this passage has been much debated,[13] for whereas in Isa 6:9–10, which is here quoted, the saying seems to describe the result (so that) of Isaiah's preaching, in MARK 4:12 it seems to describe the intent (in order that) of Jesus' teaching in parables. In other words, Mark seems to be saying that Jesus taught in parables *in order that* his readers might not understand, so that they could not repent and be forgiven. Unfortunately the translation of the *hina* as "so that" by the RSV instead of "in order that" tends to minimize the intent character of the *hina*.

Scholars have sought to explain this difficult passage in a number of ways. Some have sought to remove some of the harshness of the saying by interpreting the *hina* as "so that as a result" instead of "in order that" which is the more usual meaning of *hina*.[14] We have already mentioned that the RSV does this. This, however, not only is contrary to the usual meaning of the term but also is contradicted by the *mepote*, or "lest," found in v. 12, for this "lest" seems to indicate that the *hina* of this same verse is to be understood as revealing the intent of Jesus in teaching in parables. Other scholars have interpreted the *hina* as *hoi*, or "who," arguing that the *hina* here in Mark is a mistranslation of *de* in Aramaic, which Jesus spoke.[15] According to this reconstruction, Jesus, like Isaiah, was simply referring to the result of his teaching in parables. The passage by this reconstruction would read something like this: "To you has been given the secret of the kingdom of God, but for those outside *who* see but do not perceive and hear but do not understand everything appears in parables (riddles)." Even if one were to adopt this reconstruction, we still have the problem of the *mepote*, or "lest"! Some scholars have therefore argued that both the *hina* and the *mepote* are inauthentic, i.e., they were never uttered by Jesus but are a Markan or pre-Markan construction along Pauline lines which was then read back onto the lips of Jesus. Still other scholars have argued that the saying is authentic but occurred in a different context in the ministry of Jesus and refers to his teachings in general. The latter solution, however, instead of abating the problem simply increases its scope to all the teachings of Jesus unless like Jeremias we combine this suggestion with still another. Jeremias argues that this saying is in fact misplaced and that the *hina* expresses God's purpose, but "in the case of divine decisions purpose and fulfillment are identical."[16] According to this interpretation, the *hina* should be translated "in order that" but the meaning is "so that." Nevertheless what takes place (not perceiving and understanding) cannot simply be accidental but somehow fits in the divine purpose.

As it stands in Mark, the meaning of the passage is clear.[17] Even if one translates the *hina* as a final particle, i.e., as "so that," we still have the *mepote* ("lest") as well as the *dedotai* ("it is given") to deal with. The latter clearly states that those outside have not been given the secret of the kingdom of God and thus lack the ability to understand the parables. The parables are therefore not self-evident illustrations; they were never meant to be! Nevertheless, the question still remains, Why did Jesus teach in parables? There may be several reasons. One was to conceal his teaching from those "outside." It must be kept in mind that in the first *Sitz im Leben*[18] there were present opponents of Jesus who continually sought to find fault with him and his message and to acquire information that would be helpful in discrediting him in the eyes of the people as well as in the eyes of Rome. A message on the coming of the kingdom of God could easily be misunderstood or misused by his opponents.[19] By his use of parables Jesus made it more difficult for his opponents to bring such accusations against him. It is probable that Jesus preferred the title "Son of man" over that of Christ (Messiah) for a similar reason, for the latter title had many political and militaristic connotations and was thus liable to be misunderstood, whereas this was not the case with the title "Son of man."[20] The coming of the kingdom of God could be misunderstood in a similar way. By the Romans this could very well have been interpreted as a military or at least a political threat and challenge. As a result, Jesus frequently used parables to protect himself from such misunderstandings by "those outside."

Yet MARK 4:10–12 says more than this. It seems to say that it was the intention of Jesus to withhold his message from "those outside," in order that they might neither perceive nor understand nor turn and be forgiven. The passage is a difficult one to understand. Yet it is obvious to anyone studying the parables of Jesus that they are far from self-evident illustrations. Even the disciples of Jesus, "those given the secret of the kingdom of God," at times did not understand them. This is evident in the parable of the soils itself (MARK 4:13; cf. also Mark 4:34; MARK 7:14–18; Matt 13:36). The fact that for centuries the real meaning of the parables has been lost through allegorical interpretation and ignorance of the *Sitz im Leben* of Jesus also indicates that the parables are not self-evident illustrations. There are, furthermore, other sayings of Jesus that are parallel to MARK 4:10–12. In MATT 11:25–27, Jesus says:

> I thank thee, Father, Lord of heaven and earth, that thou hast hidden these things from the wise and understanding and revealed them to babes; yea, Father, for such was thy gracious will. All things have been delivered to me by my Father; and no one knows the Son except

the Father, and no one knows the Father except the Son and any one to whom the Son chooses to reveal him.

In Rom 11:25–32 the apostle Paul seeks to explain the unbelief of Israel in part at least by attributing this unbelief to the sovereign hardening of Israel by God, so that as a result the offer of salvation might be extended to the Gentiles. It may be unwarranted to read this interpretation into MARK 4:10–12, but as it stands the passage in Mark does seem to indicate that one of the reasons Jesus taught in parables was to conceal his message on the kingdom of God from "those outside."

A second possible reason for the use of parables by Jesus appears to contradict the first. Jesus used parables to illustrate and reveal his message to his followers. Certainly the parable of the good Samaritan illustrates "who is my neighbor" (Luke 10:29) in a most unforgettable way, even as the story of the prodigal son illustrates the love of God for sinners and his joyous welcome of the repentant in a heart-moving manner. There is therefore truth in the view that some parables at least are meant to "illustrate." Yet frequently the meaning of a parable was only available to the disciples to whom "privately . . . he explained everything" (Mark 4:34).

A third possible reason for Jesus' use of parables may have been to disarm his listeners. The famous parable of Nathan (II Sam 12:1f.) about the poor man's ewe lamb is a perfect Old Testament example of this. When the prophet Nathan approached David and told the king this parable, he was able to speak to David's situation and to his heart before David could build up any defense mechanism. Then when the message of the parable was revealed[21] it was too late for David to rationalize his actions or seek to defend himself. He had already pronounced judgment. In a similar way the parables of Jesus often disarmed his opponents, so that frequently they listened to him without raising a shield of defense only to find out too late that the parable was in effect directed toward them. An example of this is found in MARK 12:1–11 after which Mark comments, "And they tried to arrest him, but feared the multitude, for they perceived that he had told the parable against them." In this regard one should also compare Luke 15:1–2 and the resultant trilogy of parables.

THE SOURCE OF THE MATERIAL FOR JESUS' PARABLES

Where did Jesus obtain the illustrations and examples that he incorporated into his parables? As one reads the parables, one is struck by their real-life, down-to-earth character. Behind them lie the everyday experiences that Jesus had as a child, youth, and young man in Nazareth. One summer he observed two men building homes for themselves in Nazareth. The one man was wise and took great care in preparing his foundation on the bedrock; the other was in a hurry and foolishly built his home directly upon the sandy soil. When the rainy season came, the rains beat against both houses. The house on the rock stood firm, whereas the house on the sand had its foundation washed away and collapsed. Later on in his ministry Jesus remembered that incident and likened men's response to his word in a similar way. To heed the Word of God which he taught was to be like the wise man and build one's life on a firm foundation. To disobey would be to suffer disaster (MATT 7:24–27). On another occasion Jesus observed a farmer sowing seed and noticed that the results were dependent on the kind of soil the seed fell upon. In his own sowing of the Word of God he observed a similar result. His wealthy listeners did not respond favorably because of their delight in riches (MARK 4:18–19; cf. MARK 10:17–27); the people in Jerusalem were hardhearted; yet in Galilee there was often fertile soil for his preaching (MARK 4:1–20).[22]

Jesus was no doubt observant as a child and saw in incidents occurring around him examples which he later incorporated into his parables. The beauty of the lilies demonstrated for him God's loving concern for his creation (MATT 6:28–30). One day perhaps his mother sewed a patch of new material upon a tear in his old tunic, and after the garment was washed the shrinking of the new piece caused the older surrounding material to tear even worse. He remembered this and later in his ministry thought that any attempt to combine the Old Testament age with the new age (the kingdom of God) which he was bringing was like trying to sew a new piece of cloth to an old piece. It simply was not possible (MARK 2:21). The smallness of the mustard seed in contrast to its resultant product also impressed him. Yes, he later thought, the kingdom of God is like that. How insignificant it is now in the eyes of the world. Rome has no idea of what is happening, but when God brings to completion in the last day what he has now begun, how great it will be (MARK 4:30–32). Some scholars have even suggested that the parable of the lost coin (Luke 15:8–10) may have come out of an experience in his own home when his mother once lost a coin.

The material for Jesus' parables and teaching came therefore primarily from his own observations and experiences in the rural environment of Galilee. It is interesting to note that the apostle Paul also drew examples from his experiences in daily life, but in contrast to the rural imagery of Jesus, Paul drew his examples from a cosmopolitan environment. Paul therefore tends to speak of running a race, fighting a good fight, being a good soldier, the legal terminology of the courts, the theater, commerce, travel by sea, etc.[23]

THE AUTHENTICITY OF THE PARABLES

It is with the parables more than with any other form of Jesus' teaching that scholars are confident that we truly possess the actual teachings of Jesus.[24] Even the more radical Biblical critics agree that the parables, while subject to later modification, stem from Jesus and are not creations of the early church. There are several reasons for this. One reason is that the parables meet the "criterion of dissimilarity."[25] Stated simply, the criterion of dissimilarity argues that if a teaching (or in this case a form of teaching) attributed to Jesus could not have been derived either from the Judaism of Jesus' day or from the early church it must be authentic, i.e., it must stem from Jesus himself. This tool possesses certain weaknesses in that by definition it must ignore all the teachings of Jesus that he held in common with Judaism and that the early church emphasized.[26] Nevertheless, this tool is helpful in establishing a minimum of authentic material that scholars can agree upon. The parables of Jesus meet this criterion in that

we find nothing to be compared with the parables, whether in the entire intertestamental literature of Judaism, the Essene writings, in Paul, or in Rabbinic literature.[27]

We might add that we find no real parallel to Jesus' use of parables in the entire New Testament, excluding, of course, the Gospels, and in the early church fathers. This indicates that "no one" was creating parabolic stories in the early church, and thus it is difficult to argue that the parables are creations of the early church read back into the ministry of Jesus.

A second reason for acknowledging the authenticity of the parables is their Palestinian flavor. Even in the present form of the parables, this Palestinian flavor is still apparent. The unique practice of the Palestinian farmer in the time of Jesus manifests itself in the parable of the sower and the soils (MARK 4:1–20). A farmer today reading this parable might come to the conclusion that the farmer in the parable who sowed his seed indiscriminately on paths, in weeds, on rocky ground, as well as on good soil, was a rather poor as well as a wasteful farmer, but this description shows well the fact that the parable comes out of a Palestinian environment, for in Palestine the sowing of the seed preceded the plowing.[28] The path would eventually be plowed, and the weeds plowed under, and the fact is that it is not always easy to tell where the ground is rocky, because there is usually some soil covering the rock. The parable clearly arose in a Palestinian environment, and we are therefore able to trace the origin of the parable if not to Jesus at least to his environment.

Another example of the Palestinian, and in this case the Galilean, flavor of the parables is the parable of the vineyard (MARK 12:1–12). The reading of this parable often raises the natural question of why the tenants of the vineyard could ever think that killing the son would result in their possessing the vineyard. Yet placed back into the rather unique Galilean context in which absentee landlords were not uncommon and where there was much agrarian discontent, this does make sense. The coming of the son would be construed as indicating that he was the new heir due to the death of the father and that he had now come to renew the lease. His death in turn would leave the vineyard ownerless and "possession [by the tenants of course] is nine-tenths of the law"! The hiring of the servants in the parable of the laborers in the vineyard (Matt 20:1–16) likewise betrays a Palestinian environment, for elsewhere in the Roman Empire farming was usually done with the help of slaves rather than hired servants.

A third reason for acknowledging the authenticity of the parables is that in language and content they are closely related to the other sayings of Jesus which most scholars agree were uttered by Jesus. Most scholars today hold that such themes as the kingdom of God,[29] the Fatherhood of God,[30] the offer of salvation to publicans and sinners, and the emphasis on the internal motivation and not just the external appearance of an action[31] stem from Jesus, and these themes are continually found in the parables. In the light of the above, there is therefore general agreement among scholars that when we come to the parables of Jesus we arrive at the bedrock of his teachings.

THE INTERPRETATION OF THE PARABLES[32]

At first thought it might appear that there would be no need to discuss how to interpret the parables of Jesus, for such parables as the good Samaritan and the parable of the talents are self-explanatory. Yet are they self-explanatory? A history of the interpretation of the parables clearly proves otherwise.

THE EARLY CHURCH FATHERS (TO 540)

During this period the leading exegetes of the early church tended to interpret the parables in the manner of classical Greek allegorical interpretation. Some examples of the latter are the treatment of Homer's Olympian heroes, whose actions all too often left much to be desired and were therefore allegorized, and Philo's allegorization of the Old Testament whereby he sought to demonstrate that the faith of Israel was in harmony with the best of Greek philosophy.[33] Irenaeus (ca. 130–ca. 200) provides several examples of this allegorical treatment of the parables. In the parable of the hidden treasure (Matt 13:44) he interprets the field as representing the Scriptures and the treasure as representing Christ.[34] In his treatment of the parable of the laborers in the vineyard (Matt 20:1–16) he interprets the first call as referring to those called at the beginning of creation, those receiving the second call (third hour) as referring to those "after this," i.e., those under the old covenant, those receiving the third call (sixth hour) as referring to those present "after the middle of time," i.e., those present during the ministry of Christ, those receiving the fourth call (ninth hour) as referring to Irenaeus' contemporaries, and those receiving the last call (eleventh hour) as referring to those who will be present at the end time. He furthermore interprets the vineyard as symbolic of righteousness, the householder as symbolic of the Spirit of God, and the denarius as symbolic of the knowledge of the Son of God which in turn is immortality.[35]

Tertullian (ca. 160–ca. 220) allegorized the parable of the prodigal son as follows: the elder son represents the Jew who is envious of God's offer of salvation to the Gentile; the father is God; the younger son is the Christian; the inheritance is the wisdom and natural ability to know God which man possesses as his birthright; the citizen in the far country is the devil; the swine are the demons; the robe is the sonship lost by Adam through his transgression; the ring is Christian baptism; the feast is the Lord's Supper; and the fatted calf slain for the prodigal is the Savior at the Lord's Supper.[36]

With Origen of Alexandria (ca. 185–ca. 254) this method of allegorical interpretation became a "science." Origen maintained that the Scriptures contained a threefold sense, for even as Paul in I Thess 5:23 spoke of the body, soul, and spirit of man, so Origen saw the Scriptures as consisting also of a "body" (the *literal* sense of the text), a "soul" (the *moral* or *tropological* sense of the text), and a "spirit" (the *spiritual* sense of the text).[37] When applied to the parable of the mustard seed (MARK 4:30–32), this means that the mustard seed refers to three things. On the literal level it refers to the mustard seed itself. On the moral level it refers to faith, but on the spiritual level it refers to the kingdom of God. Origen also allegorized the parable of the laborers in the vineyard (Matt 20:1–16) and interpreted the first call as referring to the period between Creation and Noah, the second call as the period between Noah and Abraham, the third call as the period between Abraham and Moses, the fourth call as the period between Moses and Joshua, and the fifth call as the period between Joshua and the time of Christ. The householder also is seen as

representing God and the denarius as representing salvation.[38]
Probably the most allegorized parable of all has been the parable of the
good Samaritan (Luke 10:30–35). It reads as follows:

> A man was going down from Jerusalem to Jericho, and he fell among
> robbers, who stripped him and beat him, and departed, leaving him
> half dead. Now by chance a priest was going down that road; and
> when he saw him he passed by on the other side. So likewise a Levite,
> when he came to the place and saw him, passed by on the other side.
> But a Samaritan, as he journeyed, came to where he was; and when
> he saw him, he had compassion, and went to him and bound up his
> wounds, pouring on oil and wine; then he set him on his own beast
> and brought him to an inn, and took care of him. And the next day
> he took out two denarii and gave them to the innkeeper, saying,
> "Take care of him; and whatever more you spend, I will repay you
> when I come back."

To arrive at the deeper spiritual sense, Origen allegorized the parable.
The result was the following:[39]

The man going down to Jericho	= Adam
Jerusalem from which he was going	= Paradise
Jericho	= This world
Robbers	= Hostile influences and enemies of man such as the thieves and murderers mentioned by Jesus in John 10:8
Wounds	= Disobedience or sins
Priest	= Law
Levite	= Prophets
Good Samaritan	= Christ
Beast	= Body of Christ
Inn	= Church
Two denarii	= Knowledge of the Father and the Son
Innkeeper	= Angels in charge of the church
Return of good Samaritan	= Second coming of Christ

Later on, Augustine (354–430) allegorized the parable in an even more
fantastic way. The results of his "exegesis" were as follows:[40]

The man going down to Jericho	= Adam
Jerusalem from which he was going	= City of Heavenly Peace
Jericho	= The moon which signifies our mortality
Robbers	= Devil and his angels

Stripping him	= Taking away his immortality
Beating him	= Persuading him to sin
Leaving him half dead	= Due to sin, he was dead spiritually, but half alive, due to knowledge of God
Priest	= Priesthood of the OT (Law)
Levite	= Ministry of the OT (Prophets)
Good Samaritan	= Christ
Binding of wounds	= Restraint of sin
Oil	= Comfort of good hope
Wine	= Exhortation to spirited work
Beast	= Body of Christ
Inn	= Church
Two denarii	= Two commandments of love
Innkeeper	= Apostle Paul
Return of good Samaritan	= Resurrection of Christ

The question that these interpretations of this parable raise is not whether the theology of their interpretations is Christian or not, for certainly Adam, the fall, the devil, the inability of the law to save, the resurrection, the second coming of Christ, etc., have always been part of Christian theology. Rather, the question that they raise is whether the parable of the good Samaritan really teaches such a history of salvation. Is this parable a summary of man's fall and dilemma and of God's redemptive work from Adam to the return of Christ? The question therefore is not whether what Origen and Augustine say is true but rather whether the parable truly says this. It is evident upon a closer reading of the text that this allegorical interpretation is not what Jesus had in mind when he taught the parable. On the contrary, the parable is given in response to the question, "And who is my neighbor?" (Luke 10:29) and is concluded by Jesus with the words, "Which of these three, do you think, proved neighbor to the man who fell among the robbers?" (Luke 10:36). From the context it is clear that the parable is an "example parable" and is meant to demonstrate by way of an example what it means to be a good neighbor. Whatever else, if anything, the parable may teach is of secondary importance. The parable must be interpreted in the light of Luke 10:29 and 36! The interpretations of Origen and Augustine are therefore read into the text (*eisegesis*) rather than read out of the text (*exegesis*). They make the parable say something other than what Jesus and the Gospel writers intended, and their interpretations are therefore not to be accepted.

There was some protest in the early church against such allegorical interpretation, especially from the church fathers in Antioch. John Chrysostom (ca. 347–407), a contemporary of Augustine, protested against such interpretation, stating that it is neither wise nor correct

> to enquire curiously into all things in parables word by word, but when we have learnt the object for which it was composed, to read this, and not to busy one's self about any thing further.[41]

Yet despite such protests the allegorical method of interpretation won the field and dominated not only the interpretation of parables but all Biblical interpretation as well.

THE MIDDLE AGES (540–1500)

The main interest of church scholars during this period lay not so much in the area of Biblical exegesis as in theology, and it was during this period that complex theological systems arose. In general the scholastics of this period relied rather heavily upon the exegetical work of the early church fathers. To Origen's threefold sense, however, they added still another—the *anagogical.* Now in addition to Origen's *literal, moral,* and *spiritual* (now called simply the *allegorical*) meanings there was the *anagogical,* which sought the heavenly or eschatological significance of a passage of Scripture.[42] An example of this type of interpretation was the fourfold meaning contained in the term "Jerusalem." In the literal sense Jerusalem was understood as referring to a specific city in Judea; in the moral or tropological sense it referred to the human soul; in the spiritual sense it referred to the church; and in the anagogical sense it referred to the heavenly abode of the saints!

THE REFORMATION AND POST-REFORMATION PERIOD (1500–1888)

With the Reformation new insight was gained as to how to interpret the Scriptures. Martin Luther (1483–1546) repudiated the fourfold sense of Scripture and thought of the allegorizers as "clerical jugglers performing monkey tricks." As for Origen's exegesis, he considered it "worth less than dirt,"[43] for the Scriptures should not be treated allegorically but literally and grammatically. Luther was sound in his theory, but his practice was not always consistent with his theory in that he tended to allegorize the parables and find everywhere in them examples of the doctrine of justification by faith.

John Calvin (1509–1564) was an excellent interpreter of the parables as well as of the Scriptures in general. His *Commentary on a Harmony of the*

Evangelists: Matthew, Mark and Luke contains many lasting insights and still rewards its readers. Calvin referred to the allegorizing of the early church as "idle fooleries" and after describing the allegorical interpretation of the good Samaritan states:

> I acknowledge that I have no liking for any of these interpretations; but we ought to have a deeper reverence for Scripture than to reckon ourselves at liberty to disguise its natural meaning. And, indeed, any one may see that the curiosity of certain men has led them to contrive these speculations, contrary to the intention of Christ.[44]

Concerning the interpretation of the parable of the unjust steward (Luke 16:1–9), Calvin with great perception states:

> Here it is obvious that if we were to attempt to find a meaning for every minute circumstance, we would act absurdly. To make donations out of what belongs to another man is an action, which is very far from deserving applause; and who would patiently endure that an unprincipled villain should rob him of his property, and give it away according to his own fancy. It were indeed the grossest stupidity, if that man who beheld a portion of his substance taken away, should *commend* the person who stole the remainder of it and bestowed it on others. But Christ only meant what he adds a little afterwards, that ungodly and worldly men are more industrious and skilful in conducting the affairs of this fading life, than the children of God are anxious to obtain the heavenly and eternal life, or careful to make it the subject of their study and meditation.[45]

Unfortunately the successors of Calvin and Luther did not follow their more sound hermeneutical principles, and their insights were soon lost. As a result the allegorical method of interpreting the parables continued to dominate. Even Archbishop R. C. Trench's famous *Notes on the Parables of Our Lord* (1841) seems to owe more to the early church fathers than to Calvin and Luther. Despite a careful exegetical explanation of the parable of the good Samaritan in the context of the first *Sitz im Leben*, Trench sought to obtain "more" out of the parable, so that he allegorized the parable as follows:[46]

The man going down to Jericho	= Human nature or Adam
Jerusalem from which he was going	= Heavenly city
Jericho	= Profane city, a city under a curse
Robbers	= Devil and his angels
Stripping him	= Stripping him of his original robe of righteousness
Leaving him half-dead	= Covered with almost mortal strokes, every sinful passion

	and desire a gash from which the lifeblood of his soul is flowing—yet still maintaining a divine spark that might be fanned into flame
Priest and Levite	= Inability of the Law to save
Good Samaritan	= Christ
Binding of wounds	= Sacraments, which heal the wounds of the soul
Oil	= Christ in the human heart purifying the heart by faith—the anointing of the Holy Spirit
Wine	= Blood of Christ's passion
Placing man on beast and walking alongside	= "Reminds us of him, who, though he was rich, yet for our sakes became poor"
Inn	= Church
Two denarii	= All gifts and graces, sacraments, powers of healing, of remission of sins
Whatever more you spend	= Reward for righteous service

THE MODERN PERIOD (1888 to PRESENT)

It is with Adolf Jülicher that the modern period of parabolic interpretation begins. The first volume of his *Die Gleichnisreden Jesu*, which was published in 1888, correctly demonstrated once and for all that parables are not allegories. In an allegory each detail has meaning and significance. As a result of thinking that a parable such as the parable of the good Samaritan was an allegory, men like Origen, Augustine, and Trench saw significance in every detail of the story. Parables, Jülicher argued, are not allegories but similitudes and therefore have only one point of comparison or likeness. The details are insignificant. It is unimportant, therefore, that the man in this parable was going down from Jerusalem to Jericho. He could have been going up from Jericho to Jerusalem! This would not change the one point of comparison. The "two denarii" has no particular meaning in the parable; it could just as well have said three denarii or four! The oil and the wine have no independent significance. They simply give coloring to the story, for the wine served as an antiseptic and the oil would aid in keeping wounds from forming scabs and thus help them to drain. The parable, itself, has only one point to make. It seeks to demonstrate "who is my neighbor." Everything else is simply local coloring to aid in making this one point.

Jülicher's main contribution to the investigation of the parables was that he pointed out the difference between parables and allegories and in so doing laid to rest the allegorical method of interpreting the parables which had plagued the church for centuries. Parables are not allegories, for a parable is an extended simile and thus has only one *tertium comparationis,* or point of comparison, whereas an allegory is a chain of metaphors. Jülicher's work despite its great contribution to the interpretation of parables, however, was not without its own limitations. The first major weakness of Jülicher was that he overreacted against the former emphasis on the allegorical interpretation of the parables and denied the presence of any allegorical element in the parables of Jesus. Whenever such allegorical details or interpretations were present in the Gospels, their authenticity was denied, and they were attributed to the reworking of the parable by the early church. This reaction against the presence of allegory in the parables of Jesus is also explained by the fact that Jülicher depended on Aristotle rather than on the Old Testament for defining what a parable is. This tended to be an error of his day. Today it is evident that Jesus, as well as Paul and the early church, has much more in common with the Old Testament and with contemporary Judaism than with the Greek classical writers. As has been pointed out above,[47] not all Old Testament and rabbinic parables are similitudes, for the term *mashal* can refer to a proverb, a taunt, a riddle, a story parable, or an allegory. One cannot therefore say *a priori* that a parable cannot contain any allegorical elements or that Jesus could not have included allegorical details in his parables. Whether the parables of Jesus at times contain allegorical details and whether these details are authentic must be demonstrated on exegetical grounds, not on philosophical or *a priori* grounds. It would appear, nevertheless, to be a wise rule not to interpret the parables of Jesus or the details of the parables allegorically unless such an interpretation is absolutely necessary. We should find allegory in the parables of Jesus only when we must, not simply when we can!

The second weakness of Jülicher's work was that the one point he saw in the parables of Jesus was always a general moral truth. Jülicher was a liberal and wrote during the reign of liberal theology. It was therefore natural for him to see in the one point of Jesus' parables a general tenet of nineteenth-century liberal theology. One example of this is his treatment of the parable of the prodigal son (Luke 15:11–32), to which he devotes more space than any other. In this parable the *tertium comparationis* is seen as "an elevated revelation over a fundamental question of religion, namely 'Dare the God of righteousness accept sinners in grace?' "

(II, 363). A second example is found in the parable of the unjust steward (Luke 16:1–9), where the one main point of comparison is the generalization that "determined use of the present is a prerequisite for a happy future" (II, 511). Still another example is found in the parable of the talents (MATT 25:14–30), which has as its one main point of comparison the principle that "reward is only earned by performance" (II, 495). It is not surprising therefore to see Jesus described by Jülicher in true liberal fashion as an "apostle of progress" (II, 483).[48] Yet unlike the liberal Jesus of Jülicher who uttered general moral truths, the Jesus of the parables so disturbed and enraged some of his listeners that they sought to destroy him (MARK 12:12). They would never have bothered to do this if all he taught were general moral truths. Despite these two limitations of the work of Jülicher, however, the world of Biblical scholarship will be forever indebted to him for having broken once and for all the stranglehold that the allegorical method of interpretation held on the interpretation of parables.

It was C. H. Dodd who carried the work of interpreting the parables one step farther. In his *The Parables of the Kingdom*, which was published in 1935, Dodd pointed out that to understand the parables correctly one must seek to interpret them in their original *Sitz im Leben*. By this he meant that the parables must be interpreted in the context of the ministry of Jesus and his message and not in the context of nineteenth-century liberalism or the present situation of the believer. In other words, before one seeks to understand what the parable is saying to the believer today, one must seek the original meaning and application of the parable that Jesus intended for his listeners in the first century; or to put this in still another way, Dodd demonstrated that the question, What does the parable mean to me today? must be preceded by the question, What did the parable mean to the original audience then? To do this, one must seek to understand:

(i) . . . such ideas as may be supposed to have been in the minds of the hearers of Jesus during His ministry
(ii) . . . the general orientation of the teaching of Jesus.[49]

Dodd then proceeded to apply this insight, along with the contribution of form criticism, to the investigation of the parables. Dodd, too, had his limitations. The main limitation lay in his seeing the message of Jesus as consisting of only "realized eschatology"[50] and in interpreting all the parables of Jesus from this particular viewpoint. For Dodd, all such eschatological parables as MARK 13:28–30 (the parable of the fig tree); MATT 24:45–51 (the parable of the good and the bad servant); Matt 25:1–13 (the parable of the wise and the foolish virgins); and Luke 12:

35–38 (the parable of the waiting servants) refer not to a future eschatological judgment but to a situation and crisis in the earthly ministry of Jesus.

It seems possible, therefore, to give to all these "eschatological" parables an application within the context of the ministry of Jesus.[51]

There can be no retreat from the emphasis of Dodd that the parables must be interpreted in the light of the first *Sitz im Leben*,[52] for when this principle is applied to the parables, they breathe new life and excitement. The parable of the good Samaritan when understood in the light of the first *Sitz im Leben* is no longer simply a beautiful example but is a cutting, biting, antidiscriminatory attack against the Jewish hatred of the Samaritan,[53] for in the parable the villains are the clerical elite of Judaism (the priests and the Levites), whereas the hero is the hated Samaritan. Such a parable as the wheat and the tares (Matt 13:24–30) can also be recognized now as an anti-Zealot polemic against those who would seek to usurp the divine prerogative of judgment and seek to separate now with their own hands the wheat (the true people of God—Israel) from the tares (Rome). To the Zealot revolutionaries in his audience Jesus is saying that such judgment does not belong to men even if they be zealous for the law. Only God has the right to say, "Vengeance is mine, I will repay" (Heb. 10:30; cf. James 5:7–9). The time of the harvest (judgment) cannot be accelerated by the feverish efforts of man but lies in the hands of God (cf. also Mark 4:26–29).

Still another insight into interpreting the parables has come through the rise of redaction criticism. Since the work of Hans Conzelmann[54] and Willi Marxsen[55] in the mid-fifties, there has been a great deal of interest in the investigation of the theological context and emphases of the individual evangelist, i.e., in the investigation of the third *Sitz im Leben*. Therefore, in studying the parables we must understand them in the light of not only the situation of Jesus (the first *Sitz im Leben*) but also the situation of the early church during the oral period (the second *Sitz im Leben*) and the situation of the Evangelists (the third *Sitz im Leben*). An example of the latter is the Lukan interpretation of the parable of the pounds (LUKE 19:12–27). Generally this parable is interpreted as a parable whose main interest lies in the teaching of Christian stewardship. Yet Luke uses this parable and applies it to a particular situation and need in his own *Sitz im Leben*.

Most scholars today see in Luke's Gospel a concern by the author over a problem that disturbed many Christians in the early church. The problem involved the delay of the parousia (cf. II Peter 3:3f.). Luke in his use of this parable directs himself to this problem. He does so by reassuring his readers that such a delay is in keeping with the teachings of Jesus, for he taught that there would be such a delay. In fact, Jesus taught this very parable because his disciples "supposed that the kingdom of God was to appear immediately" (Luke 19:11). Luke seeks to point out through this parable and his redaction that Jesus himself taught that he would be away for a period of time and that during this period his disciples should concern themselves with being faithful stewards. This parable therefore has in the Lukan setting a particular emphasis that applies to the situation of Luke. That such an emphasis by Luke is not contrary to the original meaning of the parable is evident for two reasons. First, the whole principle of stewardship has meaning only if there is a period of time between the "present" and the consummation, i.e., the stewardship that Jesus taught in the parable implies—no, rather, necessitates—a delay of some sort before the consummation. Secondly, the Matthean version of the parable also contains this emphasis on the delay of the master's return, for we read in Matt 25:19, "Now *after a long time* the master . . . came and settled accounts" (italics added). Therefore, whereas the main intent of the parable may lie in the area of faithful stewardship, Luke is not misinterpreting it by his treatment of the story but rather is emphasizing for his situation that this implies a delay in the consummation.

SOME EXAMPLES IN INTERPRETING THE PARABLES

It may be helpful at this point to review the three major principles discussed above and apply them to the interpretation of certain parables. The principles are: (1) parables are not allegories but instead tend to emphasize one main point, so that parables or details in parables that do not absolutely require an allegorical interpretation ought not to be interpreted allegorically; (2) to understand the original meaning of a parable, we must seek to understand what Jesus meant when he uttered it to his listeners in the first century, i.e., we must seek to understand its meaning in the first *Sitz im Leben;* and (3) it is important also to understand how the individual Evangelists understood the parable, i.e., we should seek to understand the meaning of the parable in the third *Sitz im Leben.*[56]

> The kingdom of heaven is like treasure hidden in a field, which a man found and covered up; then in his joy he goes and sells all that he has and buys that field. (Matt 13:44)

In investigating this parable, we must remember Jülicher's contribution to the study of the parables. We should not press the details of the parable for allegorical significance but rather should look for the one main point that the parable is seeking to make. To concern ourselves therefore over the morality, or rather the immorality, of the man in the parable is to miss the point.[57] Jesus is not advocating such immoral or amoral behavior, for the deception involved certainly violates the Golden Rule (MATT 7:12). The behavior of the man in the parable simply provides the local coloring of the story. Perhaps just such an incident had recently taken place and Jesus is now using it to provide interest and flavor. The one main point that Jesus is seeking to make in the parable is clear. It is worth the surrender of all to enter the kingdom of God! Matt 13:45–46 makes this very same point and was no doubt placed alongside this parable for this reason, but here the behavior of the merchant is clearly moral.

Two other parables in which the issue of morality, if raised, can confuse the interpreter are Matt 25:1–13 and Luke 16:1–8. In the former the five maidens whom the audience is told to emulate are in a sense quite selfish in not sharing their oil,[58] but again this is only local coloring to add interest to the story. The one main point is clear. Be ready at all times, for you do not know when the consummation will take place! In the latter parable the commended servant is both a scoundrel and a thief. He is commended, however, not for his thievery but for his wisdom, because, having seen the coming judgment, he wisely prepared himself for it. "The master commended the dishonest steward for his shrewdness" (Luke 16:8). The one main point of this parable is that, seeing the impending judgment facing us, we should be wise and prepare ourselves for it. The parable tells us—Be wise for judgment is coming! Prepare! How is one to prepare for this impending judgment? A specific application is given in v. 9 that involves the wise use of money. By remembering Jülicher's contribution to the study of the parables we shall be able to focus our attention upon the main point of the parable and not err by concentrating on the details.

What man of you, having a hundred sheep, if he has lost one of them, does not leave the ninety-nine in the wilderness, and go after the one which is lost, until he finds it? And when he has found it, he lays it on his shoulders, rejoicing. And when he comes home, he calls together his friends and his neighbors, saying to them, "Rejoice with me, for I have found my sheep which was lost." Just so, I tell you, there will be more joy in heaven over one sinner who repents than over ninety-nine righteous persons who need no repentance. (LUKE 15:4–7)

Or what woman, having ten silver coins, if she loses one coin, does not light a lamp and sweep the house and seek diligently until she finds it? And when she has found it, she calls together her friends and neighbors, saying, "Rejoice with me, for I have found the coin which

I had lost." Just so, I tell you, there is joy before the angels of God over one sinner who repents. (Luke 15:8-10)

Generally the two parables above and the longer parable of the prodigal son that follows are seen as beautiful examples of the love of God for sinners, and of course they are. We gain additional insight into these parables, however, if we seek to understand them in the situation of the historical Jesus. To be sure, Jesus meant these parables to be examples of the divine love for the lost, but we must also seek to understand the context in which they were spoken. The context into which Luke places these parables is certainly a correct one. The Pharisees and the scribes are protesting the conduct of Jesus in eating with publicans and sinners (Luke 15:1-2). The incident is not unique, for this charge occurred frequently in Jesus' ministry (MARK 2:16-17; MATT 11:19; Luke 7:39; 19:7). These three parables were therefore uttered as an apology against such criticism. But what is the significance of the fact that "this man receives sinners and eats with them"? The significance of this fact is that in the ministry of Jesus, God is at work now seeking the lost sheep of Israel! This same point is made in each of the three parables in Luke 15. Understood in the context of the first *Sitz im Leben*, these parables are more than just simply examples of God's redeeming love. They are both an apology and a proclamation. They are an apology or defense of Jesus' behavior in associating with publicans, sinners, and harlots, and they are a proclamation that in this activity God is now visiting his people in fulfillment of the Old Testament promises. The eschatological significance is clear. The kingdom of God has come! God is now visiting the rejected of Israel (cf. MATT 11:4-6 with Isa 35:5-6; 61:1)! In the ministry of Jesus, God is fulfilling the Old Testament promises and now visiting the lost sheep of Israel.[59]

It can be seen from the above that when we seek to understand the parables in their original context they frequently take on new life and excitement. Admittedly, at times we cannot ascertain the exact situation in the first *Sitz im Leben* in which the parable was uttered. In such instances we shall have to be content with relating the parable to the situation of the historical Jesus in general.

A man planted a vineyard, and set a hedge around it, and dug a pit for the wine press, and built a tower, and let it out to tenants, and went into another country. When the time came, he sent a servant to the tenants, to get from them some of the fruit of the vineyard. And they took him and beat him, and sent him away empty-handed. Again he sent to them another servant, and they wounded him in the head, and treated him shamefully. And he sent another, and him they killed; and so with many others, some they beat and some they killed.

He had still one other, a beloved son; finally he sent him to them, saying, "They will respect my son." But those tenants said to one another, "This is the heir; come, let us kill him, and the inheritance will be ours." And they took him and killed him, and cast him out of the vineyard. What will the owner of the vineyard do? He will come and destroy the tenants, and give the vineyard to others. Have you not read this scripture:

"The very stone which the builders rejected
has become the head of the corner;
this was the Lord's doing,
and it is marvelous in our eyes"? (MARK 12:1–11)

The authenticity of the present form of this parable is frequently denied. There are several reasons for this. To begin with, the parable clearly contains allegorical details, and for some scholars allegorical details are always later additions and cannot be attributed to the historical Jesus. We have seen above, however, that the denial of the authenticity of all allegory in the parables of Jesus by Jülicher was based incorrectly on a classical definition of a parable and that the presence of allegorical details in Old Testament and rabbinic parables makes an *a priori* exclusion of allegory from the parables of Jesus illegitimate.[60] A second objection to the authenticity of this parable is the historical impossibility of such behavior on the part of the tenants. We have seen, however, that on the contrary such behavior fits well the historical situation of Jesus.[61] Another objection to the authenticity of this parable lies in the Christology present in the account. The portrayal of Jesus as "Son" looks to many like a reading into the parable of a later Christology of the early church. Yet it is difficult to attribute the portrayal of Jesus as "Son" in this parable to the early church, because in the parable the "Son" is killed and his body is thrown out of the vineyard presumably to rot. If the parable were created or extensively reworked by the early church, one would expect along with the death of the "Son" some sort of reference to the resurrection.

For our investigation of this parable, however, the question of authenticity is not important, because what we want to do here is to investigate how Mark understood and used the parable. The very location of the parable at this point by Mark is important.[62] Since in ch. 4 Mark gives a listing of the parables of Jesus, why did he not include MARK 12:1–12 there? Why did he place it at this point? The explanation is to be found in what the Evangelist is seeking to do in chs. 11 to 13. In Mark 11:12–26 we have an example of a Markan "sandwich." This is a frequent Markan literary device in which the Evangelist divides one story into two parts and inserts another story in between. Here we have A¹ (MARK 11:12–14—

the cursing of the fig tree), then B (MARK 11:15–19—the cleansing of the Temple), and then A² (MARK 11:20–26—the cursing of the fig tree).[63] Mark in sandwiching these two accounts indicates that they are similar in nature. As a result, the cleansing of the Temple is to be understood not as a reformatory action of Jesus but as an act of judgment. The Lord has come to the Temple expecting fruit (righteousness) and found instead nothing but leaves (hypocrisy and thievery),[64] and thus he has brought judgment on the Temple and what it represented! The Markan comment in Mark 11:13, "for it was not the season for figs," is meant to alert the readers to the fact that Jesus' action with respect to the fig tree is symbolic and thus not simply the cursing of a worthless fig tree. In ch. 13 we have the famous Markan apocalypse which speaks of the divine judgment coming upon Jerusalem (note v. 2). By placing this parable in the present context Mark reinforces this central theme of judgment on Israel. Judgment is coming upon Jerusalem/Israel. The Owner of the vineyard is about to come and destroy the tenants (the fig tree is cursed—the Temple is cleansed/judged—"There will not be left here one stone upon another, that will not be thrown down" [MARK 13:2]). In the third *Sitz im Leben* the Evangelist clearly uses this parable to reveal to his readers that God has judged Israel because of their rejection of Jesus and/or the Gospel[65] and that he will come in judgment. The Markan comment in 12:12, "And they tried to arrest him, but feared the multitude, for they perceived that he had told the parable against them; so they left him and went away," is also meant to help the readers to understand the parable in this way. This judgment did come in A.D. 70 in a most horrible way when the Romans under Titus destroyed Jerusalem, and if Mark wrote in the late sixties of the first century, he may very well have seen this coming as he wrote his Gospel.

Chapter 4

THE CONTENT OF JESUS' TEACHING: THE KINGDOM OF GOD

THE CENTRAL THEME of the teaching of Jesus is the coming of the kingdom of God. Mark states that after his baptism Jesus went

> preaching the gospel of God, and saying, "The time is fulfilled, and the kingdom of God is at hand; repent, and believe in the gospel." (MARK 1:14–15)[1]

Matthew, who also includes this verse (Matt 4:17), adds:

> And he went about all Galilee, teaching in their synagogues and preaching the gospel of the kingdom and healing every disease and every infirmity among the people. (Matt 4:23)

Luke, who has no parallel to MARK 1:14–15, nevertheless summarizes the message of Jesus as follows:

> And the people sought him and came to him, and would have kept him from leaving them; but he said to them, "I must preach the good news of the kingdom of God to the other cities also; for I was sent for this purpose." (Luke 4:42–43)

The expressions "kingdom of God" and "kingdom of heaven" are found in sixty-one separate sayings of Jesus in the Synoptic Gospels,[2] and if we include the parallels, these two expressions occur eighty-five times.[3] It is not surprising, therefore, to discover that the key to understanding the message of Jesus lies in a correct interpretation of these expressions.

One would think that there would be a consensus among scholars as to the interpretation of these expressions which are found so frequently on the lips of Jesus and make up the central theme of his proclamation. Unfortunately no such consensus exists, for Jesus never defined exactly what he meant by these expressions but assumed that his listeners would understand. As a result we come across strange and often contradictory interpretations of these expressions. It was quite popular at one time and is still not uncommon to hear someone urge believers to work together in order to build the kingdom of God. Some writers have portrayed the kingdom of God as the product of a new classless social order. Others say that the kingdom of God has nothing to do with this world but refers to "heaven." Some say in contrast that the kingdom of God refers to a millennial-like reign by God on this planet. Still others say that we must distinguish carefully between the kingdom of heaven and the kingdom of God, for the former refers to a this-worldly millennial reign on this earth for Jewish believers, whereas the latter refers to a heavenly rule for Gentile believers. Some would even teach that these two kingdoms are eternally separate, so that Jewish believers and Gentile believers always remain divided in their two eternal destinies! It is evident, therefore, that the expressions "kingdom of God" and "kingdom of heaven" are far from self-explanatory.

THE RELATIONSHIP OF THE KINGDOM OF GOD AND THE KINGDOM OF HEAVEN

It should be noted that the expression "kingdom of heaven" is found thirty-two times in Matthew, where it is the dominant expression,[4] but not at all in Mark and Luke. It is evident that the two expressions "kingdom of God" and "kingdom of heaven" are synonyms for at least two reasons. The first reason is that Matthew frequently uses the expression "kingdom of heaven" in the very same sayings in which Mark or Luke or both Mark and Luke use "kingdom of God." Some examples of this are:

Matt	*Luke*
Blessed are the poor in spirit, for theirs is the *kingdom of heaven.* (5:3)	Blessed are you poor, for yours is the *kingdom of God.* (6:20)
I tell you, many will come from east and west and sit at table with Abraham, Isaac, and Jacob in the *kingdom of heaven.* (8:11)	There you will weep and gnash your teeth, when you see Abraham and Isaac and Jacob and all the prophets in the *kingdom of God* and you yourselves thrust out. (13: 28)

Other examples of this can be found in: MATT 10:7 and LUKE 9:2; MATT 11:11 and LUKE 7:28; MATT 11:12 and LUKE 16:16; and MATT 13:33 and LUKE 13:20.

Matt	Mark
From that time Jesus began to preach, saying, "Repent, for the *kingdom of heaven* is at hand." (4:17)	Now after John was arrested, Jesus came into Galilee, preaching the gospel of God, and saying, "The time is fulfilled, and the *kingdom of God* is at hand." (1:14–15)

The interchangeable nature of these two expressions is brought out even more clearly when we compare certain sayings of Jesus that are common to all three of the Synoptic Gospels.

Matt	Mark	Luke
To you it has been given to know the secrets of the *kingdom of heaven.* (13:11)	To you has been given the secret of the *kingdom of God.* (4:11)	To you it has been given to know the secrets of the *kingdom of God.* (8:10)
The *kingdom of heaven* is like a grain of mustard seed. (13:31)	With what can we compare the *kingdom of God* . . . ? It is like a grain of mustard seed. (4:30–31)	What is the *kingdom of God* like? . . . It is like a grain of mustard seed. (13:18–19)
Let the children come to me, and do not hinder them; for to such belongs the *kingdom of heaven.* (19:14)	Let the children come to me, do not hinder them; for to such belongs the *kingdom of God.* (10:14)	Let the children come to me, and do not hinder them; for to such belongs the *kingdom of God.* (18:16)
Truly, I say to you, it will be hard for a rich man to enter the *kingdom of heaven.* (19:23)	How hard it will be for those who have riches to enter the *kingdom of God!* (10:23)	How hard it is for those who have riches to enter the *kingdom of God!* (18:24)

The above comparisons demonstrate that the expressions "kingdom of heaven" and "kingdom of God" are interchangeable and refer to the same entity. Matthew, however, prefers "kingdom of heaven" to "kingdom of God" which he found both in his Markan source and in Q.

The second reason why we know that these two expressions are synonyms is that there is a simple logical explanation for Matthew's choice of the one expression over the other. Unlike the Gospels of Mark and Luke, which were written for Gentile believers,[5] Matthew was written for Jewish believers.[6] In the Judaism of the first century, even as in Orthodox Jewish circles today, there was great reverence for the name of God. In order to protect himself from breaking the Third Commandment ("You shall not take the name of the LORD your God in vain; for the LORD will not hold him guiltless who takes his name in vain" [Ex 20:7]), the devout Jew scrupulously avoided using the sacred name of God. This practice applied primarily to the tetragrammaton, i.e., the name YHWH.[7] This name was too sacred to be uttered. In its place one would read or state instead the term "Adonai" (Lord) or "Elohim" (God). Two other means used to avoid uttering the sacred name for God were substitution and the use of the "divine passive."

There are several examples in the New Testament of the use of substitution or circumlocution to avoid the use of the name of God. After the prodigal son "came to himself" (Luke 15:17) he returned to his father and said, "Father, I have sinned *against heaven* and before you" (Luke 15:21, italics added). Here we find a clear example in this parable of the substitution of the term "heaven" for God, for the prodigal is not claiming to have sinned against the stars and planets but against God. Another example of the use of "heaven" as a substitute for the word "God" is found in MARK 11:30, where Jesus asks, "Was the baptism of John *from heaven* or from men?" (italics added). Here Jesus asks the chief priests, scribes, and elders the origin of John the Baptist's message. Is the origin divine (heavenly) or human? A different expression is substituted for the divine name in LUKE 12:8–9 when Jesus says:

And I tell you, every one who acknowledges me before men, the Son of man also will acknowledge before *the angels of God;* but he who denies me before men will be denied before *the angels of God.* (Italics added; cf. also Luke 15:10)

In Jesus' trial before the high priest we have two additional examples:

Again the high priest asked him, "Are you the Christ, the Son of the *Blessed?*" And Jesus said, "I am; and you will see the Son of man sitting at the right hand of *Power,* and coming with the clouds of heaven." (MARK 14:61–62, italics added)

Other examples that can be cited are: "Most High" (LUKE 6:35), "great King" (Matt 5:34–35), "name" (MATT 6:9), etc.[8] By this circumlocution Jesus (and the high priest in MARK 14:61) witnessed to the Jewish practice of avoiding the utterance of the tetragrammaton by substitution.

A second way in which the devout Jew sought to avoid the utterance of the sacred name of God was by the use of the divine passive. By placing an action into the passive ("they shall be comforted" [Matt 5:4]), one could avoid using the name of God ("God shall comfort them"). Other examples of this passive construction can be seen in the following:

But even the hairs of your head are all numbered. (MATT 10:30) (For "God even knows the number of the hairs on your head.")

For to him who has will more be given; and from him who has not, even what he has will be taken away. (MARK 4:25) (For "God will give more to him who has and will take away from him who has not even what he has.")

... but to sit at my right hand or at my left is not mine to grant, but it is for those for whom it has been prepared. (MARK 10:40) (For ". . . but to sit at my right hand or at my left is not mine to grant, but God will grant it to those he has chosen.")

Judge not, that you be not judged. (MATT 7:1) (For "Judge not, and God will not judge you.")

Ask, and it will be given you; seek, and you will find; knock, and it will be opened to you. (MATT 7:7) (For "Ask, and God will give it to you; seek, and God will show it to you; knock, and God will open it to you.")

Jeremias[9] lists ninety-six separate instances in the Synoptic Gospels of this use of the divine passive. It may very well be that in a number of these instances the use of the passive serves no particular function in avoiding the use of the name of God, but the number of examples we find and the clarity of many of them clearly indicates that the devout Jew frequently sought to avoid the danger of breaking the Third Commandment by means of this passive construction as well as by substitution or circumlocution.

We find then that many of the sayings in which the expression "kingdom of heaven" occurs in Matthew have parallels in Mark and Luke in which the expression "kingdom of God" is found. Secondly, we find that the pious Jew of the first century frequently sought to avoid the use of the sacred name of God by the substitution of a term such as "heaven" or by the use of the passive. Thirdly, we have pointed out that whereas Mark and Luke were writing for Gentile Christians, Matthew was writing for Jewish Christians, so that a rationale for the appearance of the expression "kingdom of heaven" is also available. In the light of this it would appear that we can conclude that the expressions "kingdom of heaven" and "kingdom of God" are synonyms and are thus used interchangeably in the Synoptic Gospels.

There is still no absolute certainty as to which of these expressions Jesus himself used. It might be argued that since Jesus was a devout Jew, he would have carefully avoided the use of the sacred name of God and would therefore naturally avoid such an expression as "kingdom of God" and use instead "kingdom of heaven." We have listed above certain instances in which Jesus himself substituted a different word for the term

"God." The use of the expression "kingdom of heaven" would be another example according to this view. Mark and Luke (or the church during the oral period), according to this interpretation, then changed the original expression of Jesus to "kingdom of God," since "kingdom of heaven" would have been meaningless to their Gentile readers. Matthew, however, although he used Mark and Q, changed the expression in his sources back to "kingdom of heaven," which Jesus had originally used. On the other hand, it is evident that, whereas Jesus at times did avoid using the sacred name of God, he did not always avoid such usage. The term "God" is frequently found on the lips of Jesus in the synoptic tradition.[10] As a result, it could be argued that Mark and Luke faithfully reproduced the actual expression of Jesus but that Matthew substituted the term "heaven" for God out of consideration for his Jewish-Christian audience. It would appear reckless at this time to be dogmatic over either position.

THE MAIN SCHOOLS OF INTERPRETATION

What is the kingdom of God? When does or did the kingdom of God come? Is the kingdom of God a present reality or a future hope? How is the kingdom of God related in time and character to the present course of this world? For the sake of simplicity we shall group the various answers given to these questions into three main schools of interpretation. Such classification, while somewhat arbitrary, will nevertheless be helpful as we seek to understand how different scholars interpret the teaching of Jesus on this subject. We shall call the three main schools: the Noneschatological School, the "Consistent" Eschatological School, and the "Realized" Eschatological School.

THE NONESCHATOLOGICAL SCHOOL

During the height of liberalism in the nineteenth century it was popular to deny or minimize the eschatological element in the teaching of Jesus. Sometimes the eschatological "husk" found in the sayings of Jesus was attributed to the disciples, who supposedly misunderstood their master's message of a spiritual reign of God and added this eschatological element. At times this element was attributed to the "apelike" eschatological heritage of Jesus which he was not able to shake off completely. What was central, however, to the teaching of Jesus concerning the kingdom of God, in contrast to the eschatological message of apocalyptic Judaism, was the inward moral ethic that Jesus emphasized. The greatest spokesman of liberal theology was

Adolf Harnack. According to Harnack, the essence of the message of Jesus could be summarized as:

The kingdom of God and its coming
God the Father and the infinite value of the human soul
The higher righteousness and the commandment of love.[11]

Harnack did acknowledge the presence of an eschatological element in the teaching of Jesus which he inherited from Jewish apocalypticism, but this was only the "husk" of his teaching and was to be discarded in favor of his real contribution. The "kernel," or essential contribution of his message, was that the kingdom of God involved the present reign of God in the heart of the believer.

This noneschatological view, which dominated theological liberalism, saw the teaching of Jesus on the kingdom of God as being totally, or in its essential features at least, noneschatological. The kingdom of God was the presence of a new principle—the present inner reign of God in the human heart. If there were any apocalyptic or eschatological elements present in his teaching, they were either discarded or interpreted symbolically to refer to this inward rule of God in the life of the believer.[12]

THE "CONSISTENT" ESCHATOLOGICAL SCHOOL

There is a sense in which we can say that Harnack's book, published in 1900, was outdated even before it came off the press, for in 1892 Johannes Weiss's *Die Predigt Jesu vom Reiche Gottes (The Preaching of Jesus on the Kingdom of God)* appeared and was soon followed in 1906 by Albert Schweitzer's *Von Reimarus zu Wrede.*[13] In these two works it was demonstrated that the eschatological element in the teaching of Jesus could not be eliminated as a subsidiary element but was fundamental to his message. Jesus in proclaiming the kingdom of God was not speaking of any ethical inward rule by God but, on the contrary, of the end of history and the supernatural installation of a new age. Eschatology was therefore not simply "husk" attached to the teaching of Jesus. On the contrary, it was the "kernel"! The noneschatological interpretations of the kingdom of God were nothing more than attempts to modernize Jesus and make him compatible with nineteenth-century liberalism.

The view of Weiss and Schweitzer is commonly referred to as "consistent eschatology" and is today the prevailing view of Continental scholarship. According to this view, the kingdom of God refers to a future reign of God which, according to Jesus, was to be inaugurated in the near future. Jesus, according to this interpretation, taught that the coming of the kingdom of God was to take place when history came to an end. At the parousia, when the Son of man would come to judge the world, the kingdom of God would be inaugurated. The end, however, was not to take place in the far-distant future, but, on the contrary, the kingdom of God would come shortly. Already the kingdom, although not present, was in the process of being realized. The signs and the powers of the kingdom were already now active and dawning, even though the kingdom itself was still future.

According to this view, and we must remind ourselves that summaries such as the above, while helpful, can never cover every related view, Jesus taught that the kingdom of God was a future eschatological reign of God which was imminent. Its arrival would mean the end of history as we know it and the inauguration of the direct rule of God. Associated with this would be the parousia of the Son of man and the judgment. It should be noted that generally in this view there is a portrayal of the ministry of Jesus as somehow closely related to the presence of the kingdom. The kingdom is sometimes thought of as proleptically present in Jesus' ministry even though still future. The shadow of the kingdom and foregleams of its splendor are frequently seen as already present in the ministry of Jesus. It is important to observe therefore that even though many scholars who hold this view deny that the kingdom of God is in any way a present reality,[14] there is a realization that somehow the ministry of Jesus is in some way uniquely connected with the kingdom of God. In essence, however, this view maintains that Jesus taught that the kingdom of God was a future entity which by its coming would bring an end to history as we know it.

THE "REALIZED" ESCHATOLOGICAL SCHOOL

Whereas the dominating view on the Continent and especially in Germany is that of consistent eschatology, in Great Britain the work of C. H. Dodd has resulted in a school of "realized" eschatology.[15] Dodd in his *The Parables of the Kingdom* argued that Jesus proclaimed that in his ministry the kingdom of God had arrived. The kingdom of God was therefore not some future manifestation of the rule of God but was a present reality in the ministry of Jesus. Already now in the ministry of Jesus the crisis of judgment had come. Already now the harvest was a reality. Already now God was asserting his sovereignty in his world. The kingdom of God had come! Already now it was a *fait accompli!*[16] Whatever futuristic eschatological material Dodd found in the teachings of Jesus he interpreted as purely symbolic descriptions of realities beyond human comprehension which were meant to portray the absolute character of the kingdom. According to Dodd and his school, Jesus taught that the kingdom of God had completely come in his ministry. There was no future unfulfilled dimension still to come.

THE BIBLICAL DATA

When one investigates the Biblical data it becomes apparent why there are such contradictory views as realized and consistent eschatology, for the material itself seems contradictory. At times the Gospel material seems to indicate that the kingdom of God is a future phenomenon and at other times that it is present now in the ministry of Jesus.

THE KINGDOM OF GOD AS A PRESENT REALITY

There are several passages in the Synoptic Gospels which claim that in the coming of Jesus the kingdom of God has already come. In LUKE 11:14–22 we read:

Now he was casting out a demon that was dumb; when the demon had gone out, the dumb man spoke, and the people marveled. But some of them said, "He casts out demons by Beelzebul, the prince of demons"; while others, to test him, sought from him a sign from heaven. But he, knowing their thoughts, said to them, "Every kingdom divided against itself is laid waste, and a divided household falls. And if Satan also is divided against himself, how will his kingdom stand? For you say that I cast out demons by Beelzebul. And if I cast out demons by Beelzebul, by whom do your sons cast them out? Therefore they shall be your judges. *But if it is by the finger of God that I cast out demons, then the kingdom of God has come upon you.* When a strong man, fully armed, guards his own palace, his goods are in peace; but when one stronger than he assails him and overcomes him, he takes away his armor in which he trusted, and divides his spoil." (Italics added)

In MATT 12:28 we have a parallel to the key statement italicized above, but instead of "by the finger of God" we read "by the Spirit of God." What Matthew has done by his redaction is to make explicit what the Lukan metaphor means, for in the casting out of demons by Jesus the Spirit is once again active in Israel. What is most important in this passage for us, however, is the claim of Jesus that in casting out demons the kingdom of God has come (*ephthasen*). The Greek verb *ephthasen* is found five more times in the New Testament. In four places (Rom 9:31; II Cor 10:14; I Thess 2:16; Phil 3:16) the meaning of the verb is clearly that something "has arrived," i.e., is already now present. The fifth instance (I Thess 4:15) has the older meaning of "come before" or "anticipate."

Some scholars have sought therefore to apply the latter meaning to LUKE 11:20, so that the verse is then interpreted as saying that the kingdom of God is "very near," so near that the powers of the kingdom are already at work in anticipation of the kingdom even though the kingdom itself has not arrived. But whereas the verb in I Thess 4:15 is in the future tense, in the other four instances as well as in LUKE 11:20 the verb is in the aorist tense and in each such instance the verb is best interpreted to mean "has arrived" or "has come." The Greek term *ephthasen* is therefore correctly translated "has come" by the RSV. According to this text, Jesus saw in his healing of the demoniacs a proof that the kingdom of God had in fact come in his ministry. It was already a present reality. Satan had already been defeated; he had already fallen (Luke 10:18);[17] he was already even now bound (MARK 3:27); and the evil spirits under his authority were already now subject to Jesus (MARK 1:27, 39; Mark 3:11) and his disciples (MARK 6:7; Luke 10:19).

In describing the relationship between John the Baptist and himself, in LUKE 16:16, Jesus sees his ministry as the beginning of a new period, the period of the kingdom of God:

> The law and the prophets were until [*mechri*] John; *since then the good news of the kingdom of God is preached.* (Italics added)

In this verse two periods of history are distinguished. The first is described as the period of the law and the prophets and lasts up to and includes John the Baptist.[18] The second period, which begins after John the Baptist, is described as the period of the kingdom of God. Although there is no one greater than John the Baptist during the old period, "he who is least in the kingdom of heaven is greater than he" (MATT 11:11), for John still belongs to the period of the law and the prophets.[19] With the coming of Jesus, however, the time of the kingdom of heaven/God begins. This distinction between the Old Testament period and the new age is also found in MARK 2:21–22:

> No one sews a piece of unshrunk cloth on an old garment; if he does, the patch tears away from it, the new from the old, and a worse tear is made. And no one puts new wine into old wineskins; if he does, the wine will burst the skins, and the wine is lost, and so are the skins; but new wine is for fresh skins.

Here we again find a radical eschatological pronouncement. The Judaism of the Old Testament is described as "old." With the coming of Jesus the Old Testament religion has been superseded by the new.[20] A second period in salvation history has come and it cannot be contained within the old order. The kingdom of God has now come!

In several instances Jesus described the Old Testament prophecies as being fulfilled by his ministry. In answer to the question of John the Baptist, "Are you he who is to come, or shall we look for another?" (MATT 11:3) Jesus replies:

> Go and tell John what you hear and see: the blind receive their sight and the lame walk, lepers are cleansed and the deaf hear, and the dead are raised up, and the poor have good news preached to them. And blessed is he who takes no offense at me. (MATT 11:4–6)

The authenticity of this incident is supported by the fact that John the Baptist, in this account, is not portrayed as a witness to the messiahship of Jesus. In his answer to John, Jesus alludes to the promises in Isaiah and especially to the good tidings which are now being given to the poor. In so doing, Jesus makes use of a traditional formula that was used to describe the days of bliss which the coming of the kingdom of God would bring. The parables of the lost sheep, the lost coin, and the lost son (Luke 15:3f.) must also be understood in this way. In the ministry of Jesus, God is seeking the hungry, the unclothed, the sorrowful, the rejected, the prodigals, the lost, etc. To these who are indeed "the poor," the good news of the kingdom of God is now being proclaimed in fulfillment of the Old Testament.

In a similar vein Jesus tells his disciples:

> But blessed are your eyes, for they see, and your ears, for they hear. Truly, I say to you, many prophets and righteous men longed to see what you see, and did not see it, and to hear what you hear, and did not hear it. (MATT 13:16–17)

In the coming of Jesus the promises of the law and the prophets are fulfilled (Matt 5:17). The disciples are now experiencing what was promised at the end time. During the former period the prophets looked forward to the time when God would establish a new covenant with his people. Jeremiah wrote:

> Behold, the days are coming, says the LORD, when I will make a new covenant with the house of Israel and the house of Judah, not like the covenant which I made with their fathers when I took them by the hand to bring them out of the land of Egypt, my covenant which they broke, though I was their husband, says the LORD. But this is the covenant which I will make with the house of Israel after those days, says the LORD: I will put my law within them, and I will write it upon their hearts; and I will be their God, and they shall be my people. (Jer 31:31–33)

In his ministry Jesus sees "those days" as having arrived, for at the Last
Supper Jesus speaks of "the new covenant in my blood" (I Cor 11:25) and
establishes a new sacrament (I Cor 11:23–26; MARK 14:22–24).

The Old Testament promises are also fulfilled in that salvation is now
being offered to the Gentiles. Although Matt 10:5–6 and 15:24 do appear
to limit the mission of Jesus to Israel, such passages as MARK 7:24–30
(Jesus and the Syrophoenician woman) and MATT 8:5–13 (the healing
of the centurion's servant) anticipate and begin just such a mission. Such
passages as MARK 11:17 (the temple as a house of prayer for all nations);
Matt 25:32 (the separation of the sheep and the goats from among the
nations); and MATT 8:11 (many from east and west sitting in the kingdom of God) envision a Gentile presence in the consummation. There is
a sense, therefore, in which the kingdom of God has already come, because already now in the ministry of Jesus salvation has begun to come
to the Gentiles, and what begins rather insignificantly and implicitly will
become explicit and most significant after the resurrection (cf. Matt 28:
18–20; Acts 1:8; Rom 1:16; etc.).[21]

Still another fulfillment of the Old Testament promises must be seen
in Jesus' selection of the twelve disciples (MARK 3:13–19), for the prevailing view in the time of Jesus was that only two and one half tribes of
Israel still remained. These were: Judah, Benjamin, and half of Levi. The
others were lost when the Assyrians destroyed Samaria in 722 b.c. and
scattered the survivors throughout the world. Only in the time of salvation, i.e., the kingdom of God, would God restore the lost tribes and
bring again wholeness to the nation. In the calling of the twelve disciples,
Jesus reveals that this time has now arrived, for the disciples clearly
represent the twelve tribes of Israel (MATT 19:28).

A final and much-debated passage that needs to be discussed in this
context is Luke 17:20–21:

> Being asked by the Pharisees when the kingdom of God was coming,
> he answered them, "The kingdom of God is not coming with signs
> to be observed; nor will they say, 'Lo, here it is!' or 'There!' for
> *behold, the kingdom of God is in the midst of* [entos] *you."* (Italics added)

This passage was frequently used to support the noneschatological interpretation of the kingdom of God as an internal rule of God in the heart
of the believer, yet

> neither in Judaism nor elsewhere in the New Testament do we find
> the idea that the reign of God is something indwelling in men, to be
> found, say, in the heart.[22]

To see in this passage the inner reign of God in the human heart is surely a modern understanding read into the text. Furthermore, the audience to which this saying is directed does not permit such an interpretation, for Jesus is certainly not saying that the inner reign of God is in the hearts of the Pharisees, and yet the "you" in whose midst the kingdom of God is present are the Pharisees! Several scholars have sought to interpret this passage as referring to a sudden future appearing of the kingdom of God in their midst. This would permit a consistent eschatological interpretation of the passage,[23] but such an interpretation would make sense only if this sudden unexpected coming of the kingdom of God were being contrasted here with a carefully calculated coming of the kingdom, and there is no evidence of the latter in this saying.[24] As it stands, the text states that the kingdom of God is now in their midst, and this is best interpreted as indicating that in the person of Jesus the kingdom of God is now present among them.

From the above it is evident that the Gospel material does portray at times a "realized eschatology." The specific sayings that teach that the kingdom of God is a present reality in the ministry of Jesus are not as numerous as those that teach a "consistent eschatology," but they are nevertheless sufficient to demonstrate that Jesus made the claim that the kingdom of God was (in some way) already present in his ministry. It was not simply proleptically present or in the process of realization. The Gospels clearly indicate that Jesus taught that in his coming the long-awaited and long-sought kingdom of God had now arrived. The kingdom of God had come! With the coming of John the Baptist the kingdom of God had drawn near. With Jesus the kingdom of God had not simply drawn nearer still but had, on the contrary, now arrived.

THE KINGDOM OF GOD AS A FUTURE REALITY

The passages that speak of the kingdom of God as a future reality are even more numerous than the ones that speak of it as a present reality. In teaching his disciples how to pray, Jesus taught them to say:

> Father, hallowed be thy name. *Thy kingdom come.* (LUKE 11:2, italics added)

To modernize the prayer and interpret the petition about the kingdom coming as referring to an inner reign of God in the believer's heart is surely to miss the point, for in Matthew the petitions that the name of God be sanctified and his kingdom come are followed by a third synonymous strophe, "Thy will be done, on earth as it is in heaven" (Matt 6:10). Here clearly the petition seeks for God to reign on earth even as he now reigns in heaven. Nothing is said here of a personal inner moral experience. The petition seeks the realization of the eschatological reign of God on earth, and the petition concerning the sanctification of the name of God and the coming of his kingdom must be understood in a similar way.

Frequently the coming of the kingdom of God is associated with the final judgment.

> Not every one who says to me, "Lord, Lord," *shall enter the kingdom of heaven,* but he who does the will of my Father who is in heaven. On that day many will say to me, "Lord, Lord, did we not prophesy in your name, and cast out demons in your name, and do many mighty works in your name?" And then will I declare to them, "I never knew you; depart from me, you evildoers." (Matt 7:21–23, italics added)

Here, entering the kingdom of heaven is to take place "on that day," i.e., on the day of judgment, when the Son of man comes to judge the world. Another passage associating the kingdom of God with the future judgment is Luke 13:22–30:

> He went on his way through towns and villages, teaching, and journeying toward Jerusalem. And some one said to him, "Lord, will those who are saved be few?" And he said to them, "Strive to enter by the narrow door; for many, I tell you, will seek to enter and will not be able. When once the householder has risen up and shut the door, you will begin to stand outside and to knock at the door, saying, 'Lord, open to us.' He will answer you, 'I do not know where you come from.' Then you will begin to say, 'We ate and drank in your presence, and you taught in our streets.' But he will say, 'I tell you, I do not know where you come from; depart from me, all you workers of iniquity!' *There you will weep and gnash your teeth, when you see Abraham and Isaac and Jacob and all the prophets in the kingdom of God and you yourselves thrust out. And men will come from east and west, and from north and south, and sit at table in the kingdom of God.* And behold, some are last who will be first, and some are first who will be last." (Italics added)

The scene here is clearly one of judgment. Those who are being excluded from the kingdom claim that in their lifetime they ate and drank in the presence of Jesus (v. 26), but alas it is too late as they *see* Abraham and Isaac and Jacob and the prophets sitting and eating in the kingdom of God. The kingdom here must therefore refer to a future realization of the reign of God. Other passages associating the kingdom of God with the future judgment are: MATT 8:11–12; Matt 5:19, 20; 25:31–46.

In the parables the kingdom of God is frequently portrayed as a future event. The parables of growth (MARK 4:30–32; MATT 13:33) and the eschatological parable found in Matt 25:1–13 portray the kingdom of God as future, all attempts by Dodd to explain them as a present reality notwithstanding. The parable of the wheat and the tares (Matt 13:24–30) likens the kingdom of God to the gathering of the tares and their destruction at harvesttime. In a similar way the parable of the marriage feast (MATT 22:1–10) contains an addendum (vs. 11–14) in which the uninvited guest is cast into the outer darkness, where men weep and gnash their teeth. The latter description is also found in Matt 8:12; 13:42, 50; 24:51; 25:30, and in each instance the scene is that of the future final judgment.

In the sacrament of the Lord's Supper there is also contained a saying in which the kingdom of God is portrayed as still future. After the drinking of the cup the Synoptic Gospels all have the following saying:

> Truly, I say to you, I shall not drink again of the fruit of the vine *until that day* when I drink it new *in the kingdom of God.* (MARK 14:25, italics added; cf. Matt 26:29 and Luke 22:18)

This future dimension is also found in the Pauline account, although instead of mention of the coming of the kingdom of God, there is mention of the coming of the Son of man.

> For as often as you eat this bread and drink the cup, you proclaim the Lord's death *until he comes.* (I Cor 11:26, italics added)

This future aspect of the Lord's Supper indicates that the kingdom of God is in some way a future reality and is associated with the coming of the Lord, or Son of man. The kingdom comes when the Son of man returns!

From the above it is evident that the Gospel materials portray the kingdom of God as a future reality whose realization the believer is to pray for (MATT 6:10) and will one day inherit (Matt 25:34) when he sits at the messianic banquet with Jesus (MARK 14:25). Entering the kingdom can furthermore be described as "entering into life" (cf. MARK 9:43–45 with v. 47), obtaining "eternal life" (cf. MARK 10:17 with vs. 23–25 and Matt 25:46 with v. 34), entering the "joy of the master" (cf. MATT 25:21, 23 with v. 14), sharing in the messianic banquet (cf. MATT 8:11; MARK 14:25; Luke 14:15), and "being saved" (cf. MARK 10:26 with vs. 23–25), and in each of these instances the kingdom of God is portrayed as coming in the future!

THE KINGDOM OF GOD—A PRESENT REALITY
AND A FUTURE INHERITANCE

After our brief look at the Biblical data, we still face the question: What is the kingdom of God? Is it a present or a future reality? If one set of data is used and the other is ignored, it can be argued that Jesus taught that the kingdom of God was a present reality and completely "realized" in his ministry. If, however, the process is reversed and the opposite set of data is used and the other ignored, one can argue that according to Jesus the kingdom of God is entirely future and thus that he taught only a "consistent eschatology." A third possibility is to weigh the data in favor of each view, see which appears more frequently in the teaching of Jesus, and decide in favor of that one. By such a process no doubt consistent eschatology would "win." There is still a fourth possibility, however, and that is to attempt to reconcile the data by seeking to harmonize it. Although such attempts are not looked upon favorably in some circles, it would seem that fairness demands that we at least make such an attempt, for perhaps Jesus taught that the kingdom of God was both present in some new and unique way as well as future.

One of the problems that arises when we seek to understand what Jesus meant by the expression "kingdom of God" is that the term "kingdom" frequently conjures up in our minds a portrait of a particular kind of kingdom. For many, a kingdom brings to mind a picture of a medieval fiefdom with its castle, its moat, its drawbridge, etc. The term "kingdom" tends to bring to the Western mind the idea of a territory or "realm." In seeking to understand the expression "kingdom of God," we must understand the key word, which is indeed the term "kingdom," but is this term to be understood statically and spatially as a "realm," whether earthly, supraearthly, or heavenly, or is it to be understood more dynamically as a "reign"?

In the Old Testament the term "kingdom," or *malkut,* can refer to a "realm" in the sense of a spatial territory, but usually it is understood dynamically as referring to the government, authority, or power of a king.[25] In the Synoptic Gospels likewise there are several instances in which the term "kingdom," or *basileia,* can only be understood in this dynamic way as referring to a "reign." In the parable of the pounds we read:

A nobleman went into a far country to receive *a kingdom* [*basileia*] and then return. . . . When he returned, having received *the kingdom* . . . (Luke 19:12, 15, italics added)

Here the term *basileia* must be understood in a dynamic rather than a static sense, for what the nobleman is receiving is not primarily a territory but a "reign" or, as the RSV formerly translated it, "kingly power." Clearly the nobleman does not return with camels laden with territory but returns with the authority to rule as king.

Several other examples of this dynamic use of *basileia* in the Synoptic Gospels are:

> Then the mother of the sons of Zebedee came up . . . [and] said to him, "Command that these two sons of mine may sit, one at your right hand and one at your left, *in your kingdom.*" (Matt 20:20–21, italics added)

The Markan parallel used by Matthew reads instead of "in your kingdom [*basileia*]" "in your glory" (MARK 10:37), so that it is clear that what the mother of James and John requests is the privilege that her sons may sit on the right and left hand of Jesus when he comes into his "reign." We have a parallel statement in the account of the crucifixion when one of the thieves appeals to Jesus and says:

> Jesus, remember me when you come *into your kingdom* [*basileia*]. (Luke 23:42, italics added)

Here again the RSV in its first edition used the expression "kingly power," translating the term *basileia* correctly in a dynamic rather than a static sense.

> But seek first *his kingdom* [*basileia*] and his righteousness, and all these things shall be yours as well. (MATT 6:33, italics added)

In this saying, the kingdom which the follower of Jesus is to seek is placed alongside the righteousness of God. Seeing that God so clothes the grass of the field and takes care of the birds of the air, the believer is to seek after the reign of God. It is with the reign of God who "reigns" over the birds and the grass that the believer is to be concerned. Here again the reign of God is seen as something dynamic and is not some present or future territory over which God is king. To these examples can also be added:

MARK 10:15 (One must receive the reign of God like a child.)

Luke 10:9 (The reign of God [not some territory] has come near.)

Luke 17:21 (The reign of God which is in the midst of you cannot be a territory.)

Matt 16:28 (The Son of man is not spoken of here as coming with a territory but coming in his kingly power.)

Cf. also Dan 6:28 (during the reign [*basileia* in the LXX] of Darius) and

Rev 17:12 (the term "royal power" correctly translates *basileia*)

Understood in this dynamic sense of the reign of God, the kingdom of God can be a present reality which has come in a unique way in and through the ministry of Jesus as well as a future more perfect realization of that reign. The kingdom of God has arrived and is present in the coming of Jesus. It has come in fulfillment of the Old Testament promises even though the consummation of the kingdom lies still in the future.[26] This twofold aspect of the kingdom is the "secret of the kingdom of God" (MARK 4:11). The kingdom has come not as most people in the time of Jesus expected, i.e., in its fullness. It has come only in part. Its fullness awaits the consummation when the Son of man returns to judge the world. This tension between the now and the not yet provides the key for understanding the teaching of Jesus concerning the kingdom of God as well as for understanding Johannine and Pauline theology. In John, eternal life[27] is both a present reality (John 3:36; 5:24; 10:28; 17:3) and a future promise (John 6:40; 11:25; 12:25; 14:1–6), and in Paul we have the well-known tension between the indicative and the imperative[28] which can be resolved only by the realization that our redemption has come in part but that its future consummation still awaits us.

Oscar Cullmann has compared these two dimensions of the kingdom of God to D-day, when the decisive battle is fought and the outcome of the war decided, and V-day, when the war is finally ended.[29] With the coming of Christ—and here, rather than thinking of one event such as the baptism, the temptation, the crucifixion, or the resurrection, we should think of the entire Christ event—Satan is defeated and the Old Testament promises are fulfilled. Yet while victory is certain, Satan is defeated, and the firstfruits of this victory already realized, the "war" is not over. D-day has come but V-day is still future. Only at the parousia will the enemy be forced to his final surrender and forever judged.[30]

This portrayal of the kingdom of God finds support in two further observations. The first is that many of the sayings which teach a "realized eschatology" indicate that what is now realized is nevertheless incomplete and awaits a more perfect consummation. In the reply of Jesus to John the Baptist (MATT 11:4–6) the presence of the kingdom is witnessed to by the blind seeing, the lame walking, the dead being raised, etc. There is present, nevertheless, an incompleteness in all this in that there are still blind and lame present and even Jairus' daughter and Lazarus must still experience the grave. The kingdom of God has indeed come in the ministry of Jesus, but the consummation is still future. In a similar way Satan is bound and in the casting out of demons by Jesus the kingdom has come (LUKE 11:20–22), but Satan has not yet been judged and "thrown into the lake of fire" (Rev 20:10).[31] A second consideration that lends support to this interpretation of the kingdom of God is the realization that Jesus expected an interval period between his ministry and the consummation, so that two stages are involved in the coming of the kingdom. In MARK 2:18–20 we read:

> Now John's disciples and the Pharisees were fasting; and people came and said to him, "Why do John's disciples and the disciples of the Pharisees fast, but your disciples do not fast?" And Jesus said to them, "Can the wedding guests fast while the bridegroom is with them? As long as they have the bridegroom with them, they cannot fast. The days will come, when the bridegroom is taken away from them, and then they will fast in that day."

In this saying Jesus envisions a period in which the bridegroom will be absent from the wedding guests. There have been numerous attempts to demonstrate that vs. 19b and 20 are inauthentic. It is doubtful, however, that the saying could ever have ended with v. 19a,[32] and even if it did, v. 19a contains the suggestion of a time when the bridegroom would be taken away and the disciples would be alone. In another important passage Jesus replies to the request of James and John:

> The cup that I drink you will drink; and with the baptism with which I am baptized, you will be baptized; but to sit at my right hand or at my left is not mine to grant, but it is for those for whom it has been prepared. (MARK 10:39–40)

The metaphors "cup" and "baptism" undoubtedly refer here to suffering and death. In this saying Jesus maintains that after his death the sons of Zebedee will experience sufferings and martyrdoms similar to those of their master. As to the authenticity of the saying, it is difficult to attribute such a saying to the early church as a *vaticinium ex eventu*, since, although James was martyred, there is little evidence that John was martyred. Furthermore, the limitation of Jesus' authority (v. 40) is contrary to what one would expect if the saying were a creation of the early church.[33] In addition to these passages the prophetic statements about the destruction of Jerusalem (cf. MARK 13:2f.; LUKE 13:34–35; Luke 19:41–44; 23:28–31) also presume an interval period before the consummation, as do the institution of the Lord's Supper (see esp. MARK 14:25) and the various sayings on discipleship (cf. MARK 8:34–36; 10:29–30; Matt 10: 17–23; 16:18–19; 18:15–20; 25:41–45; etc.).[34]

In conclusion it would appear that rather than contrasting the present and future sayings of Jesus concerning the kingdom of God and forcing an either-or decision between them, one should see in this twofold temporal description a tension between the now and the not-yet aspects of the kingdom of God which is typical of the theology of the New Testament in general.[35] The believer therefore can already rejoice in the coming of the reign of God through the life and ministry of Jesus as well as in the presence of the firstfruits of the kingdom of God which are now his present possession.[36] Nevertheless—no, rather even more so because of this—he longs for the consummation of the kingdom of God, so that instead of seeing "in a mirror dimly . . . [he will see] face to face" (I Cor 13:12) and thus he prays:

> Our Father who art in heaven,
> Hallowed be thy name.
> Thy kingdom come,
> Thy will be done,
>   On earth as it is in heaven. (MATT 6:9–10)

and

Maranatha (I Cor 16:22)—Come, Lord Jesus! (Rev 22:20)

Chapter 5

THE CONTENT OF JESUS' TEACHING: THE FATHERHOOD OF GOD

WITHIN THE GOSPELS we find several terms used by Jesus to describe God. In contrast to much of Greek philosophy which pictured God as an "unmoved mover," the "cause of all being," a "pure being," the "deity," a "world soul," etc., Jesus stood firmly within the Jewish tradition and taught that God is a Person. This is witnessed to both by the terms Jesus used to describe God and by the attributes he ascribes to him. Some of the terms used by Jesus to describe God are:

God (MARK 10:18; MATT 6:24; Matt 5:8; Luke 11:28)[1]
God of Abraham, God of Isaac, God of Jacob (MARK 12:26)
Lord (Mark 5:19; 12:29; Luke 20:37)
Lord your (our) God (MARK 12:30; MATT 4:7, 10)
Lord of heaven and earth (MATT 11:25)
Lord of the harvest (MATT 9:38)
the only God (John 5:44; 17:3)
Most High (Luke 6:35)
King (Matt 5:35)[2]

The term that is most typical of Jesus' description of God is "Father." As an address to God this term is found in all five strata of the Gospels,[3] and altogether the title "Father" is found on the lips of Jesus sixty-five times in the Synoptic Gospels and over one hundred times in John.

THE DESCRIPTION OF GOD AS FATHER BEFORE JESUS

The description of God as Father by Jesus is not unique. As early as the second and even the third millennium B.C. the deity was addressed as Father.[4] Within Judaism the term "Father" was also used as a designation for God, and in the Old Testament, God is specifically called "Father" fifteen times. At times he is described as the Father of Israel (Deut 32:6; Isa 63:16 [twice]; 64:8; Jer 3:4, 19; 31:9; Mal 1:6; 2:10) and at times

80

he is described as the Father of individuals (II Sam 7:14; I Chron 17:13; 22:10; 28:6; Ps 68:5; 89:26). At times the father-son imagery is present and God is described as a Father even though the term "Father" is not specifically used as a title (cf. Ex 4:22–23; Deut 14:1; Ps 103:13; Jer 3:22; 31:20; Mal 3:17). It must be pointed out, however, that in comparison to other designations for God in the Old Testament, such as *Yahweh* (LORD) *Elohim* (God), *El* (God), *El Elyon* (Most High God), *El Shaddai* (God Almighty), and *Adonai* (Lord), the designation "Father" for God appears surprisingly seldom, and nowhere in the entire Old Testament is God addressed as "Father" in prayer.[5]

Within the intertestamental literature of Judaism the title is found, but again the occurrences are far from abundant. The title appears six times in the Apocrypha (Wisdom of Solomon 2:16; 14:3; Tobit 13:4; Sirach 23:1, 4; 51:10),[6] eight times in the Pseudepigrapha (Jubilees 1:24, 28; 19:29; III Maccabees 5:7; 6:4, 8; T. Levi 18:6; T. Judah 24:2),[7] and once in the Dead Sea Scrolls (1QH 9:35f.).[8] It is apparent from the above data that there were amazingly few instances of the term "Father" being used in Judaism, especially in Palestinian Judaism, as a designation for God before and during the time of Jesus. This may be due to the fact that the pagan concept of the fatherhood of God was often associated with ideas of man being physically begotten from the gods. Jews may therefore have avoided this designation for God because of its association with the fertility cults of paganism. As for addressing God by the title "Father," only five instances of this exist in the entire intertestamental literature. These are: Sirach 23:1, 4; III Maccabees 6:4, 8; and Wisdom of Solomon 14:3.

THE UNIQUENESS OF THE TITLE "FATHER" FOR GOD IN THE TEACHINGS OF JESUS

In Mark 14:36 we still possess the Aramaic designation *abba* which Jesus used to address God. Elsewhere in the Gospels the Aramaic has been translated into the Greek *pater,* but in Mark 14:36 we have both *abba* and *pater.* In two epistles of Paul this Aramaic term is also found as a designation of address to God:

And because you are sons, God has sent the Spirit of his Son into our hearts, crying, "Abba! Father!" (Gal 4:6)

For you did not receive the spirit of slavery to fall back into fear, but you have received the spirit of sonship. When we cry, "Abba! Father!" it is the Spirit himself bearing witness with our spirit that we are children of God. (Rom 8:15–16)

It should be noted that Paul presupposes the use of the Aramaic *abba* not only in the prayers of his own Gentile congregations in Galatia but also in Gentile congregations such as Rome which he did not himself found. There could be only one reason for Gentile congregations using this unique Aramaic prayer of address to God, and this is that Jesus himself had used this term in his own prayers and taught his disciples to use it as well (LUKE 11:2), so that the term, although in a language foreign to these Greek-speaking congregations, had taken on a sacred significance.

The term *abba* comes from the Aramaic *ab,* "father." The *-ba* suffix was once thought to be a determinative article and thus mean "the Father," but it is now evident that the suffix is simply the exclamatory form of *ab* and that *abba* is therefore to be interpreted as the address "Father."[9] At the time of Jesus, however, the form *abba* was used rather broadly in colloquial language, so that the term could serve as a form of address, "Father"; as the emphatic determinative, "the Father"; as well as for the first person singular or plural, "my Father" or "our Father." It is therefore virtually certain that behind such designations in the Gospels as "Father" (MATT 11:27; Luke 11:2; cf. John 11:41), "the Father" (MATT 11:27; MARK 13:32; cf. John 5:36), "my Father" (MATT 11:27; Matt 16:17; 18:10), and "our Father" (Matt 6:9) lies the form *abba.*

The uniqueness of Jesus' use of this term has often been pointed out.[10] This uniqueness lies, first of all, in the frequency with which the term appears on his lips. The rarity of "Father" as a title for God in the Old Testament and the intertestamental literature stands in sharp contrast with the frequent use of this title by Jesus. It is *the* way he chose to address God, and it was *the* way he taught his disciples to address God. Secondly, the use of this term by Jesus is unique in that he gave to this designation a warmth and tenderness not found elsewhere. The term *abba* was a homely word, the address of a small child to his father. There is a statement in the Talmud that says:

An infant cannot say "father" [*abba*] and "mother" [*imma*] until it has tasted wheat [i.e., until it is weaned].[11]

It is evident from the above that *abba* was the word of a toddler whose first words were "Daddy" *(abba)* and "Mommy" *(imma).* No Jew dared address God in such a manner. It would be disrespectful. *Abba* was simply too intimate and familiar a term and was consequently thought to be unfitting as an address for God. The result is that nowhere in Jewish literature do we find *abba* used as an address for God.[12]

For Jesus, however, *abba* was the address for God, for it not only described well his own relationship with God but it also described the relationship of his disciples. It described well that God delights in forgiveness (MARK 11:25; MATT 6:12; Luke 15:1–24), and cares for (MATT

6:25–32; 7:7–11; Matt 6:8) and rewards (Matt 6:4, 6, 18) his children. In fact, this term describes the relationship which the believer has to God so well that Jesus commanded that this address should be limited to God alone.

> And call no man your father on earth, for you have one Father, who is in heaven. (Matt 23:9)

Jesus is not so much here prohibiting his disciples from calling their earthly fathers "father" but is almost certainly referring to the practice of addressing distinguished and famous men as *abba*. God alone is to have that place of intimacy and honor in the life of the believer. As *the* name for God, *abba* is a sacred word and should not be profaned. To address another man as *abba* would in effect be equivalent to addressing him as "God." The believer has but one God, whom he now has the privilege of calling *abba*, and this form of address belongs to God alone.

We have mentioned that for Jesus, *abba* was *the* address which he directed to God. In fact, we can say that it is the only way that Jesus addressed God in prayer, with one single exception. In the passion account we read:

> And at the ninth hour Jesus cried with a loud voice, "Eloi, Eloi, lama sabachthani?" which means, "My God, my God, why hast thou forsaken me?" (MARK 15:34)

In this instance there are two reasons for this different way of addressing God. The first is that Jesus is here quoting Ps 22:1, and the term in this verse is "God," not "Father." The second reason, however, is more important still, for it explains why Jesus chose to quote Ps 22:1. On the cross Jesus experienced the horror that he dreaded at Gethsemane (MARK 14:33–36). The relationship he possessed with the Father was broken. Bearing the sin of the world (MARK 10:45; MATT 26:28), Jesus felt a separation from God, a separation that sin brings (Isa 59:2). This separation, according to the New Testament, was not simply a feeling on the part of Jesus but an actual, if momentary, separation in which Jesus bore the sin of man before a holy and just God. In this moment as he died the sinner's death and experienced rejection from God, the expression "Father" would have been anachronistic, to say the least, for at that moment he became sin "who knew no sin, so that in him we might become the righteousness of God" (II Cor 5:21). Yet this abandonment by the Father was temporary, and shortly thereafter the prayer of Jesus is:

> Father, into thy hands I commit my spirit! (Luke 23:46)

THE SIGNIFICANCE OF THE TITLE "FATHER"
IN THE TEACHINGS OF JESUS

During the nineteenth century when theological liberalism reached its zenith, one tenet that became a sure result of this theology was the doctrine of the universal fatherhood of God. Closely associated with this tenet was the doctrine of the brotherhood of man. The teachings of Jesus were treasured and held in high esteem at least in part because, it was thought, Jesus not only taught but emphasized that God was the Father of all mankind and that as a result all men were brothers. In certain circles it is still popular to speak of the universal fatherhood of God which Jesus taught. Yet did Jesus in his teachings on the fatherhood of God actually teach a doctrine of the universal fatherhood of God?

Once one begins to investigate the sayings of Jesus on this subject it becomes apparent that something is amiss. In the Sermon on the Mount, Jesus refers to God as "your Father" sixteen times (MATT 5:48; 6:15, 32; Matt 5:16, 45; 6:1, 4, 6 [2], 8, 9 [our], 14, 18 [2], 26; 7:11), but it is important to note who the "you" are to whom Jesus is speaking. According to MATT 5:1–2 it was not mankind in general, i.e., the crowds whom Jesus was teaching, but rather his disciples.

> Seeing the crowds, he went up on the mountain, and when he sat down his *disciples* came to him. And he opened his mouth and taught *them,* saying . . . (Italics added)

It should also be noted that the "Our Father," or the Lord's Prayer, is not a general prayer that Jesus taught the crowds but is rather the prayer Jesus taught his disciples to pray, for the disciples had asked him to teach them a specific prayer to identify them and bind them together as a particular community even as John the Baptist (and the Pharisees and Essenes) taught his disciples a prayer.

> He was praying in a certain place, and when he ceased, *one of his disciples* said to him, "Lord, teach *us* to pray, as John taught his disciples." (Luke 11:1, italics added)

Within the early church the communitylike nature of the "Our Father" is most evident in the fact that it was associated with baptism and was part of the instruction of new converts either just before baptism or immediately after.[13] In the *Didache,* or *The Teaching of the Twelve Apostles,* which was written around the turn of the first century, it should be noted that the Lord's Prayer is found in chapter eight and that chapters one through six deal with a description of the "Two Ways," chapter seven deals with baptism, and chapters nine and ten with the Lord's Supper. Chapters one through six were almost certainly a kind of catechism for baptismal candidates, so that the teaching of the Lord's Prayer was associated with those who through baptism became part of the church. It would appear from this and other evidence that in certain parts of the early church, at least, the first recitation of the Lord's Prayer occurred at the first communion of the newly baptized when the new converts were now privileged to pray this "prayer of believers" and confess "Our Father." In so doing, they made a confession of their unique relationship to God through Jesus Christ by which they were now able to call God "Father." It is evident from Paul as well that "Father" was an address made toward God that only believers could legitimately utter, for it was as sons who possess the Spirit that the believers cried, *"Abba!* Father!" (Gal 4:6; Rom 8:15) and in this confession the Spirit himself bore witness to their sonship, that they were indeed the sons of God (Rom 8:16).[14]

It is evident, therefore, that Jesus did not teach a doctrine of the universal fatherhood of God,[15] and we do not find anywhere in the sayings of Jesus that since God is the Creator we are through creation his children and he is thus our Father. On the contrary, there are some persons who can be described as having the devil as their father (John 8:44; cf. Matt 12:34)![16] In this regard the words of Jesus in MATT 11: 25–27 are important:

> At that time Jesus declared, "I thank thee, Father, Lord of heaven and earth, that thou hast hidden these things from the wise and understanding and revealed them to babes; yea, Father, for such was thy gracious will. All things have been delivered to me by my Father; and no one knows the Son except the Father, and no one knows the Father except the Son and any one to whom the Son chooses to reveal him.

In this "Johannine thunderbolt" Jesus confesses his own unique relationship with God. He possesses a "Sonship" qualitatively different from the sonship of his disciples, for Jesus confesses to know the Father in the same way as the Father knows him. There exists between them a mutual and exclusive knowledge. One cannot help thinking here of the Johannine expression that Jesus is the "only Son" (John 1:14, 18; 3:16, 18). Yet "sonship" is available through Jesus to those who acknowledge the revelation and message he brings. He is the Mediator between the Father and man, and through Jesus the disciples are invited to become the adopted sons of God. Apart from him there is no access to the Father, for "no one comes to the Father, but by me" (John 14:6). It should also be noted that the opportunity to enter this relationship with God and thus to call him

"Abba" is not extended to the wise and understanding but rather is extended to "babes." Elsewhere Jesus states:

> Truly, I say to you, whoever does not receive the kingdom of God like a child shall not enter it. (MARK 10:15)

Only those who come as helpless small children, without claim or merit, can call God *"Abba."* The picture drawn by Jesus here is a vivid one. Even as the toddling child in trust and helplessness cries "Daddy," so the followers of Jesus must come likewise as children, trusting in the mercy of God and renouncing any claim of righteousness (MARK 2:17), and call out in simple faith, *"Abba*—Daddy—Father."

The difference between Jesus' Sonship and our sonship is also brought out by the fact that he never refers to God as "our" Father. At times he may refer to "my Father" or to "your Father" but never does he say "our Father."[17] This is revealed most clearly in John 20:17. In this verse Jesus tells Mary:

> Do not hold me, for I have not yet ascended to the Father; but go to my brethren and say to them, I am ascending to my Father and your Father, to my God and your God.

Here Jesus clearly distinguishes between his relationship with God and the relationship of his disciples with God. Both he and the disciples are "sons" of God and can call God "Father," but the disciples have become sons by adoption. Jesus is the only Son, the Son by nature.

CONCLUSION

It is evident from the above that far from seeing God as an abstract deity, a world soul, or first cause Jesus perceived of God as a Person and introduced his disciples to a unique and most intimate term of address for God. The term *abba* reveals that through Jesus the believer has entered the kingdom of God and has a new relationship with God. The term furthermore reveals the loving concern and care of the Creator for his children. Yet our "heavenly Father" is also the "Lord of heaven and earth" (MATT 11:25) through whom this planet, the solar system, the stars, the galaxies, the universe came into being. This raises the problem of how one can avoid the danger on the one hand of being irreverent and blasphemous and speaking of the Father as "Big Daddy" or "The Old Man Upstairs" and on the other hand of thinking that God as Creator is so great a deity that he is distant and far off, unconcerned and uninterested in the needs of the individual believer.

Perhaps instead of seeking to combine these two portraits and dividing by two we should permit both portraits to exist side by side. Jesus did just this. In reverence for God he avoided at times using the sacred name of God,[18] and yet he called God "Daddy." The amazing fact is that Jesus bids us through him to come to the Creator of the Universe and as babes call him *"Abba*—Daddy!"

Chapter 6

THE CONTENT OF JESUS' TEACHING:
THE ETHICS OF THE KINGDOM

AS ONE INVESTIGATES the ethical teachings of Jesus, it quickly becomes evident that any attempt to arrange them into a simple neat "system" encounters numerous problems. One such problem is that Jesus never propounded an organized ethical system. Generally the ethical teachings of Jesus are found scattered throughout the Gospels in individual pericopes and sayings, or blocks of such pericopes and sayings. What organization we do find, such as the Sermon on the Mount, is due far more to the early church and the Evangelists than to Jesus himself. Another problem one encounters is the incompleteness of the ethical teachings of Jesus. Whole areas of ethics such as economics, culture, and education are never discussed and some areas such as the individual's relationship to the state (MARK 12:13–17),[1] marriage and divorce (MARK 10:2–9), family relationships (MARK 7:5–13), and jurisprudence (Matt 5:33–37; 7:1–5) are referred to with extreme brevity and at times simply in passing, so that no comprehensive ethical system can be deduced. A third problem that the investigator encounters in his investigation of the ethics of Jesus is the apparently contradictory nature of some of his teachings. An example of this is the sayings on the apparent eternal validity of the law (MARK 12:28–34; MATT 5:17–20) and the abolition of various commandments by Jesus (Matt 5:21–48; MARK 7:1f.). Another example is the apparent conflict between the reward motif (MARK 10:21, 28–30; Matt 6:2–6, 16–18; Luke 10:25–28) and the emphasis on grace (Matt 20:1–15; MARK 2:17; cf. Jesus' emphasis on faith in MARK 2:5; 5:34; 7:29; 10:52; MATT 8:10; etc.) in the teachings of Jesus.

Still another problem that one encounters in reading the Gospels is the impossibility of much of the ethical teaching of Jesus, for what Jesus demands is that one strive not to be more loving, more truthful, more forgiving, more merciful, less lustful, etc., but to be as loving, truthful, forgiving, merciful, etc., as God himself (LUKE 6:36; Matt 18:23–35).

Jesus also demands not merely that the actions of his followers be perfect but that their motives be perfect as well (LUKE 11:33–36; MATT 5:3–8; 12:33–37; 23:25–26), and who can attain such perfection in this life? Is this not an impossible ideal? Furthermore, if one must first obtain this perfect character as a quality in this life before one can enter the kingdom of God, then is this not a "law ethic" even more condemning than the Old Testament Law? Yet we find in all of this a strange paradox, for although Jesus demanded a higher ethic than his contemporaries (Matt 5:20), he nevertheless opened the kingdom of God to tax collectors and sinners (MARK 2:15–17; Matt 21:31)!

Along with such problems several additional questions are also raised by the ethical teachings of Jesus. Some of these are: Is the ethic of Jesus universal in nature or limited to a certain people, i.e., are such teachings of Jesus as are found in Matt 19:10–12 (eunuchs for the sake of the kingdom of heaven); LUKE 14:26–27 (hating father and mother, wife and children, brothers and sisters); and MARK 10:21 (selling all one has and giving to the poor) meant for all the followers of Jesus or perhaps only for a unique spiritual elite? Are certain teachings of Jesus limited to a specific period of time and to a particular situation or are they meant to be universal ethical requirements? One can think here of: Matt 5:34–37 (Does this forever prohibit a Christian from taking an oath in a court of law?); 6:6 (Does this eliminate the possibility of corporate prayer in the church?); MATT 5:38–42 (Does this forbid physical resistance under every possible circumstance and also require giving charity to those who would use such charity to continue their slavery to drugs or alcohol?); MARK 12:13–17 (Does this require the Christian to support a government that is actively seeking to exterminate the Jews?); etc. Furthermore, are the ethical teachings of Jesus to be taken literally or must they sometimes be understood figuratively, and if we maintain that at times they are to be interpreted figuratively, is there not a danger of diluting the radical dimension of these sayings into an ethic with which we are comfortable? Finally we must raise the question of whether the ethical teachings of Jesus are to be understood as entrance requirements for the kingdom of God or as rules or laws or guides for those who have already become members of the kingdom. It is with these and similar questions that the history of interpretation has wrestled over the centuries.

VARIOUS ATTEMPTS TO INTERPRET
THE ETHICAL TEACHINGS OF JESUS

Throughout the history of the Christian church numerous attempts have been made to systematize the ethical teachings of Jesus and to seek a general concept which might prove "a" or "the" key for understanding his teachings. We shall seek to summarize these attempts under six headings, realizing full well that all these attempts do not fit perfectly under the summary headings. Nevertheless, such generalization is useful in presenting the major ways in which the ethical teachings of Jesus have been understood.

THE "CATHOLIC" INTERPRETATION

As early as the second century a two-level ethic was seen in the teachings of Jesus.[2] This two-level ethic involved a lower minimal ethic which was incumbent upon all Christians and which involved the Ten Commandments and various commandments of Jesus, such as the love commandment (MARK 12:28–34) and the Golden Rule (MATT 7:12). These commandments all Christians living in society could and had to keep. There existed, however, a higher ethic as well which was evangelical counsel for those who sought a higher and better righteousness through which rewards and merit could be earned. This higher ethic, which involved the surrender of all personal possessions (MARK 10:21; Luke 12:33), denial of family (LUKE 14:26), denial of marriage (Matt 19: 11–12), etc., was of course possible only for a minority who possessed a greater dedication and commitment. Such a twofold ethic led quite naturally to a two-dimensional Christian society. The laity who lived in this world sought to fulfill the "requirements" of the gospel, whereas the clergy, especially the monastic element, sought to fulfill the "advice" of the gospel.

Such a two-level ethic is not found, however, in the teachings of Jesus. The Sermon on the Mount cannot be divided into a lower and a higher ethic. On the contrary, it is addressed to the "disciples" of Jesus (Matt 5:1–2), i.e., to the followers of Jesus. Jesus demanded total commitment from all who would follow him, not just from the "more dedicated." The words of Jesus in MARK 8:34–38 are addressed not to a specific element in the church seeking a higher righteousness but to anyone seeking to follow him:

> If any man would come after me, let him deny himself and take up his cross and follow me. For whoever would save his life will lose it; and whoever loses his life for my sake and the gospel's will save it. (MARK 8:34–35; cf. also MATT 10:37–39)

Such terms as "any man" and "whoever" indicate that following Jesus demands a total commitment on the part of everyone who would be his disciple, i.e., become a Christian. However we understand such sayings on wealth, family, marriage, etc., we cannot see in the words of Jesus any statement that they are only "evangelical advice" for those seeking a greater righteousness. The rich young ruler who was told to sell all that he had (MARK 10:21) went away not lacking a greater righteousness but lacking any righteousness at all (MARK 10:23–26). He, as a result, failed to enter the kingdom of God altogether! It should be noted also that the command to sell all in Luke 12:33 is addressed in general to the "little flock" (v. 32). The denial of family is also directed to "any one" who seeks to follow Jesus (LUKE 14:26). Only in Matt 19:11–12 does Jesus appear to distinguish between two groups of Christians, and no hint is made here that "not to marry" results in a higher meritorious righteousness.[3]

THE "UTOPIAN" INTERPRETATION

In contrast to the "Catholic" interpretation, the "utopian" interpretation, which has been held by such groups as the left wing of the Reformation, certain Franciscan and pietistic groups, certain holiness groups, and men like Tolstoy, maintains that Jesus truly intended to give a new law for all Christians to follow and that this law was to be followed in a very literal way. The Sermon on the Mount especially was seen as a design for a new society of love and peace on this earth. Such teachings of Jesus as MATT 7:1 (judge not); 5:39–42 (resist not); Matt 5:34–37 (swear not); 19:11–12 (being eunuchs for the kingdom of heaven) were interpreted to mean that all social structures such as the police and army, judicial systems, civil authority, and in some instances marriage were to be done away with in order to allow the love, justice, and peace of the kingdom of God to be expressed. The command of love, furthermore, received a great emphasis. In emphasizing the strict literal fulfillment of the commands of Jesus, this interpretation frequently placed an emphasis on perfectionism (MATT 5:48).

It must be acknowledged that this "utopian" interpretation is correct insofar as it stresses that the commands of Jesus are binding on all Christians and not on just a spiritually elite group. It is also correct in its emphasis on the importance of Jesus' command to love. Its emphasis on the literal fulfillment of the commands of Jesus is also correct in the majority of instances. Yet it is certainly incorrect to see in the teachings of Jesus both an attack against all established social institutions and an attempt to establish the kingdom of God as a new social society in this life; "Caesar" possesses a legitimate function and deserves his due (MARK 12:13–17), and seeing the establishment of the kingdom of God as a possibility in this world loses sight of the fact that the consummation of the kingdom of God is an eschatological event that God himself establishes through the coming of the Son of man. There is also present in this interpretation of Jesus' ethic a gross disregard of the extent and intensity of sin. Certainly the Christian must seek to establish love, peace, and justice in this world, but Jesus clearly warns that despite all such efforts "nation will rise against nation, and kingdom against kingdom" (MARK 13:8). Jesus does not promise that his followers will bring about a transformation of this world into a utopian paradise but on the contrary that they will be hated (MARK 13:13) and lose their lives (MARK 8: 34–38). As to the perfection he demands, the term "perfect" in MATT 5:48 does not refer to an ethical perfection or sinlessness before God but to a wholeness of attitude toward other people. It refers to a similar attitude toward others as God himself has toward them. This means that even as God is unlimited in his goodness and graciousness toward sinners, so must our love toward our enemies be gracious and unlimited in mercy. The whole context of MATT 5:43–47, which speaks of the relationship of the Christian to his enemies, supports this interpretation. The issue of MATT 5:48 is clearly not that of an ethical perfection before God but rather that of being like God in mercy and graciousness toward other people. The parallel passage in LUKE 6:36 supports this interpretation in that instead of the term *teleios* ("perfect") we find *oiktirmon* ("merciful"):

Be *merciful,* even as your Father is *merciful.* (Italics added)[4]

THE "LUTHERAN" INTERPRETATION

According to the "Lutheran" interpretation, the Sermon on the Mount and the other ethical teachings of Jesus are an uncompromising expression of the righteousness that God demands of all men. It is furthermore maintained that this ethical demand of Jesus is impossible of fulfillment. And it is meant to be, for the ethical commands of Jesus are meant to lead man to despair and thus to him who alone fulfilled these commands, so that his righteousness may be imputed to man through faith! The ethical teachings of Jesus are therefore not intended to be a way of righteousness for man (actually any such attempt to keep the commandments of Jesus could be misconstrued as legalism or an attempt at a works-righteousness) but are meant primarily to reveal man's sin and thus, like the Old Testament Law, prepare him for the grace offered in the gospel. Through the ethical demands of Jesus, therefore, man experiences guilt and despair in order that through repentance and faith he may experience the grace of God.

It is evident that the "Lutheran" interpretation is rooted in the Reformation struggle over the doctrine of justification by faith and the struggle of Paul over the purpose of the Law (cf. Rom 3:19–20; 4:15; 5:20–21; 7:8). This interpretation nevertheless appears to be a reading into the text of the doctrine of justification by faith. The fact is that the ethical teachings of Jesus in the Gospels are not addressed to unbelievers to lead them to despair and thus to grace but are addressed to those who have already experienced that grace, i.e., the disciples (cf. Matt 5:1–2; Luke 6:20). In other words the teachings of Jesus are addressed to those who have already seen their sin and inability to keep the Law, have already fled to Jesus for grace, and thus have already been forgiven! Even as Rom 12–15 presupposes Rom 1–8, the ethical teachings of Jesus presuppose repentance and faith. The commands of Jesus, therefore, do not so much lead to grace, but on the contrary it is grace that leads to the commands.

THE "LIBERAL" INTERPRETATION

The "liberal" interpretation, which arose in the nineteenth century and is still held by many today, maintains that the essence of Jesus' ethic lies in the inculcating of principles that involve the attitudes and inward disposition of the individual.[5] Jesus never intended to place on his followers a burdensome yoke or a new legalism. On the contrary, Jesus was more concerned with what his followers should be rather than with what they should do. He was more concerned with eradicating the evil that exists in man's heart than in describing the form that the external conduct should take. As for his specific commands, many of them are "husk" and no longer applicable, but the emphasis in Jesus' teaching on the inner disposition of love in the heart is forever valid in every circumstance. The application of this inner principle was furthermore understood as primarily involving individuals rather than society and social institutions, since the latter have no "heart." Nevertheless through the individual such institutions could be influenced. A favorite text of this interpretation is Luke 17:20–21 ("the kingdom of God is in the midst of you"). Here the kernel of the teaching of Jesus on the kingdom of God was seen as a personal ethical attitude of the heart, the reign of God in the human heart. The liberal interpretation of the ethic of Jesus therefore saw this ethic as a timeless religious principle, an inward disposition of love in the heart, rather than a listing of various commandments. Many of the individual commandments of Jesus were therefore interpreted as being figurative rather than literal.

It must be acknowledged that this interpretation is correct in emphasizing that the ethical teachings of Jesus involve a new inner disposition and attitude of the heart and in seeing the use of figurative language in the teachings of Jesus. Yet "being" and "doing" go hand in hand, for to love one's neighbor involves not only or even primarily an inner feeling toward him but rather the doing of acts of love.[6] The loving man does acts of love even as a "good man out of the good treasure of his heart produces good" (LUKE 6:45). The ethic of Jesus is not simply an intention ethic. It is a doing ethic! It should also be pointed out in this respect that the use of Luke 17:20–21 to support this interpretation is illegitimate. One need only note that the statement about the kingdom of God being "in" or "in the midst of you" is uttered to the Pharisees, whose inner attitudes are repeatedly criticized by Jesus (cf. Matt 23:27–28), to realize that Jesus cannot be speaking here of a correct inner disposition.[7] As for the use of figurative language by Jesus, it is evident that he made use of such language.[8] Yet one cannot simply label every radical ethical demand of Jesus as an overstatement. It may be that the specific applications of the ethical principles that Jesus gave in the first century are as timeless as the principles themselves!

THE "INTERIM ETHIC" INTERPRETATION

The term "interim ethic" is intimately associated with Albert Schweitzer and his eschatological interpretation of the teachings of Jesus. According to Schweitzer, Jesus taught that the kingdom of God was a future, otherworldly phenomenon that was imminent and would bring history to an end. Since this future kingdom was supraethical,[9] Jesus was not concerned with giving ethical instructions for this eschatological kingdom but instead gave a temporary emergency ethic to his followers for the brief interim period before the kingdom. This interim ethic, which was concerned primarily with repentance and moral renewal in preparation for the coming kingdom, was an extraordinary ethic for an extraordinary emergency period. This explains the radical nature of such commands as MATT 5:38–42 (resist not); MATT 7:1 (judge not); and Matt 19:11–12 (being eunuchs for the kingdom of God). Jesus, however, was mistaken, for the kingdom of God did not come as he expected, and as a result his emergency ethic is both impractical and impossible and must therefore be rejected. What remained for Schweitzer was the absolute quality of the ethical demands of Jesus which, despite being inapplicable in their specific demands, call us to "heroic" actions. In the case of Schweitzer, himself, this "heroic" action led him to give up an outstanding career in theology and music in Europe in order to study medicine and work in the missionary hospital in Lambaréné.

This interpretation is correct in seeing that the ethical teachings of Jesus are intimately associated with the coming of the kingdom of God, but is the ethic of Jesus based primarily on an imminent emergency that is about to take place? At times the Christian is told, "Watch therefore, for you know neither the day nor the hour" (Matt 25:13; cf. also MARK 13:33, 35; Mark 13:37; MATT 24:44). Yet Jesus does not base his ethic primarily on the nearness of the end but bases it on the character of God (LUKE 6:32–36; MATT 6:25–34), the activity of God in creation (MARK 10:2–9), or the will of God (Matt 7:21).[10] The ethic of Jesus is therefore not so much an emergency ethic based on the nearness of the end as the ethic of a new covenant in which already the kingdom of God is realized in part, and it is based not so much on an eschatological judgment that is imminent as on the example and character of God.

THE "EXISTENTIALIST" INTERPRETATION

According to the "existentialist" interpretation, the ethical teachings of Jesus are not meant to be a system of rules for conduct but are rather an existential call for decision. The ethic of Jesus is primarily an obedience ethic in which the individual is continually confronted with the will and demand of God. Jesus never intended for his teaching to be incorporated into an ethical system whether that system was idealistic or legalistic. He intended that his teachings be understood as a radical call for obedience. Such passages as LUKE 14:26 (hating father and mother); Luke 12:33 (selling possessions); and LUKE 9:60 (leaving the dead to bury the dead) are meant to lead us to an unconditional decision and commitment that will as a result free us from bondage to a this-worldly system, i.e., from bondage to the Law.

It is obvious that this interpretation correctly sees that the teachings of Jesus involve a call to decision. Repent, believe, deny, follow, take up the cross, sell all, confess, etc., are integral to the teachings of Jesus. Jesus did call men to decision. Yet every ethical teaching of Jesus cannot be seen as only a call for decision. Many of his ethical teachings are directed to those who have already "decided" for him, the gospel, the kingdom of God. The direction and manner in which this decision is to manifest itself is also found in the teachings of Jesus, and many of the same criticisms leveled against the "liberal" interpretation can also be directed against this one.[11] Jesus did not leave his followers to decide for themselves how they should carry out their new commitment (or their new inner attitude according to the "liberal" interpretation) in every specific situation. On the contrary, he gives concrete examples as to how his followers are to live, and one cannot therefore simply claim that these concrete examples are meant to lead to an existential call for decision whose mode of action will be self-evident. Jesus frequently explained to his disciples how they were to manifest this decision in such areas as fasting (Matt 6:16–18), giving alms (Matt 6:2–4), and prayer (Matt 6:5–6). Even the love command is not considered self-evident, but numerous examples are given as to how love is to manifest itself in the life of the believer (cf. Matt 25:31–46; LUKE 6:27–36; Luke 10:29–37).[12]

THE BIBLICAL DATA

THE PREREQUISITE FOR ENTERING THE KINGDOM OF GOD

In investigating the Biblical data one becomes aware that many of the ethical teachings that Jesus proclaimed presume a new relationship between the individual and God. Such teachings as the Sermon on the Mount (Matt 5:1f.), the Lord's Prayer (LUKE 11:1–4), prayer in general (Luke 18:1, 7), humility (MARK 9:33–37), the meaning of the parables (MARK 4:10–12; Mark 4:34), and church discipline (Matt 18:15–20) are directed to those who have already entered the kingdom of God and thus had the right to address God as *"Abba—*Father." Using more technical language, we can say that the *didache* (the ethical instructions addressed to believers) assumes an earlier favorable response to the *kerygma* (the proclamation of the good news of the kingdom of God). Even as the Law was given to a people who had already experienced God's grace in their redemption out of Egypt and were already participants in a divine covenant, so too must we recognize that the ethical instructions of Jesus are addressed primarily to a people who had experienced God's grace and were participants in a new covenant. At times Jesus, of course, addressed both the crowds and his opponents, but the "existential" interpretation is correct in seeing the most basic demand of Jesus as a demand for radical unqualified decision. Only through such an unconditional unqualified decision for the kingdom of God can one become part of that kingdom and live the ethic of the kingdom.

This demand for decision appears in a multitude of forms in the Gospels. At times it appears in the form of a call for "repentance";[13] at other times as an invitation to "follow" Jesus;[14] at times it is a call to "faith";[15] at times it is a call to "deny oneself,"[16] to "take up the cross,"[17] to "confess" Jesus,[18] to "keep his words,"[19] to "take up his yoke,"[20] to "lose one's life";[21] or at times we encounter such difficult requirements as the need to "hate one's family,"[22] to "remove one's hand or eye,"[23] and to "sell all one has."[24] Rather than to see these various expressions as different requirements that Jesus demanded at various times, however, it would appear more reasonable to see them as different aspects of the same radical demand for decision and unconditional commitment to

God. At times Jesus emphasized a particular aspect of this demand, as in the case of the rich young ruler, when the situation called for it, but the same total demand of unconditional decision is implicit in each call to decision.[25]

With regard to this decision Jesus was careful to draw the attention of his prospective followers to the cost involved in such a decision:

> For which of you, desiring to build a tower, does not first sit down and count the cost, whether he has enough to complete it? Otherwise, when he has laid a foundation, and is not able to finish, all who see it begin to mock him, saying, "This man began to build, and was not able to finish." Or what king, going to encounter another king in war, will not sit down first and take counsel whether he is able with ten thousand to meet him who comes against him with twenty thousand? And if not, while the other is yet a great way off, he sends an embassy and asks terms of peace. So therefore, whoever of you does not renounce all that he has cannot be my disciple. (Luke 14:28–33)[26]

> As they were going along the road, a man said to him, "I will follow you wherever you go." And Jesus said to him, "Foxes have holes, and birds of the air have nests; but the Son of man has nowhere to lay his head." To another he said, "Follow me." But he said, "Lord, let me first go and bury my father." But he said to him, "Leave the dead to bury their own dead; but as for you, go and proclaim the kingdom of God." Another said, "I will follow you, Lord; but let me first say farewell to those at my home." Jesus said to him, "No one who puts his hand to the plow and looks back is fit for the kingdom of God." (LUKE 9:57–62)

We have already seen in Chapter 2[27] that Jesus at times employed overstatement and hyperbole in his teachings, so that certain of the demands, such as the demands to hate one's family (LUKE 14:26), to remove one's eye and hand (MARK 9:43–48), to sell all one has (MARK 10:21; Luke 12:33), must be interpreted in the context of the totality of Jesus' teachings. The love command of Jesus, which includes even one's enemies (LUKE 6:27–36), indicates that we should interpret a passage like LUKE 14:26 as an overstatement. Our knowledge of the aspective use of language by Semitic people indicates that the words of Jesus in MARK 9:43–48 must also be interpreted as overstatement.

The statements of Jesus in LUKE 9:59–62 cannot, however, in their context be interpreted as overstatements, for they are directed specifically to two individuals, and even if they are not to be universalized, they are meant to be taken literally by those individuals, even as the command to the rich young ruler (MARK 10:21) had a quite literal meaning for him.

Attempts to soften these words by interpreting LUKE 9:59 as a request by the individual to stay with his aged or dying father until he dies and is buried are readings into the text. As it stands, the text states that the young man wants to bury his father, not that he wants to wait until his father dies and then bury him.[28] It may be that since the individual himself raised a problem with regard to following him, even if it would appear to be a legitimate problem, Jesus made the "cost of discipleship" as clear and as blunt as possible. "He who loves father or mother more than me is not worthy of me" (MATT 10:37).[29]

Even if we leave room for overstatement in some of these sayings of Jesus, it is most apparent that in his proclamation of the kingdom of God Jesus demanded from his listeners an unconditional commitment. One cannot follow Jesus halfheartedly or with reservations. Jesus encouraged his audience to count the cost. He did not teach "cheap grace"! Paradoxically, however, that cost of discipleship is not "borne" or "endured" but is joyously rendered.

> The kingdom of heaven is like treasure hidden in a field, which a man found and covered up; then *in his joy* he goes and sells all that he has and buys that field. (Matt 13:44, italics added)

THE NEED FOR A NEW ATTITUDE

In seeking to describe the essence of Jesus' ethic the "liberal" interpretation emphasized the importance placed by Jesus on the attitude of the individual. To be concerned with external conduct at the expense of or apart from a correct inward attitude leads to being a "whitewashed tomb" (Matt 23:27–28; cf. LUKE 11:37–41), to being concerned about what goes into the stomach rather than that which comes out of the heart (MARK 7:5, 14–15), to losing sight of the meaning of the commandments and thus being more concerned with legalistic details than with mercy and goodness (MARK 3:4; cf. MARK 2:23–28; Luke 13:10–17; 14:1–6), etc. What is required by Jesus is not formal compliance to rules but a new attitude of the heart. The blessedness of the kingdom of God is for those who are "pure in heart" (Matt 5:8). It is the heart that must change, for out of the heart the issues of morality are decided (MARK 7:21–22). This is why riches pose so great a danger, "for where your treasure is, there will your heart be also" (MATT 6:21). It is because of their "hardness of heart" that the Pharisees opposed Jesus' healings on the Sabbath, not because of their piety (MARK 3:5)! It is because "their heart is far from [God]" that they always sought to find fault with Jesus (MARK 7:6). Yet judgment is coming and has already begun, and this judgment will be by him who knows the heart (Luke 16:15). For the hypocrite this will be disastrous, for God sees beyond the whitewashed surface and sees the dead bones of pride, arrogance, and hate. Yet for the pure in heart, God reckons even the two copper coins of the widow (MARK 12:41–44) as a great treasure in heaven, and a simple cup of cold water given out of a loving heart receives its reward (Matt 25:31–46; MARK 9:41).

The source of this new attitude is revealed in the incident recorded in Luke 7:36–50, where Jesus tells a Pharisee named Simon the following parable to explain why the woman, who was a sinner, anointed him:

> "A certain creditor had two debtors; one owed five hundred denarii, and the other fifty. When they could not pay, he forgave them both. Now which of them will love him more?" Simon answered, "The one, I suppose, to whom he forgave more." And he said to him, "You have judged rightly." Then turning toward the woman he said to Simon, "Do you see this woman? I entered your house, you gave me no water for my feet, but she has wet my feet with her tears and wiped them with her hair. You gave me no kiss, but from the time I came in she has not ceased to kiss my feet. You did not anoint my head with oil, but she has anointed my feet with ointment. Therefore I tell you, her sins, which are many, are forgiven, for she loved much; but he who is forgiven little, loves little." (Luke 7:41–47; for a similar response to God's offer of grace, see Luke 19:1–10)

It is because of her being loved by God and being forgiven of her sins that the woman now possessed a new attitude of love stemming out of gratitude toward God.[30] In a similar way it is because God has forgiven the believer that the believer is now in turn able to forgive others (MATT 6:12). It is because God has been gracious and merciful to us that we have a heart of compassion and mercy toward others (LUKE 6:36). It is because God loves us that we now seek to love (cf. John 13:34). It is because God has done for us what we had hoped and dealt with us in grace that we are now able to fulfill the Golden Rule:

> So whatever you wish that men would do to you, do so to them; for this is the law and the prophets. (MATT 7:12)

With this new attitude there also results an intensification of certain commandments. It is therefore not enough simply to refrain from killing, because this new attitude recognizes that the intention of this commandment goes deeper and thus forbids even anger (Matt 5:21–22). It is also not enough simply to refrain from adultery, for the intention of this command is seen by Jesus as going much farther. One must not even lust (Matt 5:27–28)! Likewise the commandment to love one's neighbor is intensified, so that the neighbor includes not only one's fellow Israelite but everyone—even the Samaritan (Luke 10:29–37) and the enemy (MATT 5:43–48).

It would be incorrect, however, to conceive of this new attitude as an abstract mental or emotional feeling. The separation of "thinking" and "doing" which is found in certain forms of early Christian gnosticism ought not to be read back into the teachings of Jesus. A correct attitude and correct actions go hand in hand, "for the tree is known by its fruit" (MATT 12:33).

The good man out of his good treasure brings forth good, and the evil man out of his evil treasure brings forth evil. (MATT 12:35)

It is not enough merely to hear the words of Jesus or even to assent to them in one's heart. One must do them (MATT 7:24–27).

THE LOVE COMMAND

Closely related to and giving direction to the new attitude is the love command of Jesus. It has been said that the love command is the Magna Carta of the kingdom of God, for it is the love command that best characterizes the ethical instruction of Jesus and forms its essence. When asked by a scribe which commandment is first of all, Jesus replies:

The first is, "Hear, O Israel: The Lord our God, the Lord is one; and you shall love the Lord your God with all your heart, and with all your soul, and with all your mind, and with all your strength." The second is this, "You shall love your neighbor as yourself." There is no other commandment greater than these. (MARK 12:29–31)

In so summarizing the divine demand Jesus reduced all the commandments to two. All other commands thus become a commentary on these two. Casuistry and legalism are thereby given a deathblow, for external appearance and ritual are now seen at best as of only secondary importance. By placing these two commandments side by side, Jesus also revealed that the love of God and the love of man are an inseparable unity.[31] One cannot love God and not love his fellowman, for God will not accept such love (Matt 5:23–24; cf. I John 4:20). Only when one is willing to love his neighbor can he truly love God. Yet this does not mean that the love of God and the love of man are identical. The love of God cannot dissolve into a humanism in which the love of man becomes an end in itself. God is no abstraction but a Person. The command to love God sees God as our heavenly Father who is to be loved and obeyed. Thus swearing, pride, and wickedness are evil because they violate the command to love God (MARK 7:21–22). On the other hand, the second commandment guards against a mysticism in which one ignores the needs of his fellowman for whom Christ died and seeks to concern himself only with the experience of God. Thus murder, adultery, and covetousness are evil because they violate the command to love one's neighbor (MARK 7:21–22). For Jesus, love of God and love of one's neighbor are separate and yet unseparate, different and yet one!

With regard to the command to love one's neighbor two things need to be mentioned. The first is that Jesus broadened the understanding of "neighbor" to include everyone. The follower of Jesus is to love the hated Samaritan (Luke 10:25–37), the enemy (LUKE 6:27–36), the publicans and sinners (Luke 15:1–2). Jesus removes all former limitations. The believer is to love *all*. This *all* cannot be limited in any way. The second point that must be mentioned with regard to neighbor love is that this love is not conceived of as simply an emotional feeling or empathy toward the neighbor. Love is to be understood as love demonstrated by actions. It refers not merely to feelings of love but above all to love-acts. The good Samaritan loved his neighbor not primarily because he "felt" for him but rather because he "showed mercy on him" (Luke 10:37), i.e., he performed acts of love. The righteous are told by God in the final day that they enter into life because they loved in the sense of performing acts of love.

> Then the King will say to those at his right hand, "Come, O blessed of my Father, inherit the kingdom prepared for you from the foundation of the world; for I was hungry and you gave me food, I was thirsty and you gave drink, I was a stranger and you welcomed me, I was naked and you clothed me, I was sick and you visited me, I was in prison and you came to me." Then the righteous will answer him, "Lord, when did we see thee hungry and feed thee, or thirsty and give thee drink? And when did we see thee a stranger and welcome thee, or naked and clothe thee? And when did we see thee sick or in prison and visit thee?" And the King will answer them, "Truly, I say to you, as you did it to one of the least of these my brethren, you did it to me." (Matt 25:34–40)

It is because love is understood primarily as love-acts that one can love even one's enemies (LUKE 6:27–36). It is indeed difficult to love evil men who abuse, oppress, and even kill the helpless and innocent. Some have sought to distinguish therefore between the behavior and the "souls" of such people and state that, while we do not love what they do, we can love their "souls." Despite the danger of reading a Platonic dualism into the teachings of Jesus, there is an element of truth in this view, but the command of Jesus to love one's enemies is better understood if we recognize that Jesus means by this that we are to perform acts of love toward them. The believer therefore need not wait for some emotional feeling toward his enemies but can from the beginning act lovingly toward them. That this is the correct understanding of Jesus' love command is evident from the synonymous parallelism of LUKE 6:27-28. To "love your enemies" is defined as follows:

> Love your enemies,
> do good to those who hate you,
> bless those who curse you,
> pray for those who abuse you.

To love one's enemies may involve a feeling of love toward them, but the command of Jesus, like any command, is directed to the will, not to the emotions. To love one's enemies therefore means primarily to do acts of love, such as doing good, blessing, and praying for them.

THE PLACE OF THE LAW

In comparing the various sayings of Jesus concerning the Law and the commandments one receives the impression that these sayings are inconsistent and contradictory. At times it appears as if the Law contains the basic norms of the will of God and is of permanent validity.

> Think not that I have come to abolish the law and the prophets; I have come not to abolish them but to fulfil them. For truly, I say to you, till heaven and earth pass away, not an iota, not a dot, will pass from the law until all is accomplished. Whoever then relaxes one of the least of these commandments and teaches men so, shall be called least in the kingdom of heaven; but he who does them and teaches them shall be called great in the kingdom of heaven. (MATT 5: 17-19)

> You have a fine way of rejecting the commandment of God, in order to keep your tradition! For Moses said, "Honor your father and your mother"; and, "He who speaks evil of father or mother, let him surely die." (MARK 7:9-10)

To these can also be added MARK 10:18-19; 12:28-34; 1:44; Jesus' responses in his temptations which all come from the book of Deuteronomy (MATT 4:1-11); and Matt 23:2-3 which is not to be taken sarcastically due to the second element in v. 3 which qualifies the statement. Along with these sayings we should also note Jesus' own behavior with regard to the Law. Far from being an antinomian, Jesus is seen keeping the Law not only with respect to the moral statutes but with respect to the civil and ceremonial statutes as well. He attends the synagogue on the Sabbath (MARK 1:21; 6:2; note the parallel in Luke 4:16; Luke 13:10); he joins the pilgrims on the feast days in Jerusalem (cf. John 2:13; 5:1; 7:1-14; 10:22; 12:1); he celebrates the Passover (MARK 14: 12-25). He even accepts the validity of the sacrificial system (Matt 5: 23-24) and the authority of the priest (MARK 1:44; Luke 17:14) as well as the validity of the Temple tax (Matt 17:24-27) and fasting (Matt 6: 16-18).

Yet at times Jesus seems to reject parts of the Law as well.

It was also said, "Whoever divorces his wife, let him give her a certificate of divorce." But I say to you that every one who divorces his wife, except on the ground of unchastity, makes her an adulteress; and whoever marries a divorced woman commits adultery. (Matt 5:31-32; cf. also MARK 10:2-12)

You have heard that it was said, "An eye for an eye and a tooth for a tooth." But I say to you, Do not resist one who is evil. . . . (Matt 5:38-39)

To these can also be added MARK 7:14-23, where Jesus abolishes the distinction between clean and unclean found in the Law and his attitude toward the Fourth Commandment (MARK 2:27-28; 3:1-6; Luke 13: 10-17; 14:1-6; cf. John 5:9-10).

Several attempts have been made to explain this apparent contradiction. One such attempt is the claim that what Jesus rejected was not the written Old Testament Law but rather the oral traditions which the scribes and Pharisees had added to the written Law.[32] It is clear that Jesus was bitterly opposed to the legalism of the oral traditions and utterly rejected them as binding.[33] On the contrary, these oral traditions were opposed to the Law and kept one from keeping the commandments (MARK 7:9-13). They stemmed from man not God!

You leave the commandment of God, and hold fast the tradition of men. . . . You have a fine way of rejecting the commandment of God, in order to keep your tradition! (MARK 7:8-9)

Yet it would be an oversimplification to say that Jesus was only opposed to the traditions and that he did not reject in any way the written Law, for such passages as MARK 10:2-12; Matt 5:38-39; MARK 7:14-23 clearly reveal that certain written commandments of the Law were also seen by Jesus as no longer binding.

A second attempt to explain this apparent contradiction is to distinguish between the civil and ceremonial aspect of the Law and the moral aspect of the Law. It was only the former aspect that Jesus did away with and not the latter. This solution is a very ancient one and dates all the way back to the second century.[34] It has been objected that Judaism knew of no such distinction in the Law and that all ceremonial and civil aspects of the Law were also moral aspects. Yet certainly in germinal form this distinction is present in such teachings of Jesus as MARK 7:14–23, for if Jesus no longer held to pure-impure distinctions he in effect abrogated the ceremonial aspect of the Law. Mark points this out in his comment in Mark 7:19:

(Thus he [Jesus] declared all foods clean.)

By this emphasis on the inner condition of the heart rather than on external ceremonial regulation and by his emphasis on the intent of the Law rather than on the mere civil or legal fulfillment of the Law (Matt 5:21–48; MARK 10:2–9), Jesus essentially, although of course only in embryonic form, indicated that his concern lay in the moral rather than the civil or ceremonial dimension of the Old Testament Law. To claim therefore that Judaism knew no such distinction in the Law is beside the point, for Jesus' emphasis on the need for a correct attitude and not just correct ceremonies and actions makes implicit such a distinction, and this distinction which Jesus alludes to will be developed more fully into doctrinal form in the early church (cf. Acts 10; 15; Gal 2; Rom 14).[35]

It would appear therefore that Jesus both saw the Law as a permanent valid expression of the will of God and yet believed that he possessed an authority by which he could bring to realization its original and fundamental purpose.[36] This he did at times by intensifying certain commandments (Matt 5:21–26, 27–30, 43–48) in order to arrive at the original divine intention. At other times he abrogates certain commandments which had a validity in the past but which were nevertheless temporary and accommodating. Thus divorce was permitted because of the hardness of man's heart, but now it is abrogated (MARK 10:2–9). A new period has come. The kingdom of God is already now in part a present reality, and with the coming of the kingdom comes a new covenant. The fact that it is "new" indicates that certain aspects of the old covenant are modified or eliminated; the fact that the new covenant comes from the God of Abraham, Isaac, and Jacob, i.e., the God of the "old" covenant, indicates that much of the moral teachings of the old covenant will be retained. Nevertheless it must be acknowledged that it is not always clear exactly what Jesus retained and what he modified or eliminated from the Law.[37]

GRACE AND REWARD IN JESUS' TEACHING

In the Synoptic Gospels there are several sayings of Jesus which imply that faithful service for the kingdom of God will merit reward. Two of these passages read as follows:

Thus, when you give alms, sound no trumpet before you, as the hypocrites do in the synagogues and in the streets, that they may be praised by men. Truly, I say to you, they have received their reward. But when you give alms, do not let your left hand know what your right hand is doing, so that your alms may be in secret; and your Father who sees in secret will reward you. (Matt 6:2–4)

He said also to the man who had invited him, "When you give a dinner or a banquet, do not invite your friends or your brothers or your kinsmen or rich neighbors, lest they also invite you in return, and you be repaid. But when you give a feast, invite the poor, the maimed, the lame, the blind, and you will be blessed, because they cannot repay you. You will be repaid at the resurrection of the just." (Luke 14:12–14)

To these one can also add: MARK 9:41; 10:21, 28–31; MATT 5:12, 46; 6:19–21; 24:45–51; Matt 6:5–6, 16–18. There are, furthermore, sayings in which the reward to be received varies according to the degree of faithful service rendered. For some the reward will be great (MATT 5:12; Matt 5:19), for others it will be less (cf. Matt 5:19), and for others it will mean sitting at the right or the left hand of Jesus in the kingdom of God (MARK 10:40). Certainly these passages give at first glance the notion that one's position in the kingdom of God is based on the concept of merit, for is not the offer of reward for work done essentially a concept of merit? Some scholars have as a result argued that this element of reward in the teaching of Jesus is a leftover from Judaism from which he never freed himself.

Upon closer examination, however, many of the passages listed above seem also to imply that the notion of merit has no place in this teaching of reward. The saying in Matt 6:2–4 presupposes that the disciples are not to be concerned over issues of merit but that they have detached themselves from the striving after of rewards since they are to forget whatever good deeds they have done. This same idea is brought out even more clearly in Matt 25:31–46, where those entering the kingdom of God are taken by surprise, for they are completely unaware of the good deeds they have done. As for such passages as MATT 5:12; Matt 6:5–6; MARK 9:41, it should be noted that here, too, nothing is said of "earning" or "meriting." True, there is reward, but this reward is given to those who have no thought of earning this reward. It is given therefore by God not out of debt but out of grace.

There are also, on the other hand, passages in the Gospels in which Jesus clearly repudiates the idea that man's standing before God is determined on the basis of merit. Even after serving God, the child of God can only say, "We are unworthy servants; we have only done what was our duty" (Luke 17:10b). The other passages in which the believer is portrayed as a servant/slave[38] (MARK 10:44; Matt 10:24; LUKE 12:35–45; etc.) should also be understood in this way. In his parable of the laborers in the vineyard (Matt 20:1–15), Jesus clearly reveals that the basis by which God deals with man is one of grace. It is on the basis of his "generosity" that God deals with man. The believer fortunately does not receive from God what he deserves, i.e., what God "owes" him. This was what the Pharisee, of course, hoped for, but in his blindness he never saw his sin and thus never was forgiven (Luke 18:14). The tax collector, however, who sought God's grace received grace and went away justified, for it is only on the basis of grace that the publican, the sinner, the child, etc., can enter the kingdom of God. Yet even the scribe and the Pharisee must also repent and trust in the grace of God, for forgiveness is not merited but granted (Luke 18:9–14). As for faithful service, this is rendered primarily in gratitude for God's grace and not in the hope of meriting his favor (Luke 7:40–48).

When Jesus therefore speaks of reward in the Gospels, we should not read into this the notion of merit, for the very idea of merit is incongruous in the Father-son relationship he taught. It is not out of a sense of debt that the Father rewards his children, but rather in love he gives good things to his children (cf. MATT 7:11). What the believer receives from God for his faithful service is therefore not merited pay but the gracious blessing of his heavenly Father which is meant to encourage him in his pilgrimage.[39]

A SUMMARY OF THE ETHICAL TEACHING OF JESUS[40]

In seeking to understand the essence of Jesus' ethical teaching, we must not divorce his ethical teaching from his teaching on the kingdom of God. George Eldon Ladd states:

> There is an analogy between the manifestation of the Kingdom of God itself and the attainment of the righteousness of the Kingdom. The Kingdom has come in Jesus in fulfillment of the messianic salvation within the old age, but the consummation awaits the age to

come. The Kingdom is actually present but in a new and unexpected way. It has entered history without transforming history. It has come into human society without purifying society. By analogy, the righteousness of the reign of God can be actually and substantially experienced even in the present age; but the perfect righteousness of the Kingdom, like the Kingdom itself, awaits the eschatological consummation. Even as the Kingdom has invaded the evil age to bring to men in advance a partial but real experience of the blessings of the eschatological Kingdom, so is the righteousness of the Kingdom attainable, in part if not in perfection, in the present order. Ethics, like the Kingdom itself, stand in the tension between present realization and future eschatological perfection.[41]

It is with this now and not-yet tension of the kingdom of God that Jesus' ethical demand must be understood. In the post-Pentecost situation of the early church this present in-part realization of the righteousness of the kingdom of God is described as being born again (John 3:3), being a new creation in Christ (II Cor 5:17), having died to sin (Rom 6:2), being raised from the dead (Col 2:12; cf. Rom 6:4), etc. There is a temptation to read this post-Pentecost reality back into the teachings of Jesus and see in this the realized dimension of his ethic. The New Testament does teach that during his ministry Jesus foresaw a period in which his disciples would seek to follow his teachings being indwelt by the promised Holy Spirit and thus realize, in part at least, the ethic of the kingdom (cf. John 16:5–15; Rom 8:2–5). Yet even in the pre-Pentecost situation the powers of the kingdom are present in the life of the community. Already in the ministry of Jesus the believer is granted a unique understanding of the grace and love of God as taught and revealed in Jesus, so that the outcasts of Judaism, the publicans and the sinners, have experienced the grace of God and having been forgiven much they love much (Luke 7:36–50)! Already now the Law has been modified, so that the believer is freed from the burdensome concern for the externals of the civil and ceremonial aspects of the Law and can concentrate on the inner righteousness of the heart (MARK 7:14–23).

If the ethic of Jesus bids his followers to live like sons of God (LUKE 6:35), this is because they know that through grace they have become sons of God and have the unique privilege of addressing God as "Abba."[42] If they are called upon to forgive, it is because they are assured that they have already been forgiven (Matt 18:23–35). If they sin, they have been assured that there is continual forgiveness (LUKE 11:4). If they are called upon to love their enemies (LUKE 6:27–36), it is because they, while enemies, experienced the love of God. The followers of Jesus are furthermore aware that Satan is already now defeated (MARK 3:27; Luke 10:18) and that there is therefore deliverance from the evil spirits (MARK 1: 32–34, 39; 3:11; 6:7). It is true that the promised coming of the Spirit is future, but Jesus is nonetheless present, and his presence gives both courage and strength to his followers and aids them in their attempts to live the ethic of the kingdom. Until the coming of the Spirit the ethic of the kingdom is to be lived in the presence of him who brings the kingdom! Apart from the death-resurrection of Jesus and the coming of the Spirit, the realized dimension of the kingdom of God is incomplete, but already the kingdom is manifest in the ministry of Jesus in a number of ways, and the believer is to live the ethic of the kingdom in the context of this already realized dimension of the kingdom.[43]

In the attempt to systematize the ethical teaching of Jesus it is evident that the ethic is not an ethic of regulation in which a legalistic system of commandments is put forward. On the contrary, the ethic of Jesus is an ethic of relationship in which the nucleus is provided by the love commandment. This command (MARK 12:29–31), whose second half can also be stated in the form of the Golden Rule (MATT 7:12), working through a new attitude, provides the basic principle by which the believer lives.[44] It is true that this commandment does not provide a "categorical imperative" for every hypothetical situation. Yet it would be wrong to think that the love command is contentless and simply provides a motive for service. The command to love God and one's neighbor may not always reveal how the follower of Jesus should act in every situation, but it certainly does in many. One does not need a specific rule to know what one should do for a man who has fallen among thieves. Love knows! (Luke 10:33–35.) Yet the love commandment is not given as an isolated utterance. It has a context. This context includes other ethical teachings of Jesus. Their preservation during the oral period, in the Gospels, and even in the epistles of the New Testament, reveals that the members of the early church treasured the teachings of their Lord and sought to shape their lives around them. Indeed Jesus intended this very thing (MATT 7:24–27). This context also includes the example of Jesus himself (MARK 10:42–45; cf. John 13:15). In the past perhaps too great an emphasis has been placed on the *imitatio Christi,* but certainly the example of Jesus provides direction for his followers on how the command to love is to be lived out. Through his other teachings as well as his own example, Jesus provided a specific context out of which his love command is to be interpreted.

An additional context is provided by the Old Testament. The Old Testament is not rejected by Jesus.[45] It still remains as an expression of the will of God. By expressed statements certain aspects such as the rules of purity and cleanliness are now removed, certain commands are seen as temporary concessions, and the principles and intention of the Law are expounded. But the commandments, especially the moral dimension of the commandments, are still valid.

> Whoever then relaxes one of the least of these commandments and teaches men so, shall be called least in the kingdom of heaven; but he who does them and teaches them shall be called great in the kingdom of heaven. (Matt 5:19)[46]

For the believer on this side of Easter there is still a larger context for understanding this commandment. This is the context of the New Testament.[47]

In this "context" the commandment of love does give direction and guidance for the believer. It may be objected that the command to love does not tell us how, for example, to run a government or a factory, but certainly such principles as love, justice, honesty, and truthfulness, while not giving a specific direction for every circumstance, give suggestions as well as a proper attitude by which specific directions can be reached which are "Christian." For the average follower of Jesus the love command, working in the above context, reveals the will of God for him in the vast majority of instances, and Jesus had confidence that in those rare unusual situations in which the believer possessed no teaching or principle to guide him God would reveal this to him through his Spirit (cf. MARK 13:11).

THE ORIGINALITY OF JESUS' ETHICAL TEACHINGS

Having looked at the ethical teachings of Jesus, we must raise the question as to what is unique about his teaching. That his ethic is glorious and noble is admitted by many people who make no claim to be Christians.[48] The problem with Jesus' ethic does not lie in the ethic itself but in the fact that so few Christians live this ethic. Yet despite the heavenliness of this ethic several scholars have argued that there is nothing essentially unique or original about the ethical teachings of Jesus since every teaching of his can be paralleled by statements in the Old Testament or in rabbinic Judaism.[49] We can even find parallels to the love command and the Golden Rule. The love command is not original with Jesus, since it is found in the Old Testament, in Deut 6:4–5 and in Lev 19:18. Even the placing of these two commandments side by side is not unique and can be found in Jewish literature,[50] and the Golden Rule is found not only in negative form in Judaism, as is so often claimed, but supposedly also in positive form as well.[51]

It should not be surprising that the ethics of Jesus are not completely unique. After all, Jesus did not reject the Old Testament. The kingdom of God is not a repudiation of the old covenant but its fulfillment! As a result, one would expect that the moral demands of God proclaimed by Jesus would have parallels with the moral demands of God found in the Old Testament. Jesus was no gnostic! Furthermore, to the degree to which rabbinic Judaism was faithful to the Old Testament, one would also expect to find parallels between the teachings of Jesus and rabbinic Judaism. It is to be expected therefore that the moral teachings of Jesus would have parallels in the best Jewish and even pagan moral teachings. Nevertheless, when looked at as a totality, in contrast with other ethical "systems" present in his day, the terms "unique" and "original" are not altogether inappropriate. The originality of Jesus' teaching can be seen in the following:

1. A wise selection of the key moral commandments. To say that there is nothing unique about a gold crown because that same gold is also found in a nearby mountain is to lose sight of the fact that in the mountain the gold is scattered and covered with dirt, rock, and vegetation. Certainly knowing where to find that gold, removing it from the dirt, rock, and vegetation, and then shaping it into a work of art require genius. In a similar way Jesus showed his originality by his selection of what was essential and what was not from the mountain of commandments present in his day.

2. The removal of the parasitic traditions that sought to undermine the moral teachings of the Old Testament. Like a skillful surgeon, Jesus was able to cut away the cancerous growth of the traditions that had been placed over the Word of God. It can be quite misleading to look at the parallels of Jesus' ethical teachings found in rabbinic literature and not read the context. All too often the context reveals that, although the words are similar, the spirit is quite different. As a result, although we have at times parallel statements to Jesus' sayings in ancient literature, the meaning is not the same.[52]

3. The intensification of the Law. It is true that both the Pharisees and the Essenes also intensified the Law, but the direction tends to be different, for their intensification led to legalism and elitism, whereas the intensification of the Law by Jesus led to an emphasis on the need for a new heart and to a universalism in which the command to love one's neighbor now included the Samaritan, the publican, the sinner, and the enemy.[53]

4. A new motive. To claim that all rabbinic literature was legalistic is an overstatement, but certainly legalism is a characteristic of much of rabbinic literature. The ethic of Jesus, however, was an ethic of gratitude for God's grace in contrast to an ethic of merit or achievement which is

frequently characteristic of rabbinic literature. This emphasis on the inner motivation is not altogether absent in Judaism,[54] but the emphasis in Judaism in Jesus' day tended to be on legal obedience to the letter of the Law.[55]

5. A perfect example. Jesus was unique in his moral teachings in that he proved an embodiment of his idea. Throughout the centuries Christians have seen in Jesus the perfect fulfillment of his own moral teachings. "What did/would Jesus do?", if answered correctly, is the will of God for the Christian. Unlike many of the scribes and the Pharisees, the believer can both do as Jesus said and do as he did (Matt 23:2–3).

Chapter 7

THE CONTENT OF JESUS' TEACHING: CHRISTOLOGY

THERE ARE SEVERAL WAYS in which we can seek to understand what Jesus thought of himself and of his role in history. In the past most attention was focused upon the various appellations he used to describe his mission and person. Today this method is not so popular as it once was, and at times some extremely negative claims are made in this regard.[1] As a result, more emphasis is placed on the indirect or implicit claims of Jesus rather than on his direct or explicit ones.[2] There is good reason for this because people reveal their conception of who they are not merely by the titles that they use to describe themselves but also by the way they act and what they say. In the case of Jesus his actions and sayings explain his titles even as his titles explain his actions and sayings.

In this chapter, therefore, we shall investigate the self-disclosure of Jesus as it is revealed in his actions, his words, and in the titles he used or accepted. The separation of the actions of Jesus from his words will be somewhat arbitrary, for Jesus' actions were not performed in silence. We shall, however, seek to differentiate between the two on the basis of whether the saying or the action receives the primary emphasis. Since the two classifications are meant only for convenience, absolute accuracy is not necessary.

THE ACTIONS OF JESUS

A great deal can be learned of Jesus' "self-consciousness" by noting how he acted. Frequently familiarity with the Christian tradition impairs our recognition of the great and unusual claims Jesus made by his actions, for at times his actions lay claim to a unique authority and occasionally he assumed prerogatives that belong to God alone!

THE UNIQUE AUTHORITY OF JESUS

In MARK 11:27–33[3] the following incident is related:

And they came again to Jerusalem. And as he was walking in the temple, the chief priests and the scribes and the elders came to him, and they said to him, "By what authority are you doing these things, or who gave you this authority to do them?" Jesus said to them, "I will ask you a question; answer me, and I will tell you by what authority I do these things. Was the baptism of John from heaven or from men? Answer me." And they argued with one another, "If we say, 'From heaven,' he will say, 'Why then did you not believe him?' But shall we say, 'From men?' "—they were afraid of the people, for all held that John was a real prophet. So they answered Jesus, "We do not know." And Jesus said to them, "Neither will I tell you by what authority I do these things." (Cf. also John 2:18)

Although this pericope in its present location is associated with the cleansing of the Temple, it is quite likely that the question of the opponents of Jesus involved not only Jesus' claim of authority to cleanse the Temple[4] but his other actions as well. The plural "these things" in vs. 28 and 33 seems to indicate that whereas the cleansing of the Temple was the primary question at hand, the claim of authority in Jesus' other actions forms at least a background for this question. This authority differed from that of his contemporaries not only in degree but in kind and thus the question "By what authority are you doing these things?" naturally arose. Worded differently, the question can be interpreted, "Who are you, Jesus, that you think you can do these things?" (cf. MARK 4:41). It is evident that the opponents of Jesus saw in his actions a claim to a unique authority which they challenged.

Jesus' understanding of his authority extends to several other areas besides the cleansing of the Temple. In his casting out of demons Jesus revealed that he had authority over the demons (MARK 1:27, 32–34; 5:1–13; LUKE 11:20). This authority he was even able to bestow upon his disciples (MARK 3:15; 6:7–13; Luke 10:17). Yet Jesus claimed authority not merely over the demons but over the Prince of Demons himself:

But no one can enter a strong man's house and plunder his goods, unless he first binds the strong man; then indeed he may plunder his house. (MARK 3:27)

In the parallel account in Luke this claim is sharpened, and Jesus claims to be "stronger" than Satan:

When a strong man, fully armed, guards his own palace, his goods are in peace; but when one stronger than he assails him and overcomes him, he takes away his armor in which he trusted, and divides his spoil. (Luke 11:21–22; cf. Luke 10:17–18)

Jesus here claims a unique authority. Others may also cast out demons, but Jesus possesses authority over Satan himself. His plundering of the house of Satan, i.e., his casting out of demons, indicates that he is "stronger" than Satan!

Jesus also possessed authority to perform miracles of healing. While it is true that others in the past, as well as in the present, could heal, the unique ability of Jesus to heal was recognized on numerous occasions. After Jesus healed the paralytic we read that the bystanders

were all amazed and glorified God, saying, "We never saw anything like this!" (MARK 2:12; cf. also MARK 1:27; 7:37; Matt. 9:33; and John 9:32)

It is evident that by all standards of comparison, Jesus possessed a unique authority to heal, exceeding by far any such ability on the part of his contemporaries. Even his opponents had to acknowledge grudgingly this ability and authority to heal, but they sought to discredit this by attributing his authority to Satan (MARK 3:22; Matt 9:34) or to sorcery which he had learned in Egypt.[5]

THE ASSUMPTION OF DIVINE PREROGATIVES BY JESUS

At times Jesus seems to claim authority to perform actions that are the exclusive prerogative of God. One example of this is his forgiving of sins.

And when Jesus saw their faith, he said to the paralytic, "My son, your sins are forgiven." Now some of the scribes were sitting there, questioning in their hearts, "Why does this man speak thus? It is blasphemy! Who can forgive sins but God alone?" (MARK 2:5–7)

Although some scholars have claimed that the words "Your sins are forgiven" are simply an example of the divine passive and thus possess no unique claim of authority, these words are more than a simple statement by Jesus that God had forgiven the paralytic his sins. The reaction of the scribes is proof of this, for they see in this statement of Jesus not a mere declaration that God has forgiven this man his sins but an effectuation of his forgiveness.[6] The scribes interpret Jesus' actions as the exercising of a divine prerogative, the power actually to forgive sins! His actions profess the ability to perform a spiritual as well as a physical miracle in the life of the paralytic. A similar incident and reaction is found in Luke 7:36–50. In vs. 48–49 we read:

And he said to her, "Your sins are forgiven." Then those who were at table with him began to say among themselves, "Who is this, who even forgives sins?"

That Jesus is personally forgiving the woman her sins is evident not only from these verses but from the whole pericope in general. In the pericope this woman performs loving acts upon Jesus (vs. 37–38, 43–46), and Jesus defends her actions by a parable. In the parable Jesus describes two debtors loving the one who has forgiven them their debts. In so doing he defends the woman loving him, because she has been forgiven. The analogy of the parable indicates that the debtors (or sinners) who have been forgiven love the one who forgave them. From this it is clear that the woman is performing acts of love upon Jesus because she believes that Jesus has forgiven her. Jesus must likewise understand her actions in this way, "Simon, this woman loves me a great deal because I have forgiven her much." It is difficult to interpret these words to imply that since God has forgiven this woman much, she as a result loves Jesus much. It would seem therefore most logical to interpret these passages as indicating that Jesus assumed that he possessed the authority to forgive sins. After all, his audience interpreted it in this way! This freedom which Jesus felt in going about offering the forgiveness of sins naturally raised the question:

Who then is this who can come forward as the divine pardon incarnate, proclaiming His power to lead sinful men there and then into God's presence?[7]

On several occasions Jesus equated his own actions with the actions of God himself. In Luke 15 we have a trilogy of parables which are introduced as follows:

Now the tax collectors and sinners were all drawing near to hear him. And the Pharisees and the scribes murmured, saying, "This man receives sinners and eats with them." (Luke 15:1–2)

The three parables of the lost sheep, the lost coin, and the lost son (or better "the gracious Father") are not merely examples of God's great love for the lost but are both an apology for Jesus' behavior in associating with the outcasts of Israel and a Christological proclamation. Jesus is claiming that his offering of forgiveness and pardon to the tax collectors and sinners is in reality God's reaching out and pardoning them. He explains his behavior by professing to be standing in God's stead and acting on his behalf with his authority.

It is also clear that Jesus spoke to tax collectors, who were excluded from the people of God because of their frequent contact with pagans and questionable business conduct, summoning them to fellowship at his table and thus to fellowship with God; in other words, he offered forgiveness as though he stood in the place of God. It is also certain that he promised men the kingdom of God as though he had authority to grant it.[8]

THE WORDS OF JESUS

In the words of Jesus, as well as in his actions, we find that he discloses what he thought of himself and his mission. The words of Jesus reveal that he thought he possessed an authority such as no other man had, for whereas the prophets and Moses spoke what God had revealed to them, Jesus spoke his own words which were nevertheless the Word of God. In contrast to those who had come before and proclaimed "Thus saith the Lord," the even more authoritative word of Jesus went out, "But I say to you!" We shall discuss the words of Jesus under the following headings: Jesus' authority over the Law, his use of *amen*, his "totalitarian" claims, and the comparison of himself with others.

THE AUTHORITY OF JESUS OVER THE LAW

Once again our familiarity with the sayings of Jesus and the Christian tradition tends to blunt the impact of Jesus' attitude toward the Law. It is, however, scarcely possible to exaggerate the degree to which Moses and the Law were held in veneration in the time of Jesus. The Law was the embodiment of the will of God. It was one of the few central unifying factors of Israel, for all the sects of Israel held the Law as sacred. To minimize or contradict the most minute detail of the Law was damnable.[9] It is quite possible that in no other area does the authority which Jesus claimed stand out more clearly than in his freedom to intensify, to revise, and even to reject the Law.

You have heard that it was said, "An eye for an eye and a tooth for a tooth." But I say to you, Do not resist one who is evil. (Matt 5:38–39a)

It was also said, "Whoever divorces his wife, let him give her a certificate of divorce." But I say to you that every one who divorces his wife, except on the ground of unchastity, makes her an adulteress; and whoever marries a divorced woman commits adultery. (Matt 5:31–32; cf. MARK 10:2–12)

As we have already seen,[10] although Jesus at times spoke of the permanent validity of the Law (Matt 5:17–19; MARK 7:9–10), it is clear that he, on his own authority, felt free to abolish certain aspects of the Law. There is no necessary justification at times for this claim such as a reference to the purpose of God in creation (as in MARK 10:6) or to an imminent parousia but simply a "But I say!" Jesus claimed therefore to speak with an even greater authority than Moses, who received the stone tablets from the hand of God, for Jesus believed himself to possess authority not merely to interpret the Law but to abolish it. The rabbis of his day might seek to twist the Law to fit their own interpretative scheme, but Jesus saw no such necessity. He simply placed his personal authority above it. Surely those who heard him speak thus must have been forced to ask the question, "Who is this who claims such authority over the Law of God?"

JESUS' USE OF "AMEN"

Frequently we find on the lips of Jesus the formula *"Amen* [translated as "Verily" in the KJV and "Truly" in the RSV], I say to you."

Truly, I say to you, there is no one who has left house or brothers or sisters or mother or father or children or lands, for my sake and for the gospel, who will not receive a hundredfold now in this time, houses and brothers and sisters and mothers and children and lands, with persecutions, and in the age to come eternal life. (MARK 10: 29–30)

And when you pray, you must not be like the hypocrites; for they love to stand and pray in the synagogues and at the street corners, that they may be seen by men. Truly, I say to you, they have received their reward. (Matt 6:5)[11]

The manner in which Jesus used this expression is completely new and has no parallel in Jewish literature or in the rest of the New Testament.[12] The uniqueness of Jesus' use of this term, its presence in all the Gospel strata, and its absence in the Jewish literature and the rest of the New Testament all argue strongly in favor of its authenticity. Its use by Jesus is seen as a "Christology *in nuce,"*[13] for by his use of *amen* Jesus is claiming the certainty of what is being said. The *amen* implies a finality and authority to the words that follow which is quite unparalleled and transcends that of any of the religious leaders of his day. But upon what does Jesus base the finality and reliability of his statement? Is it the Scriptures on a new revelation which he has received from God? Is it some new undeniable logic? No, it is the "I say so!" The *amen* points to the certainty of the truth of what Jesus says, but the reason it is certain is that Jesus is saying it.

Thus, when you give alms, sound no trumpet before you, as the hypocrites do in the synagogues and in the streets, that they may be praised by men. Truly, I say to you, they have received their reward. (Matt 6:2)

The force of what Jesus is saying in the last words of this quotation can perhaps be better grasped by interpreting them as follows: *Amen,* you can be certain that they [already] have their reward, because I say so! It is not surprising that such teaching brought the following response from the crowds:

And when Jesus finished these sayings, the crowds were astonished at his teaching, for he taught them as one who had authority, and not as their scribes. (Matt 7:28-29)

THE "TOTALITARIAN" CLAIMS OF JESUS

Although the term "totalitarian" has many negative connotations, Archibald M. Hunter's use of this term[14] is an accurate one and describes well the total commitment that Jesus demanded of his followers. On the lips of anyone else the claims of Jesus would appear to be evidence of gross egomania, for Jesus clearly implies that the entire world revolves around himself and that the fate of all men is dependent on their acceptance or rejection of him.

So every one who acknowledges me before men, I also will acknowledge before my Father who is in heaven; but whoever denies me before men, I also will deny before my Father who is in heaven. (MATT 10:32-33)

And blessed is he who takes no offense at me. (MATT 11:6)

If any man would come after me, let him deny himself and take up his cross and follow me. For whoever would save his life will lose it; and whoever loses his life for my sake and the gospel's will save it. . . . For whoever is ashamed of me and of my words in this adulterous and sinful generation, of him will the Son of man also be ashamed, when he comes in the glory of his Father with the holy angels. (MARK 8:34-38; cf. also Matt 10:40 and MARK 9:37)

According to Jesus, the fate of man centers around him. Rejection of him means eternal judgment; acceptance of him means acceptance by God. The pivotal point of history and salvation, Jesus claims, is himself. To obey him is to be wise and escape judgment, but to reject his words is to be foolish and perish, for his words are the only sure foundation upon which to build (MATT 7:24-27). Commitment and obedience to him must therefore take priority over all other relationships, even those of the family (MATT 10:35–37; LUKE 14:26).

Closely related to the above sayings are the various "I" sayings of Jesus:

Come to me, all who labor and are heavy laden, and I will give you rest. (Matt 11:28)

Think not that I have come to abolish the law and the prophets; I have come not to abolish them but to fulfil them. (Matt 5:17)[15]

I came not to call the righteous, but sinners. (MARK 2:17; Luke 19:10)

I came to cast fire upon the earth; and would that it were already kindled! (Luke 12:49)

Numerous other examples could be given in which we find similar statements, but the above are sufficient to demonstrate the "self-centered" aspect of the teachings of Jesus.[16] Such an ego-centered message can be viewed in several ways. It may be viewed as a repulsive egomania, but the claims of Jesus are simply too great, too all-encompassing to be interpreted as a case of a man who thinks "more highly of himself than he ought to think" (Rom. 12:3). There seem to be only two possible ways of interpreting the totalitarian nature of the claims of Jesus. Either we must assume that Jesus was deluded and unstable with unusual delusions of grandeur or we are faced with the realization that Jesus is truly One who speaks with divine authority, who actually divided all of history into B.C.–A.D., and whose rejection or acceptance determines the fate of all men. Regardless of what the individual may decide, the words of Jesus reveal a most unique and all-encompassing Christological claim.

JESUS' COMPARISON OF HIMSELF
WITH THE OLD TESTAMENT SAINTS

We find several places in the Gospels where Jesus expressly compared himself to several great men of the Old Testament and expressed his superiority over them. It has already been mentioned that Jesus professed to be greater than the prophet Jonah and the king Solomon.[17] It is also evident that Jesus by overruling the commands of Moses was claiming that he was greater than Moses as well, for each of the "You have heard that it was said. . . . But I say . . ." statements in Matthew 5 can also be understood as saying "Moses said, but I say." Thus in comparing his words to the words of Moses, Jesus was asserting his superiority over Moses. In the Gospel of John we find two other comparisons. In John 8:53 after Jesus spoke of the importance of keeping his word the response is:

Are you greater than our father Abraham, who died? And the prophets [who] died! Who do you claim to be?

In John 4:12 the contrast is between Jacob and Jesus:

Are you greater than our father Jacob, who gave us the well?

By the reply it is evident that Jesus did consider himself greater than Jacob because the "water" he provides is greater than the water Jacob provided in his well. In a similar kind of comparison Jesus professes to be greater than the Temple:

I tell you, something greater than the temple is here. (Matt 12:6)

In its present context it is evident that Matthew interprets the "something" which is greater as referring to the one who is "lord of the sabbath."

In summarizing the implications of Jesus' actions and words, we see clearly that even apart from the use of any titles Jesus lived a "Christology."

An examination of Jesus' words—his proclamation of the Reign of God, and his call for decision, his enunciation of God's demand, and his teaching about the nearness of God—and of his conduct—his calling men to follow him and his healing, his eating with publicans and sinners—forces upon us the conclusion that underlying his word and work is an implicit Christology. In Jesus as he understood himself, there is an immediate confrontation with "God's presence and his very self," offering judgment and salvation.[18]

In our discussion of the titles of Jesus we shall discover that the explicit Christology of the titles and the implicit Christology of his actions and words are not only in harmony with one another but must be understood as complementing each other.

THE TITLES OF JESUS

It is not the purpose of this section to investigate all the titles that the Gospels use to describe the person and work of Jesus. Such an undertaking would involve a far greater enterprise than envisioned in this work. Instead we shall investigate only three titles: Messiah, Son or Son of God, and Son of man. Among scholars there exists a wide variety of views as to whether Jesus actually used any of these titles to describe his mission or whether he even accepted any of these titles as a description of his person and work. Conzelmann states that all the Christological titles were conferred on Jesus by the faith of the church,[19] and Günther Bornkamm agrees with him.[20] We shall endeavor to show, however, that such views are unnecessarily negative, for the Christology implied in the words and actions of Jesus are affirmed as well by his acceptance and use of these three titles.

MESSIAH

The term "Messiah," or *mashiach,* which in Greek is translated *christos,* or "Christ," means "anointed." In the Old Testament the term occurs thirty-nine times and is used to describe kings (II Sam 1:14, 16; 19:21), priests (Ex 28:41; Lev 4:3, 5, 16), prophets (Ps 105:15; I Chron 16:22), and even the pagan king Cyrus (Isa 45:1). As time progressed, the Jewish people began to look for "the Anointed One" whom God would one day send to set all things right. In the future when God would establish his kingdom he would raise up an ideal Anointed King who would free his people from their enemies and reign in righteousness.

Behold, O Lord, and raise up unto them their king, the son of David,
　　At the time in the which Thou seest, O God, that he may reign
　　　　over Israel Thy servant.
And gird him with strength, that he may shatter unrighteous rulers,
　　And that he may purge Jerusalem from nations that trample (her)
　　　　down to destruction.
　　　　　　(Psalms of Solomon 17:23-24 in Charles, *Pseudepigrapha*)

Whereas it is possible to speak of a general "messianic" expectation in Palestinian Judaism, there was a great deal of variation concerning how this expectation would be fulfilled.[21] In some circles the Messiah was portrayed as reigning for four hundred years and then dying (II Esdras /IV Ezra 7:28-29). In the Dead Sea community at Qumran two future anointed ones were expected. One was a priestly Messiah, the Messiah of Aaron, and the other was a political Messiah, the Messiah of Israel who would come from the tribe of Judah (1QS 9:11). In rabbinic Judaism we even read of a Messiah who comes out of Benjamin.[22] In some "messianic" expectations there is not even a Messiah.[23] To the man on the street in the first century, however, the term "Messiah" tended to evoke a picture of an earthly, this-worldly political figure, a king who was David's son, who would deliver the Jewish nation from bondage to their enemies and reign in righteousness.

From the very beginning the early church associated the title "Christ" with Jesus. In fact, this title became so closely associated with Jesus that it soon ceased to be a title but became part of his name—Jesus Christ. Its use as a title, however, is found in the New Testament:

And every day in the temple and at home they did not cease teaching and preaching Jesus as the Christ. (Acts 5:42)

This Jesus, whom I proclaim to you, is the Christ. (Acts 17:3; cf. also Acts 3:20)

Numerous scholars have denied, however, that Jesus could have used a title with such political, nationalistic, and militaristic connotations to describe his mission.[24] Nevertheless there do seem to be several passages in the Gospels in which Jesus accepts this title as a self-designation, albeit with reservations.

The first passage of importance is MARK 8:27–30:

And Jesus went on with his disciples, to the villages of Caesarea Philippi; and on the way he asked his disciples, "Who do men say that I am?" And they told him, "John the Baptist; and others say, Elijah; and others one of the prophets." And he asked them, "But who do you say that I am?" Peter answered him, "You are the Christ." And he charged them to tell no one about him.

As it stands, the account is understood by all the Evangelists as an acknowledgment of the confession of Peter by Jesus.[25] Reginald H. Fuller has suggested, however, that originally the incident described a rejection of this title by Jesus. According to Fuller, in order to arrive at what actually took place in the first *Sitz im Leben*, we must remove both the command to silence (v. 30), which is a Markan theme and thus a Markan creation, and the passion prediction, which is pre-Markan but did not originally belong to the incident. Verse 32a is also seen as a church construction linking the passion prediction to Jesus' rebuke of Peter. The result of all this is that the "confession" of Peter "You are the Christ" received the response from Jesus "Get behind me, Satan!" (v. 33).[26] This hypothetical reconstruction, however, encounters several problems. For one, this reconstruction is based upon several presuppositions all of which are greatly suspect. Is it certain that every command to silence in Mark is due to the Evangelist? Certainly Mark has heightened this emphasis on the secrecy motif in his Gospel, but he did not create it *ex nihilo*.[27] Furthermore, if there is one place in all the Gospel tradition where such a command is appropriate in the first *Sitz im Leben*, it is here! Are we also to assume that every passion prediction is a *vaticinium ex eventu*?[28] Probably, however, the greatest weakness of Fuller's thesis is the assumption that the rebuke of Peter was originally associated with the account of the confession. If anything, the trend in recent research is to see this as a redactional statement by Mark, in which he sought to emphasize the dullness of the disciples and their incorrect Christology.[29] More basic to this whole reconstruction by Fuller is the question of whether historical research in the twentieth century is able to reconstruct, from three accounts in which Jesus is confessed as Messiah and accepted this appellation, an original incident in which he clearly and unequivocally denied this appellation. The present writer simply does not believe that modern historical research is capable of such a task.[30]

On the other hand, there are good reasons for maintaining that the incident is historical. It has frequently been pointed out that this incident is one of the few accounts in the Gospel tradition that is prefixed with a geographical designation. As for the designation, itself, Caesarea Philippi is never mentioned in the entire New Testament outside of this passage and its parallel in Matt 16:13. If one were simply creating a geographical site for such an account, certainly Jerusalem, Capernaum, the Mount of Olives, or better yet the Temple area would be more "suitable" for such a confession. As it is, this designation argues in favor of the historicity of the event. The preliminary answer given by the disciples also fits well with the attitudes and opinions that people held of Jesus, for elsewhere he is thought of by some as John the Baptist (MARK 6:14), Elijah (MARK 6:15), or a prophet (MARK 6:15; Matt 21:11, 46; Luke 7:16; 24:19).

The reserve with which Jesus accepted this description must be carefully noted. Peter is immediately commanded to tell no one that Jesus is in fact the Christ. It is clear that the account in Mark is not a rebuke of this appellation in that Peter is not told to tell no one "this" but to tell no one "concerning him," i.e., that Jesus was in fact the Christ. Jesus was well aware of the tremendous difference between his conception of his mission as the Messiah and the popular conception in his day of that mission. The need for secrecy is made most evident by Peter's response to the passion prediction of Jesus. Although he had been with Jesus for some time and had been taught by him, he too had a gross misconception of what Jesus' messiahship meant. If Peter found it impossible to conceive of the nonmilitaristic and apolitical messiahship which Jesus proclaimed, how much less would the crowds be able to understand! The need for silence was therefore most urgent.

A second important passage in which Jesus accepts the title of Messiah is MARK 14:61–63:

Again the high priest asked him, "Are you the Christ, the Son of the Blessed?" And Jesus said, "I am; and you will see the Son of man seated at the right hand of Power, and coming with the clouds of heaven." And the high priest tore his garments, and said, "Why do we still need witnesses?"

Having refused to answer any of the questions directed to him, Jesus is placed under an oath by Caiaphas, the high priest, who says:

> I adjure you by the living God, tell us if you are the Christ, the Son of God. (Matt 26:63)

Such an oath demanded a reply, for silence would have been a confession of guilt.[31] The accounts in the Synoptic Gospels read as follows:

Matt 26:64	*Mark* 14:62	*Luke* 22:70
Jesus said to him, "You have said so. But . . ."	And Jesus said "I am; and . . ."	And he said to them, "You say that I am."

According to the Markan account, Jesus' reply is a straightforward "I am," but both Matthew and Luke indicate that Jesus' reply possessed far more reserve, for here Jesus replies, "You have said so" (Matt) and, "You say that I am" (Luke). All three accounts agree that Jesus accepted this description of himself as the Christ, the Son of the Blessed,[32] for the response of the high priest and the Sanhedrin is identical, but the agreement of Matthew and Luke against their Markan source makes it clear that Jesus accepted this designation with great reserve. Mark is correct in describing that Jesus answered this question in the affirmative, but he was apparently not interested in describing Jesus' reserve in accepting this title. Matthew and Luke represent more accurately the actual historical situation in pointing out that Jesus did not like the particular form of the question put to him by Caiaphas. Jesus' actual reply may therefore have been something like this: You have worded this question and I will not deny that I am the Messiah, *but* I prefer, because of the misconceptions that this term raises, a different designation, which is that of Son of man, and you will see the Son of man. . . . Mark is therefore correct when he has Jesus answering in the affirmative, but Matthew and Luke preserve more carefully the original words spoken.

Closely related to this account is Jesus' appearance before Pontius Pilate. In MARK 15:2 we read:

> And Pilate asked him, "Are you the King of the Jews?" And he answered him, "You have said so."

It has been argued that if Jesus had actually replied affirmatively to such a question, Pilate would have had no reservations about crucifying Jesus.[33] This argument, however, loses sight of the reserve in which the question is answered and the complete absence of political overtones in Jesus' reply (cf. especially the account in John 18:33–37). Certainly the restrictive nature of Jesus' admission would require further examination on the part of Pilate. Dodd points out in this regard that in this situation Jesus did not even need to affirm that he was the Messiah before Pilate, for

> at this juncture a refusal to disown the title would have the same effect as an avowal, and it was a matter of life and death.[34]

The lack of a vigorous denial on the part of Jesus therefore reveals that Jesus accepted this designation as a description of his person and work, although he did so with reservations.

The strongest "historical" evidence that Jesus claimed to be the Messiah is the undeniable fact that he was crucified by the Romans as a Messianic Pretender.[35] The Romans had little interest in the theme and variations of Jewish religious beliefs. The teachings and activity of Jesus were of concern for Rome only in as much as they touched on political issues. If Jesus denied that he was the Messiah, his crucifixion is unexplainable. Yet at the crucifixion of Jesus, there was a titulus that stated the reason for his death. It was customary to have such a titulus at each crucifixion upon which the crime or crimes for which the victim was being executed were written. In the Synoptic Gospels the charge upon the titulus reads as follows:

Matt 27:37	*Mark* 15:26	*Luke* 23:38
And over his head they put the charge against him, which read, "This is Jesus the King of the Jews."	And the inscription of the charge against him read, "The King of the Jews."	There was also an inscription over him, "This is the King of the Jews."

The Johannine account of the charge in John 19:19 reads similarly: "Jesus of Nazareth, the King of the Jews." In all four Gospels the charge against Jesus that was placed upon the titulus is a political one. All read that he claimed to be the "King of the Jews," i.e., that he claimed to be the Messiah. It is difficult to attribute the wording of the titulus to the early church, since the expression is not found outside the Gospels and was not therefore a Christological title used by the early Christians to describe the person and work of Jesus. Dodd sums up the evidence as follows:

> Jesus at any rate allowed himself to be condemned to death for claiming to be (in Jewish terms) Messiah. . . . Yet a title which he would not deny to save his life cannot have been without significance for him.[36]

If we posit that Jesus was in fact crucified by the Romans on political charges and that the basis of these charges was his acceptance, with reservations, of this title, the portrayal found in the Gospel accounts of Jesus' trial and death results in a coherent picture. Jesus acknowledged that he was the Messiah, although his messiahship was totally different from the messianic conceptions of his contemporaries. Pilate's hesitancy to crucify Jesus and the fact that he nevertheless did so is understandable. Jesus' allowing himself to be crucified on political charges as the Messiah then also becomes understandable. The inscription of the titulus also fits well with this construction of the events as does the mockery of the soldiers and the crowds who ridicule Jesus' claim to be the Messiah (MARK 15:18, 32;[37] Luke 23:35–38, 39), and the other instances in which Jesus is referred to at his trial and crucifixion as the Messiah (Matt 27:17, 22) also become comprehensible. Furthermore, other events in the life of Jesus become understandable as well. His sense of "anointing" at his baptism and the subsequent sermon at Nazareth in which he emphasizes this "anointing" (Luke 4:18), his cleansing of the Temple,[38] his anointing at Bethany (MARK 14:3–9), the feeding of the five thousand and the four thousand, etc., may all then be interpreted in the light of Jesus' claim to be the Messiah. The questions that Jesus' actions and words raised (cf. John 7:40–43; 10:24) are then finally answered not only to the Baptist (MATT 11:2–6) but now to the Sanhedrin, Pilate, and as a result of the cross to the multitudes as well.

On the other hand, if we deny that Jesus ever claimed to be the Messiah, we encounter a host of insurmountable problems. Not the least of these is that we have no reasonable explanation of why Jesus was crucified as a Messianic pretender even though he denied that he was the Messiah. We then have to explain how a Jesus who denied his messiahship on several occasions to his disciples was immediately proclaimed as the Messiah after the resurrection. Are we to assume that the resurrection reversed the impression of a nonmessianic Jesus to a messianic Jesus even against Jesus' explicit denial of being the Messiah?[39] No, the resurrection is best understood as a confirmation of Jesus' claim that he was the Messiah, not the denial of his claim that he was not. Another problem which we encounter if we assume that Jesus never claimed to be the Messiah is that we must deny the historicity of a host of passages in the Gospels. Some of these are: the confession of Peter at Caesarea Philippi (MARK 8:27–30); the trial of Jesus before the Sanhedrin (MARK 14:53f.); the mockery present at the trial and at the cross (MARK 15:18, 32; Luke 23:35–38, 39); the title of the titulus (MARK 15:26 and John 19:19); various passages in John (John 4:25–26; 9:22; etc.). The difficulty involved in maintaining this extremely negative position is that one must explain not just some of the above or even most of the above passages from the perspective of a Jesus who denied that he was the Messiah, but one must explain all of them!

It would appear, therefore, that the simplest explanation is to acknowledge that Jesus did accept the appellation of Messiah, but that he did so with reservation. There are two reasons for such reservation. The first reason is that a public declaration of messiahship might cause a revolution and uprising of the people, for revolutionaries of all kinds, whether Zealot or non-Zealot, would have joined his "messianic crusade against Rome." That such a possibility existed is witnessed to by John 6:1–15. This temptation to see his mission in terms of contemporary messianic expectations Jesus encountered and rejected at the very outset of his ministry.[40] The least such an open claim would do would have been to provoke an immediate confrontation with Rome. This Jesus had no desire to do. A second reason has been suggested as to why Jesus did not openly claim to be the Messiah. According to this view, the function and work of the Messiah had to be accomplished first before the title of Messiah could be claimed. God himself must enthrone and reveal the Messiah. The individual could not do this himself.[41] The evidence given to support this suggestion is not absolutely convincing, but it is certainly not impossible that such a view did exist in Jesus' day.

SON OR SON OF GOD

One of the most ancient creedal statements of the early church was the confession "Jesus is the Son of God."[42] The title is not, however, unique to the New Testament, for it is found in the Old Testament and the intertestamental literature as well. In the Old Testament the phrase is sometimes applied to divine or heavenly beings such as the angels (Ps 29:1; 89:6; Job 1:6; 2:1; 38:7; Dan 3:25); to Israel (Ex 4:22; Deut 32:5–6, 18–19; Ps 82:6; Jer 3:19; 31:9,20; Hos 11:1); as well as to kings. The latter usage is especially important in that several of these passages were later interpreted as referring to the future Davidic ruler or Messiah.[43]

Thus says the LORD of hosts. . . . "I will raise up your offspring after you. . . . I will be his father, and he shall be my son." (II Sam 7:8, 12, 14)

I will tell of the decree of the LORD:
He said to me, "You are my son,
today I have begotten you."
(Ps 2:7; cf. also Ps 89:26–27)

Because of the idea of a physical father-son relationship between God and other divine beings or kings found elsewhere in the Orient and which is quite alien to the Old Testament,

> Israel took good care lest the designation son of God . . . be falsely linked to the physical divine sonship which was so widely spoken of in the ancient Orient. It thus employed "son of God" only when quoting the Messianic promises and elsewhere avoided this term for the Messiah.[44]

In the Apocrypha and the Pseudepigrapha the term "son of God" is found as a title for the Messiah in II Esdras 7:28; 13:32, 37, 52; 14:9; and Enoch 105:2, but all of these passages are somewhat suspect as being either post-Christian or a mistranslation of the original Hebrew term.[45] In the Dead Sea Scrolls the term is found as a designation for the Messiah but only in association with a Biblical passage such as Ps 2:7 or II Sam 7:14. The same is true with regard to the rabbinic material. As a result, there is no clear instance in pre-Christian times that Judaism used the title "son of God" alone as a designation for the Messiah, although passages in which the term "son" is found were interpreted messianically.

In the Gospels the title is found as a designation of Jesus in all the Gospel strata in MARK (13:32), Q (MATT 11:27), M (Matt 14:33), L (Luke 4:41), and John (10:36). At times the designation is directed to him by:

the demons or the demoniacs (MARK 5:7; Mark 3:11)

Satan (MATT 4:3, 6)

the disciples (Matt 14:33; 16:16)

the centurion (MARK 15:39)

the Voice from heaven—at the baptism (MARK 1:11) and at the transfiguration (MARK 9:7)

Jesus (MARK 13:32; MATT 11:27)

In contrast to its use in non-Jewish circles, the title "Son of God" in the Gospels is not associated with the miracle-working qualities of the divine men *(theios aner)* of Hellenism.[46] The difference between Jesus and the *theios aner* of paganism is evident from the fact that the pagan heroes were "sons of God" primarily because of their miraculous powers. They were thaumaturges, or wonder workers, who worked miracles. Yet this very tendency to interpret sonship as due to the possession of miraculous powers was rejected by Jesus at the temptation as Satanic.

One of the important passages in which the term "Son" is used as a self-designation is MARK 13:32:

> But of that day or that hour no one knows, not even the angels in heaven, nor the Son, but only the Father.

In this saying Jesus asserts his uniqueness by distinguishing between the "angels," the rest of mankind ("no one"), and himself as the "Son." He possesses a unique relationship to God. He is the Son! Two arguments can be put forward in support of the authenticity of this saying. The first is put forth by Eduard Schweizer, who states:

> In support of the derivation of the saying from Jesus [we should note that] the title "Son" is not primary and the goal of the statement does not lie in it.[47]

The second argument in favor of the authenticity of the saying is the difficulty of the saying in portraying Jesus as ignorant of the time of the parousia. Luke witnesses to this difficulty by omitting this verse from his Gospel. Clearly this is not the kind of saying that one would expect the early church to create and place on the lips of Jesus. "Its offence seals its genuineness."[48] Some have argued, however, that it is possible that the church would have created such a saying because of the delay of the parousia, but it is difficult to conceive of the church "solving" the problem of the delay of the parousia by creating a saying that would cause great difficulties with respect to its Christology, for how could the exalted Lord of the church not know the time of the parousia? Even P. W. Schmiedel acknowledged that MARK 13:32 was one of the "absolutely credible passages about Jesus."[49]

In MARK 12:1–9 we find a parable in which Jesus refers to a "beloved son" who is killed by the evil tenants of his father's vineyard. As a result of their action Jesus declares that the father will surely come, destroy those tenants, and give the vineyard to others. From the very beginning the Christian church has interpreted this parable allegorically and interpreted "the son" as referring to Jesus, the Son of God. For some scholars the fact that there is allegory present in the present form of the parable is sufficient to deny its authenticity, but it has already been pointed out that the presence of allegory in a parable says nothing for or against its authenticity.[50] Yet is it possible not to interpret such a parable allegorically? The very use of a vineyard as a symbol in the parable might even require that the hearer see in the parable an allegorical significance, for "a Jew could not tell a story of a vineyard without embarking upon allegory" (cf. Isa 5:7).[51] But even if some of the allegory in the parable is secondary, the original parable distinguished between the servants and the son. It would appear then that in the parable Jesus distinguished between the prophets of the Old Testament, who are "servants," and himself, the "beloved son." The treatment that the son receives in the parable is quite different from what we would expect if the parable were simply a creation of the early church, for one finds no reference at all to the resurrection in the account.[52] The parable furthermore agrees with two themes of Jesus' preaching: the coming judgment upon Israel (MARK 13:1f.; LUKE 13:34–35; Luke 23:28–31) and the final judgment being based upon man's attitude toward him.[53] The sending of the Son by the Father also brings to mind the various "I have come" sayings of Jesus:

> I came not to call the righteous, but sinners. (MARK 2:17)

> For the Son of man also came not to be served but to serve, and to give his life as a ransom for many. (MARK 10:45)

> Think not that I have come to abolish the law and the prophets; I have come not to abolish them but to fulfil them. (Matt 5:17)

> Do not think that I have come to bring peace on earth; I have not come to bring peace, but a sword. (MATT 10:34; cf. also MARK 1:38; 9:37; MATT 11:19; Matt 10:40; 15:24; Luke 19:10)

It is not difficult to see that verses such as these and MARK 12:6 led to the attributing of preexistence to the Son.

Another important passage in which Jesus asserts his "sonship" is MATT 11:25–27:

> I thank thee, Father, Lord of heaven and earth, that thou hast hidden these things from the wise and understanding and revealed them to babes; yea, Father, for such was thy gracious will. All things have been delivered to me by my Father; and no one knows the Son except the Father; and no one knows the Father except the Son and any one to whom the Son chooses to reveal him.

The authenticity of this passage has generally been denied on two grounds. The first is that the emphasis on the mutual knowledge of the Father and the Son has a Hellenistic ring to it and must therefore have arisen in a Hellenistic environment. Thus Jesus could not be the author of the saying. With the discovery of the Dead Sea Scrolls, however, such criticism is no longer valid, for in Jesus' own day the Teacher of Righteousness of the Qumran community claimed a similar knowledge of God which he was imparting to his followers.[54] Instead of being a "Hellenistic revelation saying,"[55] it is now evident that the passage is Semitic in character and originated out of a Palestinian environment.[56] The second ground for denying its authenticity is the Johannine flavor of the saying. Over a hundred years ago K. A. von Hase described this passage as a "thunderbolt fallen from the Johannine sky" because of its similarity to the teaching in John, for here, as well as in John, Jesus is clearly portrayed as the only Son of the Father, who shares in a mutual knowledge with him.

Yet Hunter rightly points out that because MATT 11:27 has parallels in John that does not in itself make it inauthentic unless

> we make it a canon of criticism that any saying in the Synoptics with a parallel in John must *ipso facto* be spurious.[57]

There is therefore no textual reason for denying the genuineness of these words as an actual saying of Jesus. Such a denial is based far more upon theological presuppositions than upon exegesis.[58]

In looking at the content of this passage we find several important Christological claims. First of all, Jesus uses as a self-designation the title "Son." This Sonship is, furthermore, unique and exclusive. It is unshared, for no one, neither the patriarchs, Moses, David, nor the prophets, truly knew the Father in the same way as Jesus, the Son, knows him. Secondly, Jesus claims the knowledge of all things.[59] He alone truly knows the Father and the Father alone truly knows him. Thirdly, Jesus states that to know the Father, one must come through Jesus, who alone mediates this knowledge. That there is a Johannine ring in all this is evident, but rather than assume that both are in error, it is more reasonable to see in this passage and in the Gospel of John a twofold witness to the unique Sonship which Jesus claimed.

The origin of this doctrine of Jesus' Sonship has been explained in several different ways. Wilhelm Bousset claimed that the title arose in the Hellenistic church and was read back into the life of Jesus and the Gospel tradition.[60] Rudolf Bultmann claimed that the title went through a two-stage development. The title was first used in the Aramaic-speaking church after the resurrection and was seen along the lines of Ps. 2:7 as a title bestowed upon the risen Christ because of his adoption and enthronement by God. Later in the Hellenistic church the title was reinterpreted along the lines of a "divine man" theology in which the term was eventually understood metaphysically.[61] More recently, Ferdinand Hahn has posited a threefold development. In the first stage it was applied by the Palestinian church after the resurrection as a fitting designation for the Messiah who had been adopted by God and enthroned in heaven. In the next stage, that of Hellenistic Jewish Christianity, the title was interpreted along the lines of a supernaturally endowed divine man who had a divine birth. Finally in the Hellenistic church the title is understood metaphysically and deification takes place. Along with deification also came the doctrine of the preexistence of the Son.[62] More recently still, Géza Vermès has argued that this entire process began in the ministry of Jesus where Jesus was seen as a son of God because of his miracle working and exorcistic power.[63]

We have seen, however, that in several important passages, which have good claim to being authentic, Jesus claims a unique and exclusive relationship to God as the "Son." Several other passages agree closely with these. We find in Luke 2:49 an account that claims that already at the age of twelve the boy Jesus sensed in a unique way that the Temple of God in Jerusalem was his Father's house. At his baptism the heavenly Voice confirms this Sonship, and at the transfiguration that same Voice reveals the uniqueness of that Sonship by contrasting between Jesus as the Son and Elijah and Moses (MARK 9:5 and 7). At his crucifixion the mockers at the cross scoff at Jesus because he is helpless and had claimed to be the Son of God (Matt 27:43).

It has already been pointed out that the unique use of the term *abba*, which has no real parallel in Judaism, reveals that Jesus understood himself to stand in a special relationship to his Father. This uniqueness is further revealed by the care that Jesus exercised in how he spoke of God as the Father, for nowhere does he ever refer to God as "our Father" but only as "your Father" and "my Father."[64] The clearest instance of this, to be sure, is in John 20:17, where Jesus tells Mary:

Do not hold me, for I have not yet ascended to the Father; but go to my brethren and say to them, I am ascending to my Father and your Father, to my God and your God.

Yet we find in the Synoptic Gospels the same distinction as well:

But I say to you, Love your enemies and pray for those who persecute you, so that you may be sons of *your* Father who is in heaven. (Matt 5:44–45, italics added)

You, therefore, must be perfect, as *your* heavenly Father is perfect. (MATT 5:48, italics added)

See that you do not despise one of these little ones; for I tell you that in heaven their angels always behold the face of *my* Father who is in heaven. (Matt 18:10, italics added)

When viewed together, the Gospel material indicates that Jesus claimed a unique Sonship. It differed from that of his followers not merely quantitatively but qualitatively, not merely in degree but in kind. It was not only one of function but of "being," for Jesus is, to use Johannine terminology, the "only Son" of God. It is therefore not surprising to discover that not only the creeds of the early church councils but even the earliest creeds and hymns of the church (cf. Phil 2:6–11; Col 1:15–20) speak of the form, essence, and preexistence of this Sonship.

SON OF MAN

Of all the titles found in the Gospels the favorite self-designation of Jesus is the title "Son of man." The title is found sixty-nine times in the Synoptic Gospels and thirteen times in John, and it is present in all the Gospel strata.[65] One striking feature of these titles is that in every instance except two the title is found on the lips of Jesus. The two exceptions are John 12:34 and Luke 24:7, but even here it should be noted that in John 12:34 Jesus' audience uses this title because Jesus had just previously used it as a self-designation (v. 23), and in Luke 24:7 the angel is simply repeating Jesus' own words. Outside the Gospels the term is found only four times: Acts 7:56; Heb 2:6 (= Ps 8:5); Rev 1:13 and 14:14 (= Dan 7:13), but in only one instance (Acts 7:56) is the title used of Jesus outside of an Old Testament reference or quotation.

There is little doubt that of all the titles found in the Gospels this is the most important one. There are at least two reasons for this. First, the frequency with which it occurs indicates that it is the prime title for understanding the person and work of Jesus. Secondly, since the title appears "only" on the lips of Jesus and was, according to the Gospels, his favorite self-designation, there is no other title that so clearly reveals the "messianic self-consciousness" of Jesus as this one. Some would even say that this title is the only Christological title whose authenticity should be taken seriously. It is therefore not surprising to discover that of all the Christological titles this is the title that is most intensely being investigated today. Yet the results of this investigation are most disappointing, for frequently we encounter the most contradictory conclusions. An example of this is the question of whether the term could be used in Aramaic as a title and/or as a circumlocution for the pronoun "I." Jeremias has denied that the Aramaic term for "Son of man" could be used as a circumlocution, but Vermès has argued that the term was never used as a title but could only be used as a circumlocution.[66] As we shall see, some scholars vigorously deny the authenticity of many or even all of the sayings in which this term appears, while other scholars just as vigorously affirm their authenticity.

Background

The term "Son of man," or *huios tou anthropou*, is a rather awkward Greek translation of the Aramaic *bar nasha* and the Hebrew *ben adam*. Within the Old Testament the term is found in the Psalms, in Ezekiel, and in Daniel. In Ps 8:4; 80:17; and 144:3 *(ben enosh)* it occurs in examples of synonymous parallelism and simply means "man," although in Ps 80:17 the "man" may be the king. In Ezekiel the expression "Son of man" occurs ninety-three times as a form of address by which God speaks to the prophet. There is general agreement, however, that the use of the title in the Gospels does not derive from this usage in Psalms or Ezekiel. Far more important is the appearance of this expression in Dan 7:13, which we shall discuss shortly.

Attempts have been made to trace the ultimate background of the term to Iranian myths of the primal man, to the Babylonian Adapa, the Egyptian sun-god Re, and the gnostic heavenly man, but whereas such investigations are important for Old Testament studies, they possess no great value for our discussion. Whatever the ultimate source of the concept may be, Jesus' usage of the term was not derived from studies in Iranian, Babylonian, Egyptian, etc., mythology. Assuming that he did in fact use the term, it could have come to him only out of Judaism or *de novo* out of his own mind. As a result, we shall confine ourselves to a brief look at the Jewish sources that use this title. The title is found in two apocalyptic works of Judaism—Ethiopian Enoch and II Esdras—as well as in the canonical Daniel. In ch. 13 of II Esdras we find several references to a figure who clearly resembles the Son of man in Daniel. The figure is called "my Son" (vs. 32, 37, 52), comes with the clouds of heaven (v. 3), comes in judgment and for deliverance (vs. 29f.), and is preexistent (v. 26). Most scholars date this work, however, around A.D. 90, so that its value as an independent witness to a pre-Christian Son of man Christology is dubious. Nevertheless, some scholars claim that despite its post-Christian date and its dependence upon Daniel, II Esdras 13 witnesses to earlier pre-Christian ideas about a Son of man figure, but this is impossible to demonstrate.

On the other hand, it is evident that the Book of Enoch is pre-Christian in origin. Since it is a composite work, the dates for various sections vary, but generally they are dated between 175 and 63 B.C.[67] Within chapters 37–71 of Enoch, which is frequently referred to as the Similitudes of Enoch, we have numerous references to a Son of man figure. In Enoch the term is clearly used to describe a preexistent messianic figure who is divine and revealed at the end of history (Enoch 48:2f.; 62:9), who comes in judgment (46:4; 62:11; 69:27–29), and who rules over the elect in peace (52:8–9; 62:13–16; 71:17). It appears then that the first clear pre-Christian use of the term "Son of man" as a messianic description and title is found in Enoch 37–71.

At least two objections have been raised against this view, however.

The first involves the dating of the Similitudes of Enoch. Even before the discovery of the Dead Sea Scrolls, some scholars expressed their doubts over the pre-Christian dating of the Similitudes,[68] and the discovery of the Dead Sea Scrolls has raised additional doubts. The reason for this is that although fragments representing five different Aramaic manuscripts have been found for Section I (chs. 1–36), fragments from four manuscripts for Section III (chs. 72–82), fragments from five manuscripts for Section IV (chs. 83–90), and fragments from one manuscript for Section V (chs. 91–104), not a single fragment has been discovered that comes from the Similitudes.[69] Can it be purely an accident that no fragment of the Similitudes has been found at Qumran or does this fact argue in favor of the view that the Similitudes are post-Christian? To be sure, many scholars still argue for a pre-Christian dating of Enoch,[70] but it would seem precarious in the light of these doubts to argue that the use of the term by Jesus was in any way dependent on a knowledge of the Similitudes.[71]

The second criticism leveled against the use of Enoch 37–71 as a source for the pre-Christian utilization of this term as a title is that even in Enoch it is not certain that the term is actually a title.[72] This criticism does not seem too weighty, however, because the term, even though it is always qualified, is used so frequently that the reader of the Similitudes does receive the impression that the figure is a "Son of man-like person" and to give this figure the title "Son of man" would appear a natural thing for the reader to do.

The final Jewish reference to the title "Son of man" that must be discussed is Dan 7:13–14:

> I saw in the night visions,
>   and behold, with the clouds of heaven
>   there came one like a son of man,
>   and he came to the Ancient of Days
>   and was presented before him.
>   And to him was given dominion
>   and glory and kingdom,
>   that all peoples, nations, and languages
>   should serve him;
>   his dominion is an everlasting dominion,
>   which shall not pass away,
>   and his kingdom one
>   that shall not be destroyed.

Although the expression "one like a son of man" is not an explicit title in Dan 7:13, it would appear that this passage forms the background for understanding the use of this term in the Gospels, for there exist at least six passages in the Synoptics in which a reference to Dan 7:13 is to be found: MARK 8:38; 13:26; 14:62; Matt 10:23; 19:28; 25:31.[73] There is furthermore no other Jewish source for the apocalyptic understanding of the role of the Son of man in the Gospel tradition, since Jesus did not know the Similitudes of Enoch and could not have known II Esdras 13. It should also be noted in this regard that neither Ezekiel nor the Psalms provides an apocalyptic setting for this term, since both describe man primarily in his frailty. It has been objected that since the "one like a son of man" in Dan 7:13 must be understood corporately as referring to Israel (cf. vs. 18, 22, 27), this passage cannot be the source of this title in the Gospels. Some scholars have sought because of this to give to the title a corporate interpretation even within the New Testament,[74] but the biggest problem with this objection is that it assumes that Dan 7:13 was interpreted in this corporate manner in the first century. It is evident, however, that Judaism always interpreted the "one like a son of man" in Dan 7:13 as a messianic figure and not as a corporate entity.[75] Since therefore the Gospels on several occasions tie the title "Son of man" to Dan 7:13 and since elsewhere Jesus' acquaintance with Daniel 7 is evident,[76] the burden of proof is surely with those who deny that this was the source for the New Testament's use of the term. It is nevertheless quite clear that there was not present before the time of Jesus a well-defined Christology in Judaism which spoke of a messianic figure called the Son of man. It may even be that there was no messianic concept of the title "Son of man" at all before the time of Jesus![77] The use of this term by Jesus in his ministry would not necessarily therefore have been interpreted as a messianic claim. It would also not immediately have evoked the picture of a glorious Son of man as found in Dan 7:13 who comes from heaven to judge the world.

The Use of the Title "Son of Man" in the Gospels

The usual method of classifying the Son of man sayings is to arrange them into three groups. The first group consists of those sayings which speak of the Son of man as he is presently engaged in his earthly ministry; the second consists of those sayings which describe the Son of man in his future suffering, dying, and resurrection; and the third consists of those Son of man sayings in which he is portrayed in his future glorious return.[78] If we arrange the various passages in which the term "Son of man" is found according to these three classifications, we obtain the following:[79]

Group A—The Son of Man in His Earthly Ministry

MARK	Q	M	L
MARK 2:10	MATT 8:20	Matt 13:37	Luke 6:22
MARK 2:28	MATT 11:19	Matt 16:13	Luke 19:10
MARK 10:45	MATT 12:32		

Group B—The Son of Man in His Future Suffering

MARK	Q	M	L
MARK 8:31		Matt 26:2	Luke 22:48
MARK 9:12			Luke 24:7
MARK 9:31			
MARK 10:33			
MARK 10:45			
MARK 14:21 (2)			
MARK 14:41			

Group C—The Son of Man in His Future Coming

MARK	Q	M	L
MARK 8:38	MATT 12:40	Matt 10:23	Luke 12:8
MARK 9:9	MATT 24:27	Matt 13:41	Luke 17:22
MARK 13:26	MATT 24:37	Matt 16:28	Luke 18:8
MARK 14:62	MATT 24:39	Matt 19:28	Luke 21:36
	MATT 24:44	Matt 24:30	
		Matt 25:31	

Although there are some problems in dividing all the Son of man sayings in this manner, this classification shall be used both because of its convenience and because most of the discussion on the subject has made use of this classification.

There have been three main attempts to deny the authenticity of some or all of the Son of man sayings. These can be described as the Linguistic Attempt, the Psychological Attempt, and the Exegetical Attempt. The Linguistic Attempt, which attempts to deny the authenticity of all the Son of man sayings, goes back to Hans Lietzmann and Julius Wellhausen. According to Lietzmann, the term *bar nasha* was a generic term and simply meant "man." It therefore could not have been used as a title by Jesus, because his listeners would and could have only thought that Jesus was referring to "man" and not to the "Son of man."[80] Thus on linguistic or philological grounds he denied that the term *bar nasha* could have been used by Jesus as a title.[81] More recently, Vermès has once again raised this objection to the use of *bar nasha* as a title.[82] There is general agreement today that *bar nasha* does in general mean "man," but the conclusion that Lietzmann drew from this, that it could not therefore be used as a messianic title, does not follow, for in apocalyptic contexts especially "the man" would be understood in a messianic sense as a description and as a title.[83]

Vermès also seems justified by the evidence he has collected in saying that *bar nasha* could be and was used as a circumlocution for "I." The evidence he cites demonstrates this.[84] To argue from this, however, that the term could not be used as a circumlocution when the speaker referred to his uniqueness or made statements that were true only with respect to himself[85] does not follow. Vermès, himself, lists as an example of circumlocution the following example:

A certain man came to Rabbi Yose ben Halafta and said to him: It has been revealed to *that man* (= me) in a dream. . . .[86]

Here the expression "that man," or *bar nasha*, is used as a circumlocution by the man speaking to Rabbi Halafta even though he is claiming a unique experience. God in a unique way had revealed to him (alone) something in a dream! Whether the expression *bar nasha* was ever used as a circumlocution for "I" can be determined only by observing the evidence. Our evidence is not great, but it is clear that it was used in this way. Whether it could be used in statements when the speaker meant "I and no other" can likewise be determined only by observation. It should be pointed out that it is dangerous in the light of the paucity of evidence to be dogmatic here, but it seems fairly clear that in the example cited by Vermès and quoted above, *bar nasha* is used to refer to this man exclusively, i.e., "him and no other." The man did not claim that to me *(bar nasha)*, and every one else as well, God has revealed in a dream the following . . ., but rather he was saying, "To me [*bar nasha*] in a unique way God has revealed in a dream the following. . . ." That Jesus thought of himself as unique has already been demonstrated and there is no *a priori* reason why Jesus could not have used the term *bar nasha* in a similar way as a circumlocution for "I" when he was emphasizing his uniqueness.

It must also be pointed out that even if *bar nasha* was not used as a title before the time of Jesus, this says nothing whatsoever concerning whether Jesus could have used it as a title. If the expression can be used as a title in Aramaic, and it could, then someone somewhere had to create the first instance of its use as a title. Why could this not have been Jesus? The use of such a term would be simply another *mashal* which those outside would hear but not understand but which nevertheless revealed a messianic claim to those who had eyes to see.

The Psychological Attempt to deny the authenticity of the Son of man sayings proceeds as follows:

PREMISE 1—For anyone to claim to be the apocalyptic Son of man would be insane.

PREMISE 2—Jesus was not insane.

CONCLUSION—Therefore Jesus never claimed to be the Son of Man.[87] This entire line of reasoning contains several *a priori* assumptions which are at least questionable. For one, it assumes that a rational man could not claim to be the Son of man, but it is evident from Enoch 71:14, where Enoch is called the Son of man, that a "man" could be given this title. The Enoch literature therefore, because of its high view of its hero, is able to identify a historical person as the apocalyptic Son of man. Premise 1 is therefore open to question. Another assumption that this line of reasoning presupposes is that Jesus was not qualitatively different from others and therefore not just "anyone." One cannot prove this. It must be taken by faith! Finally it might be claimed that since the evidence in favor of the authenticity of the Son of man sayings is stronger than that against it,[88] another perhaps more "logical" solution based upon these premises is as follows:

PREMISE 1—For anyone to claim to be the apocalyptic Son of man would be insane.

PREMISE 2—Jesus claimed to be the Son of man.

CONCLUSION—Therefore Jesus was insane.

It is indeed a poor example of objective research when one predetermines what Jesus could or could not have said about himself without having to look at the passages that make such a claim. Whether or not Jesus referred to himself as the Son of man cannot be determined on the basis of *a priori* presuppositions as to the psychological makeup of Jesus which in turn is itself based upon a naturalistic presupposition! Such a conclusion can and must be made only on the basis of exegetical investigation!

The third attempt to deny the authenticity of part or all of the Son of man sayings is the Exegetical Attempt. Whereas in the former attempts the main tools employed were linguistic and psychological, the main tool employed here is the critical-historical method and especially form-critical and redaction-critical analysis. Since the critical-historical method is concerned with linguistic analysis, it is not surprising to find some overlapping in these two attempts to deny the authenticity of some or all of the Son of man sayings. One of the more popular positions in recent discussions is the view that only the C sayings (the Son of man in his future coming) are authentic and that Jesus when he refers to the Son of man in these sayings is not referring to himself but is referring to someone else. The authentic C sayings can therefore be ascertained quite easily, because in these sayings Jesus clearly distinguishes between himself and the Son of man. This is most noticeable in the text, for when Jesus speaks of himself he uses the first person, but when he speaks of the Son of man he uses the third person. Some examples of this are:

> For whoever is ashamed of me and of my words in this adulterous and sinful generation, of him will the Son of man also be ashamed, when he comes in the glory of his Father with the holy angels. (MARK 8:38)

> And I tell you, every one who acknowledges me before men, the Son of man also will acknowledge before the angels of God. (Luke 12:8; cf. also MARK 14:62; Matt 19:28)

Since the A and B sayings differ from the C sayings both in subject (In A and B, Jesus is the Son of man, whereas in C someone other than Jesus is the Son of man) and in theme (In A and B, the Son of man is a humble and abused individual, whereas in C he is glorified divine Being), the A and B sayings cannot be authentic. Additional support for claiming that the B sayings are inauthentic is the fact that they are prophetic statements of Jesus' forthcoming death. As a result, many scholars conclude that they are all *vaticinia ex eventu,* or prophecies after the fact, which the church later placed on the lips of Jesus.[89] There are several objections, however, to claiming that all the sayings of Jesus that speak of his forthcoming death must be predictions later placed on the lips of Jesus by the church. First, the view that there can be no such prophecy is based on an antisupernaturalistic premise which itself is an act of "faith." Secondly, on purely historical grounds one cannot claim that all prophecies of a man's forthcoming death must be dismissed as unhistorical in that there have been incidents of men who have "prophesied" not only their deaths but the events that would attend their deaths.[90] Thirdly, it would have been rather strange for Jesus never to have thought that his preaching which so antagonized the religious authorities might not lead to death in that his own cousin had experienced martyrdom for just such preaching. Finally, it must be pointed out that there are certain passages in which Jesus speaks of his death which do not appear to be church creations because of the problems involved in the prophecies.[91]

A number of criticisms must be raised against the view presented above that only the C sayings in which Jesus supposedly refers to someone else are authentic. The first is that nowhere else in the teachings of Jesus is there the slightest hint that he expected someone greater than himself who would come after him. On the contrary, his actions and sayings reveal quite clearly that there could not come one greater than he.[92] Furthermore, such a passage as MATT 11:5f. would have been impossible, for Jesus would not have been able to reply in the affirmative to John the Baptist's question but would have had to say: "No, I am not. There is one coming after me." Yet such a saying as Matt 5:17 reveals that Jesus thought of himself as the fulfiller of the Old Testament promises. A second problem that this view encounters is that it presumes the existence of a fairly precise Son of man Christology in contemporary Judaism to which Jesus could refer. If, as we have maintained, there did not exist a well-defined concept of the Son of man in Jesus' day, how could Jesus have referred so furtively to such a figure and expected his listeners to understand about whom he was speaking?[93] On the other hand, if the term "Son of man" could be used as a circumlocution for "I" and was used in delicate situations such as referring to one's death,[94] why should it be strange for Jesus to use this circumlocution when he referred, in his modesty, to his role as the Son of man? Does not Paul in II Cor 12:2f. use the third person even though he is referring to himself? Finally, it should be noted that although Jesus frequently exhorts his followers to wait for and be prepared for the coming of the Son of man, he never includes himself among those who are to await his coming.[95]

The second view that shall be discussed is the view that all the Son of man sayings in the Gospels are inauthentic.[96] This view has gained numerous adherents of late.[97] A number of arguments are presented in support of it. It is argued that *bar nasha* without the demonstrative "this" is never a self-designation, so that Jesus could never have referred to himself in a unique way as the Son of man. We have already seen the weakness of this argument. It is also argued that since there was no pre-Christian Son of man concept, Jesus could never have used *bar nasha* as a titular self-designation. Yet who can say what title Jesus could or could not have used for himself? Could not a creative genius create such a term or take such a term and use it for a self-designation? The whole "criterion of dissimilarity" assumes just such a creative capability on the part of Jesus. One thing we know about Jesus is that he did not let the forms and thinking of his day limit him! Can the twentieth-century exegete dogmatically say to the Jesus of history, "You cannot use this term *bar nasha* to describe yourself"? Why should modern scholarship hesitate to acknowledge that Jesus transcended the thought forms of his day in the area of Christology? It has no such hesitation in permitting him to do so in the area of ethics.

Another argument sometimes raised against the authenticity of this term is that nowhere in Judaism or in Jesus' teachings are the concepts of the kingdom of God and the Son of man brought together, for in fact they are irreconcilable.[98] I. H. Marshall points out that although such links are rare, such links do exist and he lists Dan 7:13f. and Enoch 69:26–28 as examples.[99] If it is objected that Dan 7:13 does not refer to a messianic individual but refers to the people of Israel in general, it must be pointed out that in the first century the "one like a son of man" was interpreted as an individual messianic figure and this figure is clearly associated with the kingdom of God (cf. Dan 7:14, 18, 23f.). In Enoch 69:26–28 it should also be noted that the Son of man sits on the throne and exhibits all the functions of kingship! In two of the three apocalyptic sources of Judaism in which the expression Son of man occurs, therefore, *bar nasha* is in fact associated with the kingdom of God. Again the rarity with which the term "Son of man" is found in Jewish literature ought to warn us against making such hasty conclusions. As to the Gospel materials, it may well be that the terms "Son of man" and "kingdom of God" do not appear in the same sayings. They certainly do appear, however, in the same sources, contexts, and even in the variant forms of parallel sayings![100] As for the Evangelists, it is quite apparent by their use of the "Son of man materials" and "kingdom of God materials" that they saw no inconsistency or incoherence in placing them together, and if they could place these two concepts together, why is it considered impossible that Jesus could do the same? On the other hand, it appears in some ways at least that rather than being inconsistent, Jesus' teachings about the kingdom of God and the coming of the Son of man are quite consistent. Both are portrayed as taking place unexpectedly (cf. Matt 25:1–13 and MATT 24:37–41) and both involve judgment (cf. LUKE 19:11–27 and MATT 24:37–41). Instead of seeing a conflict we could more easily see in these two expressions two different ways of expressing the same reality.

Finally, it has been argued that there is not a single Son of man saying whose authenticity is absolute and which cannot be doubted. It is certainly true that the authenticity of every Son of man saying can be doubted. What is there that cannot be doubted? The question, however, is not whether the authenticity of any Son of man saying can be doubted but rather whether the authenticity of every Son of man saying can be doubted. This is an entirely different question.

The Authenticity of the Son of Man Sayings
The case for the authenticity of the title "Son of man" as a self-designation will be divided into two parts. The first will involve general considerations, and the second will involve the investigation of several passages in which the title appears. During the last few decades, the single most

important tool for ascertaining authentic sayings of Jesus has been the "criterion of dissimilarity."[101] This tool has proved a most valuable one. It has been criticized at times because it eliminates the great bulk of the Gospel traditions from consideration, since by definition it must eliminate any material that could possibly have been derived from Judaism or from the early church. Nevertheless, there has been almost universal agreement that when a saying of Jesus in the Gospels meets the criterion of dissimilarity it is almost certainly authentic. Yet many scholars who apply this tool in their research still deny the authenticity of the Son of man sayings even though the sayings satisfy the criteria established by this tool.

The first criterion that the Son of man sayings satisfy is that they could not have arisen out of a Jewish environment, for we do not possess a single clear example of the use of this title in pre-Christian Jewish literature.[102] The title furthermore meets the second criterion because there is no evidence that the title could have arisen out of the Christian church. This second criterion is, of course, disputed, but the evidence that is given to refute this statement all comes from the Gospels, not from the rest of the New Testament. When we eliminate the Gospel data from consideration, there exists only one passage in the entire New Testament in which we find this term used as a title—Acts 7:56.

It might be objected, however, that the Gospel passages ought not be eliminated as sources for the church's Christological views. Yet there are at least two reasons why in this instance they must be. The first reason is to avoid as much circular reasoning as possible. To assume that some or all of the Son of man sayings are inauthentic and thus reveal a Son of man Christology in the early church partly at least on the presupposition that there was such a Christology in the early church raises numerous questions. If indeed there did exist such a Christology in the early church, it should be visible elsewhere. Yet where does one find this term in any creedal formulation? The answer is "Nowhere!"[103] Such evidence is found only in the texts of the Gospels. Secondly, it should be noted that in other instances where the authenticity of a saying or teaching is accepted, such as Jesus' use of the term *Abba*, his teaching in parables, and his claim over the Law, no one denies that they meet the criterion of dissimilarity because there exist other passages in which the term *Abba*, or a parable, or a claim over the Law, etc., is found in the Gospels on the lips of Jesus. No, in these other instances these areas of Jesus' teachings are said to meet the second aspect of the criterion of dissimilarity because they are not found elsewhere in the New Testament or in the early church fathers. When it comes to the title "Son of man," however, the Gospels themselves become the source of a widespread Son of man Christology which becomes the basis for rejecting the authenticity of the term. To argue in this circular manner seems far from objective.

It is interesting in this regard to observe how the Gospels treat one of the favorite titles of the early church's Christology. In the New Testament, apart from the Gospels, the title "Christ" is used over four hundred and fifty times. Its popularity is such that for the most part it has become part of the name of Jesus—Jesus Christ. In the Gospels, however, this title is found only seven times as a self-designation on the lips of the historical Jesus.[104] Certainly there seems to be a remarkable reserve in reading back this Christological title upon the lips of Jesus, even though this was probably the favorite title which the church used to describe the person and work of Jesus. Yet when it comes to the title "Son of man," we find it used only once in the rest of the New Testament, but as a self-designation of Jesus sixty-nine times in the Synoptic Gospels. Such a phenomenon is incredible if the early church created this title! Such a phenomenon would have required a "conspiracy" of vast proportions. This "conspiracy" would then have exercised great care to see to it that all these Son of man sayings would appear only on the lips of Jesus and in all the Gospel strata. Yet the fact that the church did not read back the title "Christ" upon the lips of Jesus even though it was their favorite title argues conclusively against their having read back the title "Son of man" upon the lips of Jesus when it was not a favorite title and perhaps even a misunderstood title for Jesus. The simplest explanation for the appearance of this self-description upon the lips of Jesus is that Jesus did in fact use this term to describe himself and his mission.[105]

It should also be pointed out that the number of Son of man sayings in the Gospels is really quite impressive. When we eliminate the repetition of a specific saying from the sixty-nine instances in the Synoptic Gospels, we still have some forty individual sayings in which the title "Son of man" is found. Morna D. Hooker correctly states in this regard:

> It is comparatively easy to argue against the authenticity of any one particular saying considered in isolation; the arguments look less convincing when they are weighed against the total evidence of all the Son of man sayings.[106]

Viewed just from a statistical point of view, whereas the chance of a particular Son of man saying being inauthentic may be fairly high, the chance that all of them are inauthentic would appear extremely low.

Still another argument in favor of the authenticity of this title as a self-designation of Jesus is the inadequacy of any reasonable argument as to where this title could have originated if Jesus did not use it. Some, who have argued that only the C sayings (the Son of man in his future coming) are authentic but that Jesus was referring to someone else, have suggested that after the resurrection the early church identified Jesus as the Son of man and read the title back into his ministry as a self-designation. This reconstruction, however, rests upon two presuppositions, both of which are quite questionable. The first is that the Son of man was a distinct pre-Christian messianic title, and the second is that Jesus saw himself only as a forerunner of a greater messianic figure who was to come after him. Both of these presuppositions are doubtful, so that this reconstruction does not seem reasonable. Others have argued that after the resurrection the early church in its investigation of the Old Testament discovered this title and interpreted the resurrection and exaltation of Jesus in the light of Dan 7:13. This reconstruction also presupposes that the Son of man existed as a messianic title or it credits the church with the ingenious *de novo* creation of the title. Yet could the church have flooded the Gospels with this title, so that it would appear in all the Gospel strata, and, if it did, could it have prevented a backwash of this title from entering the rest of the New Testament? This seems doubtful. Furthermore, if the church possessed sufficient creativity to assign this title to Jesus, why could not Jesus have done so himself? Finally it must be noted that the translation of the Gospel materials from Aramaic into Greek took place in a bilingual environment (cf. Acts 6:1f.). As a result, it is not easy to explain the origin of this title as due to a mistranslation of the Aramaic *bar nasha.*[107]

The second part of the argument for the authenticity of this title as a self-designation of Jesus involves certain texts that possess a good claim for being actual sayings of Jesus. One of these texts is MATT 11:18–19:

> For John came neither eating nor drinking, and they say, "He has a demon"; the Son of man came eating and drinking, and they say, "Behold, a glutton and a drunkard, a friend of tax collectors and sinners!"

This saying is an important one in that there are several strong arguments that favor its authenticity. For example, it should be noted that Jesus as the Son of man seems to be placed on the same level as John the Baptist. This would be strange if the passage were a church creation since the early church continually stressed the subordination of John the Baptist to Jesus. If the church were responsible for this passage, therefore, one would expect some indication that Jesus was superior to John. The derogatory language used to describe Jesus also speaks in favor of its authenticity. It would be strange for the church to create a passage in which Jesus is called a glutton and a drunkard, even if these words are the expression of his enemies. They simply would have found such words too offensive.

Still another argument in favor of its authenticity is the fact that the description of Jesus given in these verses corresponds well with what we know about Jesus. There is no doubt that Jesus was in fact accused of being a friend of tax collectors and sinners and that he saw his ministry not as a time of fasting but of feasting. It therefore need not be doubted that the above saying is "an authentic dominical saying."[108] It goes without saying that in this instance *bar nasha* cannot mean "man" but must be a self-designation.

Another Son of man saying that has a strong claim for authenticity is Matt 10:23:

> When they persecute you in one town, flee to the next; for truly, I say to you, you will not have gone through all the towns of Israel, before the Son of man comes.

Several difficulties arise if one seeks to argue that this verse is a church creation. The first is that it is difficult to see why the early church would create a prophetic saying and place it upon the lips of Jesus even though that prophecy does not appear to have been fulfilled. It is clear that the majority of the Jewish church never had to flee Judah or Galilee (the Hellenists of Acts 6:1f. are the exception that proves the rule) and no major persecution came upon the Gentile church until the end of the first century. Even here the scope of this persecution under the emperor Domitian is not clear, and the persecution under Nero again is the exception which proves the rule. As for the Jewish War in A.D. 66–70, this time of flight for the Jewish Christian church is too late, for the cities of Judah and Galilee had long ago been "gone through" and evangelized. One would expect that with the delay of the coming of the Son of man there would be a tendency within the early church not to create such sayings but rather to eliminate them because of their difficulty. It should also be noted that this missionary commission does not mention a mission to the Gentiles but seems to imply that Jesus was only interested in a mission to the Jews.

> Only as an authentic dominical saying can Mt. 10:23 have survived the tendency, which is particularly clear in Mt., to ascribe to Jesus a work among the Gentiles.[109]

Viewed as an individual text apart from other considerations, there does not seem to be any reason to deny the authenticity of this verse. Again it should be observed that *bar nasha* can hardly refer here to "man" in a generic sense.

There are several other passages whose cases for authenticity are also convincing. MARK 2:10 makes a strong claim for being a saying of Jesus, and the view that *bar nasha* means "man" here seems to be refuted by the response of those who hear this word of Jesus. The criticism of Jesus in this pericope is due not to his claim that "man" in general can forgive sins but that "this man Jesus" can forgive sins. His audience took his words as referring to his being able to forgive sins! Nowhere do we find in Jesus' teaching the idea that "man" can forgive sins. Here as in Luke 7:49 the audience interprets Jesus as making the unique claim that he can forgive sins, and they attack him on that basis rather than on having made a general statement that "man" can forgive sins. MATT 8:20 likewise seems to be a saying of Jesus rather than a creation of the church.[110] It is also difficult to see why the church would have created a Son of man saying for Jesus' reply to the high priest in MARK 14:62, for why would they not frame an answer to the question "Are you the Christ?" using the title "Christ," since it was one of the favorite titles of the church? Instead we find a reference to the Son of man, which is not a popular title in the early church to describe the person and work of Jesus.

The Meaning of the Title "Son of Man" for Jesus

It seems clear from the above that Jesus did use the expression *bar nasha* to describe his role and function. The question must be raised at this point as to why he chose this self-designation rather than another such as "Christ." One reason seems to be the ambiguity surrounding the term. A public self-designation as the "Christ" would have had political consequences which Jesus clearly sought to avoid. The situation simply did not permit his using such a title. On the other hand, there did not exist a clear, well-known "Son of man Christology" which might be misunderstood. On the contrary, the title was a *mashal* which both concealed and revealed. Like the parables,[111] the term *bar nasha* concealed from those outside and was itself understood only by his followers, to whom Jesus explained everything privately (cf. MARK 4:34). A second reason why Jesus chose this self-designation was that it revealed well his origin and unique relationship with God. "The Son of man is come" described well that he had come from God and that he had a special relationship with God that man through faith might also share in. Finally, the title revealed that even though the kingdom of God had become a present reality through his coming, the consummation lay still in the future. It too would come, and it would also be ushered in by the same Son of man who introduced its present realization. The Son of man came and through his ministry, death, and resurrection the kingdom of God has become realized in history. The Son of man will come and with his glorious return the kingdom of God will be consummated. Jesus used this title in part then because he saw it as a means by which the entirety of his mission could be expressed.

CONCLUSION

In this chapter we have tried to demonstrate that by his actions, his words, and the titles he used or accepted, Jesus made a unique and amazing claim. That he was like mankind and truly man is, of course, true, and the creeds of the church have always proclaimed him as "very man of very man." Yet the church in its creeds was also careful to assert the uniqueness of Jesus, for there was a qualitative difference between Jesus and man, and the church expressed this by describing Jesus as "very God of very God." Whatever may be our attitude toward the way the early church creeds expressed the uniqueness of Jesus, the fact remains that Jesus made claims, spoke, and acted in a way that makes him different from other men. One cannot simply admire Jesus as a great man or even as a great prophet. One must either acknowledge his claim of Lordship or reject it. Even today we can either kneel before him and say, "My Lord and my God!" (John 20:28) or deny him by means of apathy or anger. Jesus did not seem to permit any other option.[112]

Notes

Chapter 1. Jesus the Teacher

1. See Vincent Taylor, *The Names of Jesus* (St. Martin's Press, Inc., 1953), who lists forty-two.

2. MARK 5:35 (Luke 8:49); 9:17 (Luke 9:38); 10:17 (Matt 19:16; Luke 18:18); 12:14 (Matt 22:16; Luke 20:21); 12:19 (Matt 22:24; Luke 20:28); 12:32 (Luke 20:39); 14:14 (Matt 26:18; Luke 22:11)
Mark 4:38; 9:38; 10:20, 35; 13:1
MATT 10:24 (LUKE 6:40); 10:25 (LUKE 6:40); 22:36 (LUKE 10:25)
Matt 8:19; 9:11; 12:38; 17:24; 23:8
Luke 7:40; 11:45; 12:13; 19:39; 21:7
John 1:38; 3:2; 11:28; 13:13, 14; 20:16
For the significance of MARK, Mark, MATT, Matt, LUKE, and Luke, see Abbreviations.

3. MARK 14:45 (Matt 26:49); Mark 9:5; 10:51; 11:21; Matt 26:25; John 1:38, 49; 3:2; 4:31; 6:25; 9:2; 11:8; 20:16; cf. also Matt 23:8.

4. See Joachim Jeremias, *Jerusalem in the Time of Jesus*, trans. by F. H. and C. H. Cave (Fortress Press, 1969), pp. 233–245, for a description of the normal process by which one became a rabbi.

5. Apparently at this time the title was used more freely than at a later time. Jeremias, *Jerusalem in the Time of Jesus*, p. 236.

6. See below, pp. 27–32.

7. See Chapter 2.

8. For additional parallels, see Rudolf Bultmann, *The History of the Synoptic Tradition*, trans. by John Marsh, rev. ed. (Harper & Row, Publishers, Inc., 1968), pp. 105–108.

9. See John L. McKenzie, "Reflections on Wisdom," JBL, Vol. 86 (1967), p. 2, for the view that MARK 7:24–30 represents a "typical wisdom duel of wits." McKenzie states furthermore that "the debates between Jesus and the scribes and Pharisees are generally couched in wisdom style" *(ibid.).*

10. It is true that the *pleion* is neuter and is therefore better translated as "something" rather than "someone," but the "something" that is greater is

149

brought by a "someone" greater as well, so that the following analogy still has validity, for the point of comparison is with the wisdom of Solomon not his kingdom.

11. I am indebted to my colleague, John Piper, for this insight.

12. It is not our concern here to deal with the question of whether Jesus ever considered himself to be "the" eschatological prophet who would come at the end time (cf. Matt 21:11; John 6:14, 7:40; Acts 3:22–26). For a discussion of this, see Oscar Cullmann, *The Christology of the New Testament*, trans. by Shirley C. Guthrie and Charles A. M. Hall (The Westminster Press, 1959), pp. 13–50.

13. Joachim Jeremias, *New Testament Theology*, trans. by John Bowden (Charles Scribner's Sons, 1971), p. 4.

14. See Jeremias, *New Testament Theology*, p. 6, n. 4.

15. According to Jeremias, *New Testament Theology*, p. 6, n. 10, the use of the plural *sabbata* to denote a single sabbath cannot be explained from Greek usage but only from Aramaic.

16. See Jeremias, *New Testament Theology*, pp. 3–8, for an excellent discussion of this subject.

17. See Jeremias, *New Testament Theology*, pp. 6–7, and Vincent Taylor, *The Gospel According to St. Mark* (London: Macmillan and Co., Ltd., 1959), pp. 55–66.

18. Bar Cochba was the messianic pretender who led the Jewish revolt against Rome in A.D. 132–135.

19. See J. A. Emerton, "The Problem of Vernacular Hebrew in the First Century A.D. and the Language of Jesus," JTS, Vol. 24 (1973), pp. 1–23, and Matthew Black, *An Aramaic Approach to the Gospels and Acts*, 3d ed. (Oxford: At the Clarendon Press, 1967), pp. 41–49.

20. T. W. Manson, *The Teaching of Jesus* (Cambridge: At the University Press, 1931), p. 48, n. 1, mentions that there are eighty-seven quotations of the Old Testament found on the lips of Jesus. He also gives an example on pp. 82–83 to demonstrate the "intimate and detailed" knowledge that Jesus possessed of the Hebrew Scriptures.

21. See above, pp. 1–2.

22. Jeremias, *New Testament Theology*, p. 7.

23. Cf. also John 12:20f.

24. For an excellent discussion on the entire question of the languages of Jesus, see Joseph A. Fitzmyer, "The Languages of Palestine in the First Century A.D.," CBQ, Vol. 32 (1970), pp. 501–531, and Pinchas Lapide, "Insights from Qumran Into the Languages of Jesus," RQ, Vol. 8 (1975), pp. 483–501.

Chapter 2. THE FORM OF JESUS' TEACHING

1. For the significance of MARK, Mark, MATT, Matt, LUKE, and Luke, see Abbreviations.

2. Compare I Maccabees 4:46; 9:27; 14:41; II Baruch 85:1–3; b. Yoma 21b; and Tos. Sota 13:2 which states: "Since the last prophets Haggai, Zechariah, and Malachi died, the Holy Spirit has ceased in Israel."

3. Compare the Matthean parallel in MATT 10:37 which reads: "He who loves father or mother more than me is not worthy of me; and he who loves son or daughter more than me is not worthy of me."

4. We should note that the context of this overstatement in Matthew deals with lust (cf. Matt 5:27–28).

5. Compare MARK 7:21–23. It is true that the saying in MATT 5:29–30 speaks of the right eye and the right hand "causing" one to sin, but this is to be understood as a picturesque way of speaking. Only if one were to accept a crass Platonic dualism in which evil stems from and is caused by matter (the eye, the hand, the muscles, the bones, etc.), can one interpret these words literally. Jesus, however, speaks out of a Hebraic environment that uses such terms aspectively. For a discussion of this aspective understanding of man, see George Eldon Ladd, *A Theology of the New Testament* (Wm. B. Eerdmans Publishing Company, 1974), pp. 457–478.

6. A good example of the use of overstatement in which this form is no longer effective is modern advertising. Here understatement is often more effective!

7. See below, p. 97, for a discussion of the necessity of interpreting such statements in the entire context of Jesus' teaching.

8. In LUKE 6:29 the order of the garments is reversed and the outer cloak is mentioned first. This is due to the fact that the situation in Luke involves robbery and, of course, the outer garment would be taken first. In Matthew we are dealing with a courtroom scene where the defendant is forced to give up his dispensable undergarment and is advised by Jesus to give up the outer one as well.

9. For examples of the idea of an elephant going through the eye of a needle in rabbinic literature, see b. Baba Metzia 38b; b. Erubin 53a; and b. Berachoth 55b.

10. See Luke 19:1–10 (esp. v. 2); MARK 15:42–46 with Matt 27:57; Luke 8:1–3.

11. In Greek also the same term *pneuma* can mean both "wind" and "spirit."

12. See Black, *An Aramaic Approach to the Gospels and Acts*, pp. 218–223.

13. For other suggested examples, see Black, *An Aramaic Approach to the Gospels and Acts*, pp. 160–185, 217–218, and Géza Vermès, *Jesus the Jew* (London: Wm. Collins & Co., Ltd., 1973), p. 29.

14. See below, pp. 34–39.

15. See Archibald M. Hunter, *Interpreting the Parables* (The Westminster Press, 1961), p. 9.

16. See Hunter, *Interpreting the Parables*, pp. 121–122, and Manson, *The Teaching of Jesus*, pp. 66–68, for a listing of the parables.

17. Aristotle in his *Rhetoric* 2, 20, 2ff. (III. iv. 1) defines the difference between a simile and a metaphor as follows: "The simile also is a metaphor; for there is very little difference. When the poet says of Achilles, 'he rushed on like a lion,' it is a simile; if he says, 'A lion, he rushed on,' it is a metaphor; for because both are courageous, he transfers the sense and calls Achilles a lion" (Loeb).

18. See the discussion below on pp. 34–39.

19. Hunter, *Interpreting the Parables*, pp. 121–122, lists the following examples given above as parables: MARK 2:17, 19–20; MATT 6:22; 7:16–20; 9:37–38; Matt

5:13, 14–16. Manson, *The Teaching of Jesus*, pp. 66–68, lists the following as parables: MARK 2:17, 19–20; 7:26–27; 8:15; MATT 7:16–20; 9:37–38; Matt 5:14–16; 7:6.

20. These are not to be confused with the " 'I'—Sayings" listed by Bultmann, *The History of the Synoptic Tradition*, pp. 150–166.

21. See above, pp. 2–3.

22. What MARK 4:10–12 states about parables could also be said of riddles. Cf. MARK 7:17, where the riddle of v. 15 is specifically called a parable.

23. Jeremias, *New Testament Theology*, p. 30, would also include as examples MARK 9:31; MATT 11:4f.; 12:40; LUKE 11:49.

24. See above, pp. 17–18.

25. For the frequent appearance of the triad "deaf and dumb, weak-minded, and under-age" in rabbinic literature, see Jeremias, *New Testament Theology*, p. 227, n. 2.

26. Jakob Jónsson, *Humour and Irony in the New Testament* (Reykjavik: Bokautgafa Menningarsjods, 1965), lists numerous other examples in the Gospels, but the vast majority of them are not convincing to the present writer.

27. It should be remembered that the Jews during the Maccabean period had decided that to save their lives they would "profane" the Sabbath (I Maccabees 2:29–41, esp. v. 34) and fight. In so defending themselves, they would both save life (their own) and kill (their enemies). Jesus, however, sought only to save life and to harm no one!

28. See below, pp. 57–59.

29. The Lord's Supper has not been included in this listing of the parabolic actions of Jesus because of the necessary verbal element involved in explaining the bread and the cup. Cf. MARK 9:36–37 and 12:15–17 for other examples of Jesus' use of physical objects as a means of instruction.

30. C. F. Burney, *The Poetry of Our Lord* (Oxford: At the Clarendon Press, 1925), pp. 15–16, attributes the first three classifications to Bishop Lowth.

31. Jeremias, *New Testament Theology*, pp. 15–16, lists 138 different examples of antithetical parallelism in the Synoptic Gospels. Burney, *The Poetry of Our Lord*, p. 83, states that "this form of parallelism characterizes our Lord's teaching in all the Gospel-sources [MARK, Q, M, L, JOHN]." Jeremias, *New Testament Theology*, p. 18, agrees.

32. See Jeremias, *New Testament Theology*, pp. 15–16, for a complete listing of examples in the Synoptic Gospels. Jeremias lists 30 examples in MARK; 34 in Q (MATT-LUKE); 44 in Matt; and 30 in Luke.

33. Burney, *The Poetry of Our Lord*, pp. 89–90.

34. Cf. also John 8:44.

35. Cf. Rom 2:7–10, where v. 7 = a, v. 8 = b, v. 9 = B, v. 10 = A; I Cor. 4:10, where we find an ab/ab//BA pattern; Phil 1:15–17, where v. 15a = a, v. 15b = b, v. 16 = B, v. 17 = A; and Rom 11:22. For a description of chiasmus in Paul, see Joachim Jeremias, "Chiasmus in den Paulusbriefen," ZNW, Vol. 49 (1958), pp. 145–156.

36. The same can also be said for the parables and to a lesser degree perhaps for the other forms used by Jesus.

37. See Harald Riesenfeld, *The Gospel Tradition*, trans. by Robert Kraft (Fortress Press, 1970), pp. 1–29, and Birger Gerhardsson, *Memory and Manuscript* (Lund: C. W. K. Gleerup Publishers, 1961), pp. 324–335.

38. Certainly the mission of the twelve (MARK 6:7f.) provides a natural situation in the life of Jesus for the memory and transmission of Jesus' words. Cf. also Luke 10:1f.

39. For examples of personification, see MATT 11:21–24; Luke 11:49; 19:40; Matt 6:3; 10:15; cf. John 3:8. For additional rhythmic forms, see Burney, *The Poetry of Our Lord*, pp. 100–146, and Jeremias, *New Testament Theology*, pp. 20–27. For the presence of alliteration, assonance, and paronomasia in the sayings of Jesus, see Burney, *The Poetry of Our Lord*, pp. 147–175; Black, *An Aramaic Approach to the Gospels and Acts*, pp. 160–185; and Jeremias, *New Testament Theology*, pp. 27–29.

40. It is therefore entirely beside the point to argue that the mustard seed is not the smallest seed on earth (MARK 4:31), for this would be to demand scientific accuracy from an impressionistic portrait!

41. In this regard nineteenth-century liberalism frequently distinguished between the "husk" of Jesus' message which was to be discarded and the real "kernel" of his message which was the divine message.

Chapter 3. THE PARABLES OF JESUS

1. Archibald M. Hunter, "The Interpreter and the Parables: The Centrality of the Kingdom," *New Testament Issues*, ed. by Richard A. Batey (Harper & Row, Publishers, Inc., 1970), p. 71.

2. For the significance of MARK, Mark, MATT, Matt, LUKE, and Luke, see Abbreviations.

3. See the discussion of simile and metaphor above on pp. 14–17.

4. Note Ezek 17:2–10; 24:3–5; Isa 5:1–7; II Sam 12:1–4. For examples of allegorical details in rabbinic parables, see Hunter, *Interpreting the Parables*, pp. 113–116, and C. K. Barrett, *The New Testament Background: Selected Documents* (Harper & Row, Publishers, Inc., 1961), pp. 148–151.

5. Eta Linnemann, *Parables of Jesus*, trans. by John Sturdy (London: SPCK, 1966), p. 3.

6. *Ibid.*, p. 4.

7. *Ibid.*

8. For a discussion of Adolf Jülicher's contribution to the interpretation of parables, see below, pp. 51–53.

9. For a discussion of allegorical interpretation of the parables by the early church, see below, pp. 45–49.

10. Linnemann, *Parables of Jesus*, p. 8.

11. Joachim Jeremias, *The Parables of Jesus*, trans. by S. H. Hooke (rev. ed., Charles Scribner's Sons, 1963), p. 20, states that such attempts at classification and distinction are "a fruitless labour in the end," since the Hebrew *mashal* and the Aramaic *mathla* embraced all these categories and many more without distinction. Cf. also C. H. Dodd, *The Parables of the Kingdom* (London: James Nisbet & Co., Ltd., 1935), p. 18.

12. Hunter, "The Interpreter and the Parables," p. 74, estimates that there are approximately 55 parables in the Gospels of which 25 are similitudes (figurative sayings and proverbs). Manson, *The Teaching of Jesus*, pp. 66–68, lists 65.

13. Taylor, *The Gospel According to St. Mark*, p. 257, states: "This interpretation of the purpose of parables is so intolerable that from earliest times it has been questioned." Cf. also Manson, *The Teaching of Jesus*, p. 76, who states: "As the text stands it can only mean that the object, or at any rate the result, of parabolic teaching is to prevent insight, understanding, repentance, and forgiveness. On any interpretation of parables this is simply absurd."

14. See C. H. Peisker, "Konsekutives *hina* in Markus 4¹²," ZNW, Vol. 59 (1968), pp. 126–127.

15. Manson, *The Teaching of Jesus*, p. 78.

16. Jeremias, *The Parables of Jesus*, p. 17.

17. See Black, *An Aramaic Approach to the Gospels and Acts*, pp. 213–214.

18. The expression *Sitz im Leben* is frequently used to describe the various stages through which the Gospel traditions passed. The first *Sitz im Leben* refers to the situation in which Jesus uttered the saying or in which the incident occurred. The second *Sitz im Leben* refers to the period in which these traditions were passed on orally, and the third *Sitz im Leben* refers to the situation in which the Evangelists wrote their Gospels.

19. Note how the opponents of Jesus misused his statement about the destruction of the "temple" in MARK 14:58.

20. For use of these titles by Jesus, see below, pp. 121–127, 133–148.

21. Note that Nathan's parable was not self-evident but required the explanation—"Thou art the man!"

22. It seems to the present writer that the emphasis on this parable falls not so much on the abundant harvest (so Jeremias) as on the kinds of soils or the different receptions Jesus' preaching of the Word of God received.

23. See Adolf Deissmann, *Paul*, 2d ed. rev. and enl., trans. by William E. Wilson (Harper & Brothers, 1957), p. 71.

24. Sometimes the terms *ipsissima verba* (the actual words [of Jesus]) or *ipsissima vox* (the actual voice [of Jesus]) are used in this regard.

25. See Norman Perrin, *Rediscovering the Teaching of Jesus* (Harper & Row, Publishers, Inc., 1967), pp. 39–43.

26. An application of this principle to the teachings of Martin Luther, for instance, would only accept as authentic that material in which he differed with the Roman Catholicism of his day and early Lutheranism. The result, while correct in part, would nevertheless present a distorted picture of his teaching.

27. Jeremias, *New Testament Theology*, p. 29.

28. Jeremias, *The Parables of Jesus*, pp. 11–12. Cf. also Jubilees 11:11 for an example in which sowing precedes plowing.

29. See below, pp. 60–79.

30. See below, pp. 80–87.

31. See below, pp. 98–100.

32. The author is heavily indebted to the following works for this section: Adolf

Jülicher, *Die Gleichnisreden Jesu* (Tübingen: J. C. B. Mohr, 1910), Vol. I, pp. 203ff.; and Hunter, *Interpreting the Parables,* pp. 21–41.

33. Philo, of course, did not live in the classical Greek period but lived in the first century of our era. He is mentioned here, however, because of his heavy use of allegory in interpreting the Old Testament and his Alexandrian origin. Origen, who made such allegorical interpretation most popular in the early church, came from the city of Alexandria.

34. Irenaeus, *Against Heresies* IV. xxvi. 1.

35. *Ibid.,* IV. xxxvi. 7.

36. Tertullian, *On Modesty,* Ch. 9.

37. Origen also used the Septuagint translation of Prov 22:20–21 to support this idea of a threefold meaning in Scripture. See *De Principiis* IV. i. 11–13.

38. See Chr. A. Bugge, *Die Haupt-Parabeln Jesu* (Giessen: Töpelmann, 1903), p. 283.

39. Commentary on Luke 10:30–35 (Origen, Homily XXXIV). Another example of Origen's allegorical interpretation of the parables is his treatment of the parable of the unforgiving servant (Commentary on Matthew 18:23–35 [Matt XIV, Book 6–8]). Origen interprets the lord as referring to the Son of God, the servants as the stewards of the Gospel, the reckoning as the final judgment, and the unforgiving servant as the Antichrist or Devil.

40. Augustine, *Questiones Evangeliorum* 2.19.

41. John Chrysostom, *Matt Hom* lxiv. 3. Unfortunately the large work against the allegorizing of the Alexandrian school by Theodore of Mopsuestia, another member of the Antiochian school, has not survived, but his view can be found in his commentary on Gal 4:24.

42. For a defense of this fourfold sense, see Thomas Aquinas, *Summa Theologica,* Part I, Question 1, Article 10.

43. See Frederic W. Farrar, *History of Interpretation* (London: Macmillan and Co., Ltd., 1886), p. 328.

44. John Calvin, *Commentary on a Harmony of the Evangelists: Matthew, Mark and Luke,* trans. by William Pringle (Wm. B. Eerdmans Publishing Company, 1949), Vol. III, p. 63.

45. *Ibid.,* Vol. II, p. 177.

46. Richard Chenevix Trench, *Notes on the Parables of Our Lord* (New York: Appleton, 1866), pp. 258–264.

47. See above, pp. 34–36.

48. Jülicher, *Die Gleichnisreden Jesu,* Vol. II. For additional examples of Jülicher's tendency to read nineteenth-century liberal dogma into the parables, see Dodd, *The Parables of the Kingdom,* pp. 24–25, and Hunter, *Interpreting the Parables,* pp. 38–39.

49. Dodd, *The Parables of the Kingdom,* p. 32.

50. Realized eschatology maintains that Jesus taught that the kingdom of God had come in its completeness in his ministry. See below, pp. 67–68.

51. Dodd, *The Parables of the Kingdom,* p. 174.

52. It was Joachim Jeremias who most effectively applied this principle to the

interpretation of the parables. His work, *The Parables of Jesus,* will no doubt be the standard text for the study of the parables for many years to come.

53. Over the centuries the Jewish-Samaritan hatred had grown. The Jew thought of the Samaritan as a rebel (they had rebelled against God's anointed, Solomon's son Rehoboam, and thus divided the kingdom) and a half-breed heretic (after the fall of Samaria in 722 B.C. many Israelites intermarried with the Gentiles who had been resettled in the area), whereas the Samaritan remembered the Jewish rejection of their offer to help rebuild the Temple in Jerusalem (Ezra 4) and the Jewish destruction of their own temple on Mt. Gerizim in 128 B.C. by John Hyrcanus. The profaning of the Temple by certain Samaritans during a Passover sometime between A.D. 6 and 9 (see Josephus, *Antiquities,* 18. 2. 2) likewise did not help Jewish-Samaritan relations.

54. Hans Conzelmann, *The Theology of St. Luke,* trans. by Geoffrey Buswell (Harper & Brothers, 1960).

55. Willi Marxsen, *Mark the Evangelist,* trans. by James Boyce, Donald Juel, William R. Poehlmann with Roy A. Harrisville (Abingdon Press, 1969).

56. It should be mentioned here that one can also investigate the meaning of the parables in the second *Sitz im Leben,* for the parables were also interpreted by the church during the oral period.

57. For an attempt to defend the morality of this action, see J. D. M. Derrett, "Law in the New Testament: The Treasure in the Field (Mt 13:44)," ZNW, Vol. 54 (1963), pp. 31–42.

58. The author can still remember attending a church service in which this passage provided the text for the morning message. The pastor focused heavily on the detail of the five maidens not sharing their oil. The point he obtained from the parable was that Christians were not to be like the five maidens who possessed oil but would not share it! In so doing, the pastor turned the meaning of the parable completely around. If Jülicher's point had been followed, this error would not have been made.

59. See below, pp. 114–116.

60. See above, pp. 35–36, 52.

61. See above, p 45.

62. One of the positive contributions of form criticism is the recognition that in general the Gospel traditions circulated as independent oral units before being incorporated into the Gospels. Some material, however, was collected into larger complexes such as Mark 1:21–39 (45); 2:1 to 3:6; and 4:1–34 before being incorporated into our Gospels.

63. Other examples of Markan "sandwiches" are:
Mark 3:22–30 into Mark 3:19b–21 and 31–35
Mark 5:25–34 into Mark 5:21–24 and 35–43
Mark 6:14–29 into Mark 6:6b–13 and 30f.
Mark 14:3–9 into Mark 14:1–2 and 10–11.

64. Whatever the motivation for such business in the Temple may have been, it is clear that the money changers and merchants were not there as nonprofit agencies.

65. Note that in Mark 8:35 these terms are equivalent.

Chapter 4. THE CONTENT OF JESUS' TEACHING: THE KINGDOM OF GOD

1. For the significance of MARK, Mark, MATT, Matt, LUKE, and Luke, see Abbreviations.

2. Jeremias, *New Testament Theology*, p. 31, lists 13 instances in MARK, 9 in MATT/LUKE (Q), 27 in Matt, and 12 in Luke.

3. The expression "kingdom of God" also occurs twice in John—John 3:3 and 5.

4. Matt 3:2; 4:17; 5:3, 10, 19 (2), 20; 7:21; 8:11; 10:7; 11:11, 12; 13:11, 24, 31, 33, 44, 45, 47, 52; 16:19; 18:1, 3, 4, 23; 19:12, 14, 23; 20:1; 22:2; 23:13; 25:1.

5. See Donald Guthrie, *New Testament Introduction* (London: Inter-Varsity Fellowship, 1970), pp. 59–61, 93–96; Paul Feine; Johannes Behm; and Werner Georg Kümmel, *Introduction to the New Testament*, trans. by A. J. Mattill, Jr. (Abingdon Press, 1966), p. 97; Alfred Wikenhauser, *New Testament Introduction*, trans. by Joseph Cunningham (Herder & Herder, Inc., 1958), pp. 169–170, 219–221.

6. See Guthrie, *New Testament Introduction*, pp. 25–29; Kümmel, *Introduction to the New Testament*, pp. 79–81; Wikenhauser, *New Testament Introduction*, pp. 195–196.

7. YHWH is frequently mispronounced as "Jehovah," but the more correct pronunciation is "Yahweh."

8. For additional examples, see Jeremias, *New Testament Theology*, pp. 9–10. For examples of this in the Dead Sea Scrolls, see Helmer Ringgren, *The Faith of Qumran*, trans. by E. T. Sander (Fortress Press, 1963), pp. 47–48.

9. Jeremias lists in *New Testament Theology*, p. 11, 21 instances in MARK, 23 in MATT/LUKE, 27 in Matt, and 25 in Luke.

10. Jeremias, *New Testament Theology*, p. 97, n. 2, states that the term is found on the lips of Jesus 35 times in Mark, 33 in Matthew, and 65 in Luke.

11. Adolf Harnack, *What Is Christianity?* trans. by Thomas Bailey Saunders (G. P. Putnam's Sons, Inc., 1908), p. 55.

12. It is interesting to note that existential theologians do something quite similar when they acknowledge the apocalyptic element in the teaching of Jesus but maintain that what Jesus intended by his preaching of the kingdom of God was to place an existential demand on human existence at the present moment. Jesus in his preaching confronted his hearers with the immediate presence of God and the call to decision or to put it in other words—the end of the world. Thus the twentieth-century existentialist removes the eschatological "husk" from the teaching of Jesus through demythologizing in order to arrive at the existential kernel of his teaching, whereas the liberal eliminated that husk outright in order to arrive at his religion of the heart.

13. The even more famous English translation of Schweitzer's *Von Reimarus zu Wrede, The Quest of the Historical Jesus,* appeared in 1911.

14. Cf. Rudolf Bultmann, *Theology of the New Testament*, trans. by Kendrick Grobel (Charles Scribner's Sons, 1951), Vol. I, p. 22, who states that the view that

the kingdom of God is a present reality in the teaching of Jesus "cannot be substantiated by a single saying of Jesus, and it contradicts the meaning 'God's Reign.' " Later Bultmann apparently wavered somewhat on this and saw Jesus as standing "between the times."

15. George Eldon Ladd, *Jesus and the Kingdom* (Harper & Row, Publishers, Inc., 1964), pp. 17–20, includes Dodd under the noneschatological interpretations. We shall list Dodd and his school under a third and separate category for two reasons. First, this school is frequently placed over against the school of consistent eschatology and is therefore probably best dealt with as an independent entity. Secondly, Dodd sees the kingdom of God as associated with certain events such as the death, resurrection, ascension, and parousia of Jesus which are certainly eschatological events.

16. Hunter, *Interpreting the Parables*, p. 40.

17. Compare the Assumption of Moses 10:1, where the fall of Satan is associated with the coming of the kingdom of God.

18. "Until" *(mechri)* must be understood inclusively, i.e., up to and including, for in Luke the kingdom of God begins after John the Baptist. See Acts 1:5; 10:37; 13:24f.; 19:4.

19. Some scholars have argued that in MATT 11:13, John the Baptist is placed in the new age rather than in the old, in that the "until" *(heos)* is exclusive, i.e., "up to but not including." (So Jeremias, *New Testament Theology*, pp. 46–47.) Matt 11:12 seems to support this view, but Matt 11:11 seems to argue the opposite, for here John is not part of the kingdom! What is important for us here, however, is to note that whether the kingdom of God begins after John or whether he overlaps somewhat in the kingdom period, the kingdom of God is portrayed as a present reality that is now suffering violence!

20. Jeremias, *New Testament Theology*, p. 106, points out that "from earliest times in the East, vine and wine have been symbols of the new age."

21. See Jeremias, *New Testament Theology*, pp. 245–247, for a discussion of the offer of salvation to the Gentiles by Jesus.

22. Jeremias, *New Testament Theology*, p. 101.

23. So *ibid.*, pp. 100–101.

24. See Werner Georg Kümmel, *Promise and Fulfilment*, trans. by Dorothea M. Barton (Alec R. Allenson, Inc., 1957), pp. 34–35.

25. Jeremias, *New Testament Theology*, p. 98.

26. Ladd, *Jesus and the Kingdom*, p. 303.

27. It should be noted that in the Synoptic Gospels "eternal life" is a synonym for the kingdom of God. Compare MARK 10:17 with 10:23–25 and Matt 25:46 with 25:34.

28. Compare Rom 6:6, 11, 14 with 12–13; 6:17–18 with 19; 8:9–11 with 12–13; I Cor 5:7b with 7a; Gal 5:25a with 25b; Col 3:1a with 1b; 3:3a with 5; 3:9b–10 with 9a.

29. Oscar Cullmann, *Christ and Time*, trans. by Floyd V. Filson (London: SCM Press, 1951), pp. 84–88.

30. A common schematization frequently used to portray this is as follows:

THE KINGDOM OF GOD

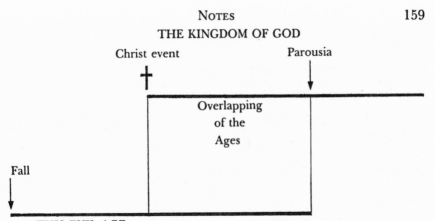

31. One should note a similar two-step binding and judging of Satan in Revelation 20.

32. Kümmel, *Promise and Fulfilment*, p. 76.

33. Contrast Matt 28:18; Phil 2:10; Col 1:15–20.

34. The authenticity of many of these sayings on discipleship is questioned, but the denial of the authenticity of all such sayings would be due less to exegetical grounds than to *a priori* presuppositions.

35. For an excellent and succinct discussion of this now–not-yet tension in the teaching of Jesus on the kingdom of God, the Johannine teaching on eternal life, and the Pauline teaching on justification, see George Eldon Ladd, *The Pattern of New Testament Truth* (Wm. B. Eerdmans Publishing Company, 1968).

36. It may be useful at this point to list some of the ways in which the kingdom of God is a present reality in the coming of Jesus. In doing this we shall begin with the evidence found in the Gospels and then proceed to the New Testament epistles. The realized dimension of the kingdom lies in the fact that:

a. The promised Spirit has once again become active in Israel in the ministry of Jesus (LUKE 11:14–23 [MATT 12:28]); MARK 3:28–29; Luke 4:18).

b. The Spirit now comes upon every believer in fulfillment of Joel 2:28–32 (MARK 1:8 [MATT 3:11]; LUKE 11:13; these passages should be interpreted in the light of John 7:39; Acts 2:1f.).

c. The Spirit represents the guarantee (earnest) and seal of our redemption (II Cor 1:22; 5:5; Eph 1:13–14), the firstfruits of our salvation (Rom 8:23).

d. Satan has been defeated (MARK 3:27; Luke 10:18; the exorcisms) and we are thus delivered from the evil powers (Eph 2:1–7; Col 1:13) even if we must still resist them (Eph 6:12; I Peter 5:8–9).

e. The Old Testament prophecies are fulfilled (LUKE 7:22–23; Luke 4:18–21; MATT 13:17; Matt 5:17).

f. A new covenant is made in fulfillment of Jer 31:31–34 (MARK 14:24), so that the old covenant of circumcision (Acts 7:8) is now abolished (Matt 5:21f., 27f., 31f., 33f., 38f., 43f.; MARK 7:14f. [Note esp. the Markan comment in v. 19]; II Cor 3:6; Heb 7:22; 8:8; 9:15).

g. The resurrection of the dead has begun (MARK 8:31; 9:9, 31; 10:33–34; 16:6; I Cor 15:20, 23).

h. The resurrection life has already begun, for the higher ethic of Jesus found in Matt 5:20, 21f., etc., is being realized (Col 2:12; Rom 6:1f.; II Cor 3:18).

Chapter 5. THE CONTENT OF JESUS' TEACHING: THE FATHERHOOD OF GOD

1. For the significance of MARK, Mark, MATT, Matt, LUKE, and Luke, see Abbreviations.

2. For various circumlocutions used by Jesus to avoid the sacred name of God as well as his use of the divine passive, see above, pp. 62–64.

3. MARK 11:25; 13:32; 14:36

MATT 5:48; 6:9, 32; 11:25–27

Matt 5:16; 6:1, 8; 16:17

Luke 12:32; 22:29; 23:34, 46

John 11:41; 12:27; 17:1, 5, 11, 21, 24–25

4. Cf. the Hymn to the Moon-God in James B. Pritchard (ed.), *Ancient Near Eastern Texts Relating to the Old Testament* (Princeton University Press, 1955), pp. 385–386.

5. Isa 63:16 (2); 64:8; Jer 3:4; Ps 89:26 are statements not prayerful addresses.

6. There seem to be some textual problems, however, with Sirach 23:1 and 4. See Joachim Jeremias, *The Prayers of Jesus*, trans. by John Bowden (Alec R. Allenson, Inc., 1967), pp. 28–29.

7. There is a possibility, however, that T. Levi 18:6 and T. Judah 24:2 may be Christian interpolations.

8. For a discussion of the title "Father" as a designation for God in rabbinic literature, see Jeremias, *The Prayers of Jesus*, pp. 16–19.

9. G. Schrenk, *"Pater,"* TDNT, Vol. 5, p. 985, and Jeremias, *The Prayers of Jesus*, pp. 58–59.

10. Jeremias, *New Testament Theology*, p. 36, states: "The use of the everyday word *abba* as a form of address to God is the most important linguistic innovation on the part of Jesus."

11. b. Sanhedrin 70b.

12. Joachim Jeremias, probably the greatest authority on this term, states in "The Lord's Prayer in Modern Research," *New Testament Issues*, ed. by Richard Batey (Harper & Row, Publishers, Inc., 1970), p. 95: "With the help of my assistants I have examined the whole later Jewish literature of prayer, and the result was that in no place in this immense literature is this invocation of God to be found."

13. Joachim Jeremias, *The Lord's Prayer*, trans. by John Reumann (Fortress Press, 1964), pp. 1–5.

14. "There is no surer sign or guarantee of the possession of the Holy Spirit and the sonship than this: that a man 'makes bold' to repeat this one word *Abba.*" (Jeremias, "The Lord's Prayer," p. 96.)

15. H. F. D. Sparks, "The Doctrine of the Divine Fatherhood in the Gospels,"

Studies in the Gospels, ed. by D. E. Nineham (Oxford: Basil Blackwell & Mott, Ltd., 1955), p. 260, states: "In spite of what is commonly supposed, there is no ground whatever for asserting that Jesus taught a Doctrine of 'The Fatherhood of God and the Brotherhood of Man.' "

16. Bruce M. Metzger, *The New Testament* (Abingdon Press, 1965), p. 146, sums this up well when he writes:

"One must be beware, however, against reading into Jesus' teaching more than the records warrant. So far from teaching the multitudes that God is the Father of all, there is general agreement among all the sources that Jesus spoke of this subject only to his disciples. When Jesus addressed the general public, he seems almost never to have referred to God as Father. In fact, of all the passages where Jesus mentions the fatherhood of God, in only one is he represented as speaking to the crowds as well as to his disciples: 'You have one Father, who is in heaven' (Matt. 23:9, compare vs. 1). From the mass of evidence, therefore, it appears that, instead of teaching the universal fatherhood of God, Jesus spoke of God as Father only (1) in terms of his own relation to God and (2) in terms of the relation of his disciples to God. Apparently, therefore, Jesus restricted the right to call God 'Father' to those who had shown by their loyalty to himself to be entitled to regard themselves as children of God."

17. The "our Father" in Matt 6:9 is no exception, for Jesus tells his disciples, "When *you* pray, say 'Our Father. . . .' "

18. See above, pp. 62–65.

Chapter 6. THE CONTENT OF JESUS' TEACHING: THE ETHICS OF THE KINGDOM

1. For the significance of MARK, Mark, MATT, Matt, LUKE, and Luke, see Abbreviations.

2. See Tertullian, *To His Wife*, 2.1 and Origen, Commentary on Romans 3.3. Cf. also *Didache* 6.2.

3. The exact meaning of Matt 19:11–12 is far from certain. The problem lies with the question of what "this precept" refers to. It can refer either prospectively to v. 12 or retrospectively to vs. 4–9. For the view that it refers to divorced people who have put away their wives on the grounds of adultery, see Quentin Quesnell, " 'Made Themselves Eunuchs for the Kingdom of Heaven' (Mt 19, 12)," CBQ, Vol. 30 (1968), pp. 335–358. Although Quesnell's thesis is not particularly convincing, he does have a good discussion on the difficulty in interpreting these verses as a call to virginity. See pp. 344–345.

4. Cf. also the parallel in b. Shabbath 133b: "Be thou like Him; just as He is gracious and compassionate, so be thou gracious and compassionate."

5. This "liberal" interpretation must be understood in the light of the ethical philosophy of Kant and of philosophical idealism in general.

6. Note the fourfold enumeration of the six most important works of love in Matt 25:31–46. Here love is seen not in the attitude of the individual but in his actions.

7. For the more probable explanation of this passage, see pp. 71–72.

162
162 NOTES

8. See Chapter 2.

9. The church fathers spoke of man as *non posse peccare* or "not able to sin" in the final state.

10. Note here also that Matt 25:31-46 does not mention that these acts of love were done because the end was near.

11. Thaddäus Soiron, *Die Bergpredigt Jesu* (Freiburg: Verlag Herder, 1941), p. 43.

12. Harvey K. McArthur, *Understanding the Sermon on the Mount* (Harper & Brothers, 1960), pp. 105–148, contains a helpful summary and discussion of the various interpretations given above. See also Soiron, *Die Bergpredigt Jesu*, pp. 1–96.

13. MARK 1:15; Mark 6:12; MATT 11:20-21; 12:41; Luke 5:32; 13:3, 5; 15:7; 16:30.

14. MARK 1:16-20; 2:14-15; 8:34; 10:21, 28; MATT 8:18-22; 10:38; LUKE 5:11; cf. John 1:43; 12:26.

15. MARK 1:15; 2:5; 5:34; 10:52; MATT 8:10; Luke 7:50; 8:12; 17:19; and esp. John 3:12, 15, 16, 18, 36, etc.

16. MARK 8:34.

17. MARK 8:34; MATT 10:38.

18. MATT 10:32; cf. MARK 8:38.

19. MATT 7:24-27.

20. Matt 11:28-30.

21. MARK 8:35; MATT 10:39; cf. John 12:25.

22. LUKE 14:26.

23. MARK 9:42-47.

24. MARK 10:21; Luke 12:33; cf. MATT 6:19-21.

25. It is quite common to see the call of Christ portrayed as a two-stage call. According to this view, one at conversion receives Jesus as "Savior" and thus enters into the kingdom of God. Later he should then receive Jesus as "Lord" and surrender his whole life to him. Such teaching finds no support in the words of Jesus. Certainly the call to decision demanded a total unconditional commitment. The rich young ruler (MARK 10:17-31) knew of no two-stage commitment. Furthermore, the invitation to salvation as proclaimed by the early church involved believing and confessing the *Lord* Jesus Christ (cf. Acts 16:31; Rom 10:9).

26. The context of Luke 14:28-33 should be noted. In the previous verses we have the demand to "hate" parents and family.

27. See above, pp. 8-12.

28. The demand of Jesus in v. 62 is not quite so difficult to understand as the one in v. 59, for the kingdom of God does not demand any less commitment than the Old Testament prophets. Cf. Elijah's demand in I Kings 19:20.

29. In the light of such sayings as MARK 7:9-13 and 10:19 and the love and compassion of Jesus, this saying still remains difficult to understand. This difficulty lies not so much in the absoluteness of the demand of Jesus but in seeking to reconcile such a demand with a passage like MARK 7:9-13.

30. At first glance it appears that the woman's sins are forgiven *because* she loved. Yet Jeremias, *New Testament Theology*, p. 218, has pointed out that both

Aramaic and Hebrew have no term such as "gratitude" and thus must use terms such as "love," "praise," or "bless" to express this. It was therefore because of her gratitude toward God's offer of forgiveness, i.e., because of her grateful acceptance of God's grace, that she was forgiven. That this is the correct interpretation is shown by Luke 7:47, "but he who is forgiven little, loves little," as well as the parable itself which speaks of the two *forgiven* debtors loving the creditor. It was because the woman was forgiven much that she loved much! Nevertheless, the causal relation between God's forgiveness and our new attitude is so close that at times man's response can be spoken of as paralleling (LUKE 11:4), preceding (MARK 11:25), or following the divine forgiveness (Matt 18:23–35).

31. There is a sense in which these two commands can be conceived as two sides of one command. Note MARK 12:31: "There is no commandment greater than these."

32. These oral traditions, which supposedly came from Moses himself (Pirke Aboth 1:1f.) and which fill the "gaps" left by the Old Testament Law, were finally written down around A.D. 200 and form what is called the Mishnah. This along with its commentary, the Gemara, make up the Talmud. The Palestinian Talmud, which is also called the Jerusalem Talmud, was completed around A.D. 400 and the Babylonian Talmud around A.D. 500.

33. See Robert J. Banks, *Jesus and the Law in the Synoptic Tradition* (Cambridge: At the University Press, 1975), p. 238.

34. See Justin Martyr, *Dialogue with Trypho*, 44,2, and Irenaeus, *Against Heresies* IV. xiv.3, xv.1–2.

35. Another attempt to explain this apparent inconsistency in the teachings of Jesus is to see a development in Jesus' attitude toward the Law, but any attempt to see a change from an attitude of acceptance of the Old Testament to one of rejection faces two major problems. The first is that the apparently contradictory statements are found both at the beginning and the end of the Gospels; the other is that the difficulty of knowing where such statements fit into the chronology of Jesus' life is such that one cannot be sure exactly when such statements were uttered.

36. See Banks, *Jesus and the Law in the Synoptic Tradition*, p. 131.

37. W. D. Davies, *The Setting of the Sermon on the Mount* (Cambridge: At the University Press, 1964), p. 101, n. 1, explains this ambiguity as follows: "I have argued . . . that the ambiguity which our sources reveal in the attitude of Jesus to the Law, namely, that he appears to uphold it and to annul it at the same time, is to be understood in terms of a distinction which Jesus himself drew between the time before and the time after his death. While in principle the Law had passed away during his ministry, it was not until Jesus had sealed the New Covenant in his death that it could openly be declared to have done so."

38. The term *doulos* can mean either servant or slave. In ancient society the difference between the two was not as great as we tend to think.

39. Jeremias, *New Testament Theology*, p. 217, makes a distinction between merit and recompense and uses the latter term to describe Jesus' teaching on reward. He states: "Merit has an eye to human achievement; recompense looks to God's

faithfulness. That God is trustworthy and offers recompense stands assured."

40. The question is often raised as to whether an attempt to systematize Jesus' ethical teachings is legitimate, since Jesus himself never did so. The failure of Jesus to do this, however, does not invalidate such attempts, providing that such a schematization is faithful to his teaching.

41. Ladd, *Jesus and the Kingdom*, pp. 287–288.

42. See above, pp. 84–86.

43. Joachim Jeremias, *The Sermon on the Mount*, trans. by Norman Perrin (Fortress Press, 1963), pp. 34–35, has an excellent summary on this issue which deserves to be quoted at length: "The sayings of Jesus which have been collected in the Sermon on the Mount are not intended to lay a legal yoke upon Jesus' disciples; neither in the sense that they say: 'You must do all of this, in order that you may be saved' (perfectionist conception); nor in the sense: 'You ought actually to have done all of this, see what poor creatures you are' (theory of the impossible ideal ["Lutheran" interpretation]); nor in the sense: 'Now pull yourself together; the final victory is at hand' (interim-ethic). Rather, these sayings of Jesus delineate the lived faith. They say: You are forgiven; you are the child of God; you belong to his kingdom. The sun of righteousness has risen over your life. You no longer belong to yourself; rather, you belong to the city of God, the light of which shines in the darkness. Now you may also experience it: out of the thankfulness of a redeemed child of God a new life is growing. This is the meaning of the Sermon on the Mount."

44. Manson, *The Teaching of Jesus*, p. 306, states that the objection that these commandments are vague in their specific application "is met by the provision of the precept which is commonly known as the Golden Rule."

45. Luke 16:16 should not be interpreted as a rejection of the Old Testament by Jesus but must be interpreted in the context of salvation history. "The law and the prophets" refers to the old covenant, not to the commandments of the Pentateuch. These are evidently still valid for Luke. See Luke 16:17.

46. Another aid that Jesus alludes to in passing which is a helpful aid for understanding the will of God is the "conscience" (cf. Luke 12:57). It would be unwise, however, to attempt to build on this a "natural theology."

47. Cf. John 16:13.

48. Joseph Klausner, *Jesus of Nazareth* (Beacon Press, Inc., 1964), p. 414, ends his work as follows: "If ever the day should come and this ethical code be stripped of its wrappings of miracles and mysticism, the Book of the Ethics of Jesus will be one of the choicest treasures in the literature of Israel for all time."

49. Klausner, *Jesus of Nazareth*, p. 363, states: "Without any exception he [Jesus] is wholly explainable by the scriptural and Pharisaic Judaism of his time."

50. See T. Dan 5:3; T. Issachar 5:2; 7:6; Philo, *Spec Leg*, II, 63.

51. It appears in negative form in Tobit 4:15 and in b. Shabbath 31a and supposedly in positive form in Letter of Aristeas 207, but the latter can also be understood as being in negative form: "As you wish that no evil should befall you, but to be a partaker of all good things, so you should act on the same principle towards your subjects and offenders" (*Apocrypha and Pseudepigrapha of the Old*

Testament, Vol. II, ed. by R. H. Charles [Oxford: At the Clarendon Press, 1913]).

52. Contrast Tobit 4:15 ("And what you hate, do not do to any one") with Tobit 4:17 ("Place your bread on the grave of the righteous, but give none to sinners").

53. Contrast Josephus, *The Jewish War* II. viii. 7, which states that the Essenes swore an oath to hate the unrighteous as well as 1QS 1.9, which states that the members of the sect are "to love all the sons of light, each according to his lot in the counsel of God, and to hate all the sons of darkness, each according to his guilt in the vengeance of God."

54. Cf. T. Gad 6:3; T. Benjamin 8:2.

55. Metzger, *The New Testament*, p. 166, states this very well when he says: "Both he [Jesus] and contemporary scribes spoke of the law of God, but the latter commonly stressed the word 'law' while he emphasized the word 'God.' "

Chapter 7. THE CONTENT OF JESUS' TEACHING: CHRISTOLOGY

1. See below, pp. 120–121.

2. See Fred L. Fisher, *Jesus and His Teaching* (The Broadman Press, 1972), p. 85.

3. For the significance of MARK, Mark, MATT, Matt, LUKE, and Luke, see Abbreviations.

4. For the view that the cleansing of the Temple was a Messianic act, see below, note 38.

5. See Justin Martyr, *Dialogue with Trypho*, 69; Origen, *Against Celsus*, I, 28; b. Sanhedrin 43a.

6. The attempt of Vermès, *Jesus the Jew*, pp. 65–69, to demonstrate that "there is nothing outstandingly novel or unique in the words of Jesus, 'My son, your sins are forgiven' " flounders upon the reaction of the scribes in MARK 2:7 and the parallel story in Luke 7:48–49.

7. Archibald M. Hunter, *The Work and Words of Jesus* (The Westminster Press, 1950), pp. 87–88.

8. Eduard Schweizer, *Jesus*, trans. by David E. Green (John Knox Press, 1972), p. 14; cf. also Jeremias, *The Parables of Jesus*, p. 132.

9. See b. Sanhedrin 99a.

10. See above, pp. 102–104.

11. Jeremias, *New Testament Theology*, p. 35, lists 13 examples in MARK, 9 in MATT-LUKE, 9 in Matt, 3 in Luke, and 25 in John. In John the expression is always doubled.

12. *Ibid.*

13. H. Schlier, *"Amen,"* TDNT, Vol. I, p. 338.

14. Hunter, *Work and Words*, p. 88.

15. This verse has been interpreted in several ways. The most common are: (a) Jesus lived in perfect obedience to the Law; (b) Jesus fulfilled the promises of the Old Testament in his coming; (c) Jesus brings the Law to its fuller and ultimate meaning as revealed in Matt 5:21–48; and (d) Jesus came to bring the Law to its completion or end. Regardless of how one interprets this verse, there is still present a strong Christological claim.

166   Notes

16. Cf. also MATT 10:16; 23:39; Matt 16:18–19; MARK 14:27, 58.

17. See above, p. 3.

18. Reginald H. Fuller, *The Foundations of New Testament Christology* (Charles Scribner's Sons, 1965), p. 106; cf. also Günther Bornkamm, *Jesus of Nazareth*, trans. by Irene and Fraser McLuskey with James M. Robinson (Harper & Brothers, 1960), p. 178.

19. Hans Conzelmann, *Jesus*, trans. by J. Raymond Lord (Fortress Press, 1973), p. 49.

20. Bornkamm, *Jesus of Nazareth*, p. 172, states: "For this is the truly amazing thing, that there is in fact not one single certain proof of Jesus' claiming for himself one of the Messianic titles which tradition has ascribed to him." Cf. also Schweizer, *Jesus*, p. 21, who states: "In any case, Jesus did not assume any current title with an exalted meaning."

21. See Cullmann, *The Christology of the New Testament*, pp. 111–112; Vermès, *Jesus the Jew*, pp. 130–140.

22. A. S. van der Woude, *"Christos,"* TDNT, Vol. 9, pp. 526–527.

23. See Sigmund Mowinckel, *He That Cometh*, trans. by G. W. Anderson (Abingdon Press, 1956), pp. 280–281.

24. Vermès, *Jesus the Jew*, p. 149. See above, notes 19 and 20.

25. Among certain circles of redaction critics an attempt has been made to portray MARK 8:27–30 as a rejection by the Evangelist of this confession by Peter. See Theodore J. Weeden, *Mark—Traditions in Conflict* (Fortress Press, 1971), pp. 32–34, 64–65. The very fact that Mark introduced his Gospel with the words, "The beginning of the gospel of Jesus Christ, the Son of God," however, indicates that Mark was in no way embarrassed by the terms "Messiah" or "Son of God" as a description of the person and work of Jesus.

26. Fuller, *The Foundations of New Testament Christology*, p. 109.

27. For a somewhat dated but still excellent discussion of the Messianic secret in Mark in which the author argues for the historicity of the secret in the life of Jesus, see Vincent Taylor, "W. Wrede's The Messianic Secret in the Gospels," ExpT, Vol. 65 (1953–54), pp. 246–250.

28. For an excellent discussion of the passion sayings of Jesus, see Jeremias, *New Testament Theology*, pp. 276–299.

29. See Weeden, *Mark—Traditions in Conflict*, p. 33.

30. C. S. Lewis' essay "Fern-seed and Elephants," in *Fern-seed and Elephants and Other Essays on Christianity* (London: Wm. Collins & Co., Ltd., Fontana Books, 1975), pp. 104–125, should be required reading in this regard.

31. The Fifth Amendment may guarantee that Americans can remain silent in such circumstances, but the Old Testament Law did not. Cf. Lev 5:1; I Kings 22:16; Prov 29:24.

32. The term "Son of the Blessed" is an example of substitution for the divine name (see above, p. 63) and is the equivalent of "Son of God." This term was not a reference or claim to deity such as we find in the Nicene Creed, however, but was an appositive for "Messiah." This is evident from the fact that this expression was understood in contemporary Judaism solely in a messianic sense.

See William L. Lane, *Commentary on the Gospel of Mark* (Wm. B. Eerdmans Publishing Company, 1974), p. 535. See especially note 133.

33. Cullmann, *The Christology of the New Testament*, p. 121.

34. C. H. Dodd, *The Founder of Christianity* (London: Macmillan and Co., Ltd., 1970), p. 102.

35. So Fuller, *The Foundations of New Testament Christology*, p. 110; Otto Betz, *What Do We Know About Jesus?* trans. by Margaret Kohl (London: SCM Press, Ltd., 1968), pp. 84–85; W. Grundmann, "Christos," *TDNT*, Vol. 9, p. 528.

36. Dodd, *The Founder of Christianity*, pp. 102–103.

37. It is difficult to believe that the church would have created such an account in which their Lord is reviled and mocked while hanging on the cross. It is far more likely that the church here preserved such a painful account because it was historical.

38. See Bertil Gärtner, *The Temple and the Community in Qumran and the New Testament* (Cambridge: At the University Press, 1965), p. 105, who states: "One aspect of the work of the Messiah in the last days was believed to be the renewal of the temple."

39. See Betz, *What Do We Know About Jesus?* pp. 84–85, for an excellent discussion of this.

40. See Jeremias, *New Testament Theology*, pp. 70–75, for the view that the essence of the temptation of Jesus in the wilderness was to emerge as a political Messiah.

41. See J. C. O'Neill, "The Silence of Jesus," *NTS*, Vol. 15 (1968), pp. 165–167, and Richard N. Longenecker, *The Christology of Early Jewish Christianity* (Alec R. Allenson, Inc., 1970), pp. 71–73.

42. Cullmann, *The Christology of the New Testament*, p. 290.

43. E. Lohse, "*Huios*," *TDNT*, Vol. 8, p. 360; Vermès, *Jesus the Jew*, p. 197.

44. Lohse, "*Huios*," p. 360.

45. *Ibid.*, p. 361.

46. Cullmann, *The Christology of the New Testament*, p. 277, states: "The only story in which Jesus is called 'Son of God' in a sense which corresponds to the Hellenistic concept is Matthew's version of Jesus' walking on the sea, after which the disciples cry out as a result of the miracle, 'Truly you are the Son of God' (Matt 14:33) . . . [and] even within Matthew itself it has no special significance whatsoever."

47. Eduard Schweizer, "*Huios*," *TDNT*, Vol. 8, p. 372.

48. Taylor, *The Gospel According to St. Mark*, p. 522.

49. P. W. Schmiedel, "Gospels," *Encyclopedia Biblica*, ed. by T. K. Cheyne and J. Sutherland Black (London: Black, 1914), col. 1881.

50. See above, pp. 35–36, 52, 58.

51. C. K. Barrett, *Jesus and the Gospel Tradition* (Fortress Press, 1968), p. 27.

52. See Taylor, *The Gospel According to St. Mark*, p. 472.

53. See above, pp. 118–119.

54. 1QH 4:5–33.

55. Bultmann, *The History of the Synoptic Tradition*, p. 159.

56. Jeremias, *New Testament Theology*, pp. 57–61.
57. Archibald M. Hunter, *"Crux Criticorum—Matt. XI. 25–30—A Reappraisal,"* NTS, Vol. 8 (1961), p. 245.
58. Hunter, *"Crux Criticorum,"* p. 245, deserves to be quoted here. He states: "We conclude that, if men reject this logion, they reject it not because they have proved it a Hellenistic revelation word, or because its Johannine ring condemns it, but because they have made up their minds, *a priori*, that the Jesus of history could not have made such a claim."
59. The term *panta*, or "all things," is best understood in this context to mean "all knowledge" rather than "all power."
60. Wilhelm Bousset, *Kyrios Christos*, trans. by John E. Steely (Abingdon Press, 1970), p. 97.
61. Bultmann, *Theology of the New Testament*, Vol. I, pp. 50, 121–133.
62. Ferdinand Hahn, *The Titles of Jesus in Christology*, trans. by Harold Knight and George Ogg (The World Publishing Company, 1969), pp. 279–317.
63. Vermès, *Jesus the Jew*, pp. 211–212.
64. The "exception" in Matt 6:9 is not really an exception, for Jesus is teaching his disciples to pray. When they pray, *they* are to say, "Our Father . . ."
65. The eighty-two occurrences (including the parallels to MARK and MATT references) are found as follows:
    MARK 2:10, 28; 8:31, 38; 9:9, 12, 31; 10:33, 45; 13:26; 14:21 (2), 41, 62
    MATT 8:20; 11:19; 12:32, 40; 24:27, 37, 39, 44
    Matt 10:23; 13:37, 41; 16:13, 28; 19:28; 24:30; 25:31; 26:2
    Luke 6:22; 12:8; 17:22; 18:8; 19:10; 21:36; 22:48; 24:7
    John 1:51; 3:13, 14; 5:27; 6:27, 53, 62; 8:28; 9:35; 12:23, 34 (2), 13:31
66. Jeremias, *New Testament Theology* p. 261; Vermès, *Jesus the Jew*, pp. 163–177.
67. See Otto Eissfeldt, *The Old Testament: An Introduction*, trans. by Peter R. Ackroyd (Harper & Row, Publishers, Inc., 1965), pp. 619–620; D. S. Russell, *The Method and Message of Jewish Apocalyptic* (The Old Testament Library) (The Westminster Press, 1964), pp. 51–53.
68. See J. Y. Campbell, "The Origin and Meaning of the Term Son of Man," JTS, Vol. 48 (1947), pp. 145–155; C. H. Dodd, *According to the Scriptures* (Charles Scribner's Sons, 1953), pp. 116–117.
69. Vermès, *Jesus the Jew*, p. 176; William S. LaSor, *The Dead Sea Scrolls and the New Testament* (Wm. B. Eerdmans Publishing Company, 1972), p. 104, points out that a total of eleven different manuscripts of Enoch have been found at Qumran.
70. Fuller, *The Foundations of New Testament Christology*, pp. 37–38.
71. C. F. D. Moule, "Neglected Features in the Problem of 'Son of Man' " in *Neues Testament und Kirche*, ed. by Joachim Gnilka (Freiburg: Verlag Herder, 1974), p. 416, points out that in the light of the absence of the Similitudes of Enoch at Qumran it would be "unscientific" to assume an early date for this work.
72. C. Colpe, *"Ho Huios tou Anthropou,"* TDNT, Vol. 8, pp. 423–429; Vermès, *Jesus the Jew*, p. 175; Ragnar Leivestad, "Exit the Apocalyptic Son of Man," NTS, Vol. 18 (1971), p. 246.

73. For an excellent discussion of these verses in relation to Dan 7:13, see R. T. France, *Jesus and the Old Testament* (London: Tyndale Press, 1971), pp. 139–144.

74. This is the view of such scholars as T. W. Manson, V. Taylor, C. E. B. Cranfield, A. M. Hunter, O. Cullmann, C. F. D. Moule, M. D. Hooker, C. K. Barrett.

75. Colpe, *"Ho Huios tou Anthropou,"* p. 430.

76. See Jeremias, *New Testament Theology*, p. 265, for examples of the use of other passages in Daniel 7 by Jesus.

77. So Dodd, *The Founder of Christianity*, pp. 110–111; Barnabas Lindars, "Re-enter the Apocalyptic Son of Man," NTS, Vol. 22 (1975), pp. 52–53. Does John 12:34 suggest this or does it refer to a particular interpretation of the role which the Son of man was to fulfill?

78. It should be pointed out that the threefold division of these passages says nothing for or against their authenticity unless we presuppose that Jesus could not have viewed his life as consisting of three dimensions: now (his present ministry), soon (his coming death and resurrection), and future (his glorious return). Such a presupposition, however, is not based on exegetical grounds but upon one's preconceptions.

79. The chart follows primarily Reginald H. Fuller, *The Mission and Achievement of Jesus* (London: SCM Press, Ltd., 1954), pp. 96–97. The main difference is that M and L present here not only the sources used by Matthew and Luke but their editorial work as well.

80. There are several examples in the Gospels where scholars believe such a confusion is revealed. In MARK 2:27–28, for example, it has been suggested that Jesus might have originally said: "The sabbath was made for man [*bar nasha*], not man [*bar nasha*] for the sabbath; so man [*bar nasha*] is lord even of the sabbath." Other suggested passages in which *bar nasha* may have originally meant "man" in the generic sense but was mistranslated as "Son of man" into Greek are: MARK 2:10; MATT 8:20; 11:19; 12:32.

81. Hans Lietzmann, *Der Menschensohn* (Leipzig: J. C. B. Mohr, 1896), p. 85.

82. Vermès, *Jesus the Jew*, p. 176.

83. Colpe, *"Ho Huios tou Anthropou,"* p. 404.

84. Vermès, *Jesus the Jew*, pp. 163–168, and his appendix on the Son of man in Black, *An Aramaic Approach to the Gospels and Acts*, pp. 310–328.

85. So Hendrikus Boers, "Where Christology Is Real," *Interpretation*, Vol. 26 (1972), p. 307.

86. Vermès, *Jesus the Jew*, p. 163.

87. Some of the scholars who have attacked the authenticity of the Son of man sayings on psychological grounds are Bultmann, *The History of the Synoptic Tradition*, p. 137; Morton Scott Enslin, *Christian Beginnings* (Harper & Brothers, 1938), p. 163; Frederick C. Grant, *The Gospel of the Kingdom* (The Macmillan Company, 1940), pp. 63, 67–68; A. J. B. Higgins, *Jesus and the Son of Man* (Fortress Press, 1964), p. 199; and Howard M. Teeple, "The Origin of the Son of Man Christology," JBL, Vol. 84 (1965), p. 221, who states: "Enslin has noted that if Jesus had believed either that he was or would be transformed into the Son of man,

his mental state would have been so far from normalcy as to be psychopathic. Historical scholarship leads to the conclusion that Jesus shared some of the mistaken views of his age, but that he was normal."

88. See below, pp. 142–147.

89. Bultmann, *Theology of the New Testament*, pp. 29–30.

90. See Frederick Houk Borsch, *The Son of Man in Myth and History* (The New Testament Library) (The Westminster Press, 1967), pp. 330–331.

91. Such passages as Luke 13:32–33 (The designation of Jesus as a prophet would be rather unusual in a church creation); 12:49–50 (The allusive character of this saying about his death argues for its authenticity); MARK 2:18–20 (The early church did not understand itself as living in a period of fasting and mourning); Matt 12:40 (The three days and three nights does not fit well the period between the crucifixion and the resurrection); and MARK 10:38–40 (The claim that this is a *vaticinium ex eventu* encounters great difficulty in the fact that there is no evidence that both James and John experienced martyrdom) argue strongly that Jesus in one way or another did predict that he was going to die in Jerusalem. See also Eduard Schweizer, "The Son of Man," JBL, Vol. 79 (1960), pp. 120–121.

92. See above, pp. 112–120.

93. See Lindars, "Re-enter the Apocalyptic Son of Man," p. 66, n. 1.

94. See Vermès, *Jesus the Jew*, pp. 163–164; Lindars, "Re-enter the Apocalyptic Son of Man," pp. 53–54.

95. So Fuller, *The Mission and Achievement of Jesus*, p. 103.

96. The view of Schweizer, "The Son of Man," pp. 119–129, that the A sayings have the greatest claim for authenticity has not received any significant following.

97. Some of the scholars who hold this view are P. Vielhauer, H. Braun, H. Conzelmann, E. Käsemann, H. M. Teeple, H. Boers, N. Perrin.

98. This argument was apparently first brought forward by Henry Burton Sharman, *Son of Man and Kingdom of God* (Harper & Brothers, 1943), but has been developed more fully by Philipp Vielhauer in "Gottesreich und Menschensohn in der Verkündigung Jesu," in W. Schneemelcher (ed.), *Festschrift für Günther Dehn* (Neukirchen: Verlag des Buchhandlung des Erziehungsvereins, 1957), pp. 51–79.

99. I. H. Marshall, "The Synoptic Son of Man Sayings in Recent Discussion," NTS, Vol. 12 (1965), p. 336.

100. Some of the contexts in which these terms appear together are: MARK 8:38 to 9:1; LUKE 21:27, 31 (Note here that the Matthean parallel uses "he" [the Son of man] whereas Luke speaks of the kingdom of God coming!); Luke 17:21–22; Matt 13:37, 43; 25:31, 34. At times one Evangelist will use one term, such as the kingdom of God, whereas the other Evangelist will use the other term, such as the Son of man. Cf. MATT 19:28; 24:33. For an excellent discussion of this, see Heinz Eduard Tödt, *The Son of Man in the Synoptic Tradition*, trans. by Dorothea M. Barton (The New Testament Library) (The Westminster Press, 1965), pp. 332–336.

101. For a description and discussion of the "criterion of dissimilarity," see above, p. 44.

102. Lindars, "Re-enter the Apocalyptic Son of Man," p. 65, argues as a result

that since there existed no clearly defined concept from which this title could have arisen, it must be traced back to Jesus himself.

103. So Jeremias, *New Testament Theology*, p. 266.

104. MARK 8:29–30; 14:62; Mark 9:41; Matt 23:10; 24:5; John 4:25–26; 17:3. Counting the parallels, the title "Christ" appears 11 times in the Gospels as a self-designation.

105. Jeremias in his *New Testament Theology*, pp. 262–264, has argued that of the 51 different Son of man sayings found in the Gospels, 37 of them have a competing tradition in which the title is not found. He also concludes that in every instance in which a competing form of the tradition lacks the title this competing form is more original. In so doing Jeremias, of course, narrows down considerably the number of Son of man sayings that he believes are authentic. Although specific examples could be debated (The Son of man saying in LUKE 12:8–9 seems to be more original than the parallel in MATT 10:32–33 which lacks the title), the main difficulty with Jeremias' reasoning lies elsewhere. It is evident that the term "Son of man" came to the Evangelists as a kind of technical term for Jesus. It is not therefore surprising that they sometimes substituted the first person for the title (cf. MATT 5:11 with LUKE 6:22; MARK 8:31 with MATT 16:21), so that despite Jeremias' statement to the contrary, the reverse process of Son of man to "I" also took place. This is not the least bit surprising, for if the church believed that Jesus and the Son of man were one and the same, and it did, they would have felt free to substitute "Son of man" for "I" or vice versa and still feel faithful to the tradition. As a result, Morna D. Hooker's statement in *The Son of Man in Mark* (Montreal: McGill University Press, 1967), p. 79, is correct. In investigating the question of the authenticity of the Son of man sayings, we must consider the total usage of this title in all the Gospels and not just investigate individual sayings in isolation from the others.

106. Hooker, *The Son of Man in Mark*, p. 79.

107. Borsch, *The Son of Man in Myth and History*, p. 24, states: "Even granting the difficulty of understanding the idioms of ancient languages, it was hard to *hear* Jesus so frequently speaking in such a roundabout way, harder still to imagine that all four of the evangelists could have completely misunderstood the idiom when there must still have been a few *ear*-witnesses who could have corrected the error, or at least several persons who knew both Greek and Aramaic."

108. Colpe, *"Ho Huios tou Anthropou,"* p. 431.

109. *Ibid.*, p. 437.

110. *Ibid.*, p. 432.

111. See above, pp. 39–42

112. C. S. Lewis, *Mere Christianity* (London: Wm. Collins & Co., Ltd., 1956), pp. 52–53, states this well: "I am trying here to prevent anyone saying the really foolish thing that people often say about Him: 'I'm ready to accept Jesus as a great moral teacher, but I don't accept His claim to be God.' That is the one thing we must not say. A man who was merely a man and said the sort of things Jesus said would not be a great moral teacher. He would either be a lunatic—on a level with the man who says he is a poached egg—or else he would be the Devil of Hell.

You must make your choice. Either this man was, and is, the Son of God; or else a madman or something worse. You can shut Him up for a fool, you can spit at Him and kill Him as a demon; or you can fall at His feet and call Him Lord and God. But let us not come with any patronising nonsense about His being a great human teacher. He has not left that open to us. He did not intend to."

Index of References

173

Index of Authors and Subjects

185